TRUTH

Michael Shermer

TRUTH

What It Is, How to Find It, and Why It Still Matters

Johns Hopkins University Press
Baltimore

Printed in the United States of America on acid-free paper
9 8 7 6 5 4 3 2 1

Johns Hopkins University Press
2715 North Charles Street
Baltimore, Maryland 21218
www.press.jhu.edu

Library of Congress Cataloging-in-Publication Data

Names: Shermer, Michael author
Title: Truth : what it is, how to find it, and why it still matters / Michael Shermer.
Description: Baltimore : Johns Hopkins University Press, 2026. | Includes bibliographical references and index.
Identifiers: LCCN 2025017553 | ISBN 9781421453729 hardcover | ISBN 9781421453736 ebook
Subjects: LCSH: Truthfulness and falsehood
Classification: LCC BJ1421 .S54 2025 | DDC 121–dc23/eng/20250818
LC record available at https://lccn.loc.gov/2025017553

A catalog record for this book is available from the British Library.

Special discounts are available for bulk purchases of this book. For more information, please contact Special Sales at specialsales@jh.edu.

EU GPSR Authorized Representative
LOGOS EUROPE, 9 rue Nicolas Poussin, 17000, La Rochelle, France
E-mail: Contact@logoseurope.eu

To Daniel Dennett

Friend, colleague,
and fellow traveler
on the journey
in search of truth

■ We alone can be wracked with doubt, and we alone have been provoked by that epistemic itch to seek a remedy: better truth-seeking methods. Wanting to keep better track of our food supplies, our territories, our families, our enemies, we discovered the benefits of talking it over with others, asking questions, passing on lore. We invented culture. Then we invented measuring, and arithmetic, and maps, and writing. These communicative and recording innovations come with a built-in ideal: truth. The point of asking questions is to find *true* answers; the point of measuring is to measure *accurately*; the point of making maps is to *find your way* to your destination.

—**Daniel Dennett, "Postmodernism and Truth,"** *Proceedings of the Twentieth World Congress of Philosophy*

■ If we do not have the capacity to distinguish what's true from what's false, then by definition the marketplace of ideas doesn't work. And by definition our democracy doesn't work. We are entering into an epistemological crisis.

—**Barack Obama,** *The Atlantic*

CONTENTS

PROLOGUE

Why Truth Matters Skepticism as an Agent of Reason Against Organized Irrationalism

■ Imagine you are at work and you get a call from one of your neighbors to inform you that there is something suspicious going on at your home—possibly burglars casing the place and looking like they may want to break in. You call the police. They send a squad car over and report back that they didn't see anything unusual. You phone your neighbor, relate what the police said, and ask him to double-check. Minutes later, the neighbor calls back to report that there is now a big truck backing up to the rear of your house. Frantic, you call 911 again and plead with the dispatcher to send the cops back to recheck what is going on there. Minutes tick by, and you finally get a return call from the police, who say they circled the neighborhood and the only truck they could see was what looked like a utility vehicle possibly servicing electricity poles. You relax momentarily, but your neighbor calls again to report that now he can see people moving around inside your home.

What would you do? If you couldn't count on the authorities to get to the truth about what is happening at your house, would you jump in your car and return home to get to the bottom of it yourself? Sure you would. That would be a rational response to an apparently real threat to your home.

Now, put yourself into that mindset, only this time your home is the US Capitol building in Washington, DC, and your neighbor is the president of the United States, who is reporting that your country, your democracy, your election are being stolen before your very eyes. This is, in essence, what a great many people believed on January 6, 2021, when they stormed the Capitol to disrupt the Electoral College procedure of confirming Joe Biden as the forty-sixth president of the United States. Clubs were swung, flagpoles were thrust, doors and windows were shattered, and the result was five dead, many more wounded, and considerable property damage, not to mention the psychological scarring of the people inside who feared for their lives and were whisked off to safety.

What drove these protesters to violence? It was the false belief that the 2020 election was stolen from Donald J. Trump (and by proxy, themselves), who in a speech earlier that day had cajoled his supporters to "be strong," "fight like hell," and go over there to "stop the steal," or else "our country will be destroyed, and we're not going to stand for that."[1] Figure P.1 illustrates the power of belief in action.

To what extent President Trump is responsible for the mob actions of his followers is debatable, and at the time of this writing, many of the protesters have been tried, convicted, and imprisoned for insurrection (most of whom were pardoned and released by Trump at the start of his second term). Trump didn't tell the crowd to break into the Capitol, which is protected by police, nor did he direct them to be violent. In fact, at one point in his speech that morning near the Capitol dome, he said, "I know that everyone here will soon be marching over to the Capitol building to peacefully and patriotically make your voices heard." Most free speech scholars I've consulted on the matter tell me that making a legal case for a speech being an "incitement to violence" is difficult to do, as the bar has been set very high through precedence.[2] Nevertheless, it seems evident enough that even with qualifications in Trump's words, it was too little, too late, as he had just spent the previous hour working up the crowd into a fever pitch through his claim that forces inside the Capitol building were stealing the

Figure P.1. Illustration of the power of belief in action on January 6, 2021, with the storming of the United States Capitol. Wikimedia Commons, source DSC09254-2

election and destroying America.[3] What did he think they were going to do? Encircle the Capitol and sing "We Shall Overcome"?

Though we may deplore what happened that day—and there is little doubt that it was one of the most shocking direct assaults on our democracy in US history—when considered from the perspective of the rioters and insurrectionists, their actions were based on a certain logic. If you truly believed that the 2020 election was stolen and that the officials in charge weren't doing anything about it, then it is understandable why you might protest; unfortunately, peaceful protests can easily morph into violent rioting when emotions wrest control from reason. Did these people genuinely believe that the election was rigged and that Trump was the real winner? Most did, yes, and they explained why in their own words while standing in court before a judge at their hearings. If that isn't convincing enough, watch Alexandra Pelosi's HBO series *The Insurrectionist Next Door*, in which several of these guys boast of their bravery for going up against the deep state in defense of their beloved president and, even after serving time in prison, still proclaim, "Trump won!"[4]

Since people often act on their convictions, the truth or falsity of such beliefs matter. Thus, truth matters. In this book, I make the case that science, reason, and empiricism are the best tools we have for getting to the truth. To be sure, in science, there are no Truths with a capital *T*, but that does not mean there are no objective facts or that all opinions are equal. The popular saying that "everything is relative" is false; otherwise, what would be the objective standard by which to assess that everything is relative? The same reasoning applies to the claim that we are living in a post-truth world. That can't be true, because if it were, there would be no method by which to conclude that we're living in a post-truth period. Likewise for fake news: It can't all be fake, for if it were, then we would have no journalistic standards by which to fact-check news claims as true, false, or uncertain. Such assertions are like the liar's paradox: "This sentence is false." If true, then it is false, but it states that it is false, so it must be true, and so on.

■

Truth, the book before you, is about the search for objectivity and what we should believe. There are many different kinds of truths whose outline roughly follows the contents of this book: post-truth truths, how we know what is true, the truths of science and rationality, the truths of religion and spirituality, the truths of mythology and history, the truths of extraterrestrial flying objects and intelligence, the truths of morals and values, and the truths about consciousness, free will, God, and existence.

In the context of recent assaults on truth in the form of populism, postmodernism, and anti-science, we begin in chapter 1 by considering whether we are, in fact, living in a post-truth world of fake news, alternative facts, and anti-science. As I shall argue, we are not. Justified true belief about objective reality is possible, even if it is often obscured by the fog of uncertainty that results from our many biases, expectations, and prejudices. Scientific observations and rational conclusions lead to provisional truths about the world for which we can reach consensus, the subject of chapters 2, 3, and 4, on how to define truth and how to determine it. Here we address the issues of epistemology (the study of how reliable knowledge is established) and ontology (the study of the nature of reality) and what tools scientists and philosophers use to get at the truth about anything. We will consider how scientists and philosophers employ the tools of rationality and empiricism, such as the scientific method, Bayesian reasoning, correlation and causation, signal detection theory, double-blind experiments, randomized controlled trials, natural experiments, and so forth to help us come to some consensus on what is probably true, probably false, or undetermined at this time.

Many miraculous and religious truths, on the other hand, are altogether different from those in science and philosophy, and these we address in chapter 5. There may be religious historical facts, such as whether Jesus of Nazareth was a real person who lived in first-century Rome and was crucified. Most historians accept these assertions as historical truths. The proposition that Jesus died for our sins, by contrast, is a faith-based truth claim with no purchase on valid knowledge. You may accept it as true for you and your faith, whereas, for example, Jews and Muslims do not accept it as true for them and their faiths. There's no experiment we can run or set of propositions for testing whether this claim is "really" true in a scientific sense.

Historical truths, the subject of chapter 6, are yet another area with different methods of establishing justified true belief, because the past already happened, and we cannot reconstruct it in all its richness of causal connections. And the farther back in time we go, the worse this problem becomes. Yet historical truths can be established—indeed, *must* be established—because if they couldn't, then deniers who say the Holocaust never happened would have the same claim to valid truth as historians who assert that it did. And even the most extreme postmodern historical relativists do not concede that point.

Then there are truths related to morals and values—namely, determining right and wrong in some objective sense. Many of these truths are necessarily personal and subjective, and yet, because of human nature, there are some objective truths even in these realms. In chapter 7, I outline my theory propounding that facts and values overlap, that we can derive an *ought* from an *is*—that is, figuring out what we ought to do by studying the way the world is—and that this is the foundation of an objective morality, a science of values.

In chapter 8, we consider the claims by generals, pilots, and government officials that unidentified flying objects, unidentified aerial phenomena, and aliens are true in some objective sense—that is, the search for extraterrestrial intelligence is over because we have made contact. If true, this would be the biggest story of the past millennium, if not of all human history. And, unlike religious and mythic truths, this one could be scientifically true. As a lifelong student of the subject, I must confess that I would *like* it to be true; but is it *in fact* true?

In the final part of the book, chapters 9, 10, 11, and 12, we explore the limits of human knowledge and consider some of the greatest mysteries of all—*consciousness*, *free will*, *God's existence*, and *why there is something rather than nothing*—in the context of our evolved cognitive limitations as bipedal primates living on a single planet in a cosmos so vast and complicated that we have only begun to understand it and ourselves. I am calling these *known unknowables*. The verbiage—and the parts dividing the chapters in this book—was inspired by Secretary of Defense Donald Rumsfeld, who, at a February 12, 2002, news briefing, explained the limitations of intelligence reports: "There are known knowns. There are things we know we know. We also know there are known unknowns. That is to say, we know there are some things we do not know. But there are also unknown unknowns, the ones we don't know we don't know."[5] Rumsfeld's phrasing may be tongue-twisting, but his epistemology was sound enough to make it the subject of a documentary film by Errol Morris called *The Unknown Known*, result in Rumsfeld's memoir being titled *Known and Unknown*, and spark a

Wikipedia page with the heading "There are unknown unknowns."[6] The philosopher Slavoj Žižek added a fourth category—*the unknown known*—or that which we intentionally refuse to acknowledge that we know (lies of omission). The German sociologists Christopher Daase and Oliver Kessler added their own fourth category of "what we do not like to know" (denial).

Here I add a fifth category: *known unknowables*. For centuries, the greatest minds of our species have grappled to gain purchase on the vertiginous ledges of these great mysteries, ascending nowhere near the thin air of their peaks. Unlike other inscrutable problems we have faced, from the small-scale organization of the atom and large-scale structure of the cosmos to the molecular assembly of cells and organs and social aggregation of societies—for which we have made stunning achievements of understanding—these mysteries (*consciousness*, *free will*, *God*, and *existence*) seem to recede ever farther from enlightenment, even as we race ever faster to catch them in our scientific nets. I would like to suggest that there may be some things we can never know unless we ourselves become gods, and this possibility I consider in the epilogue.

■

I end this prologue with an insightful observation of the late Harvard paleontologist and historian of science Stephen Jay Gould, which he made in the foreword to my first book, *Why People Believe Weird Things*:

> Only two possible escapes can save us from the organized mayhem of our dark potentialities—the side that has given us crusades, witch hunts, enslavements, and holocausts. Moral decency provides one necessary ingredient, but not nearly enough. The second foundation must come from the rational side of our mentality. For, unless we rigorously use human reason both to discover and acknowledge nature's factuality, and to follow the logical implications for efficacious human action that such knowledge entails, we will lose out to the frightening

> forces of irrationality, romanticism, uncompromising "true" belief, and the apparent resulting inevitability of mob action. Reason is our potential salvation from the vicious and precipitous mass action that rule by emotionalism always seems to entail. Skepticism is the agent of reason against organized irrationalism—and is therefore one of the keys to human social and civic decency.[7]

Amen, brother.

PART I

KNOWN KNOWNS

■ Thinking is skilled work. It is not true that we are naturally endowed with the ability to think clearly and logically—without learning how, or without practicing. People with untrained minds should no more expect to think clearly and logically than people who have never learned and never practiced can expect to find themselves good carpenters, golfers, bridge players, or pianists.

—**Alfred E. Mander,** *Logic for the Millions*

1

The Truth About Post-Truth Truthiness

Why We Are Not Living in a Post-Truth, Postmodern, Fact-Free World

■ Words embody ideas, and their changing usage and meaning are tracked by lexicographers in dictionaries, which therein become barometers of cultural trends. In 2006, for example, the American Dialect Society and *Merriam-Webster's Dictionary* both chose as their word of the year the neologism *truthiness*, introduced by the comedian Stephen Colbert on the premiere episode of his satirical mock-news show *The Colbert Report* (on which I appeared twice), meaning "the truth we want to exist."[1] It was a prescient comedic bit, as a decade later, three examples of truthiness entered our lexicon.

After Donald Trump's presidential inauguration on January 22, 2017, his special counselor Kellyanne Conway concocted the term *alternative facts* during a *Meet the Press* interview while defending White House Press Secretary Sean Spicer's inaccurate statement about the size of the crowd that day: "Our press secretary, Sean Spicer, gave alternative facts to that [the inaugural crowd size], but the point remains that—" NBC correspondent Chuck Todd cut her off: "Wait a minute. *Alternative facts?* . . . Alternative facts are not facts. They're falsehoods."[2] German linguists deemed it the "un-word of the year" (*Unwort des Jahres*) for 2017. Later that year, the related term *fake news* became common parlance, leaping in usage by 365%

and landing on the "word of the year shortlist" of *Collins Dictionary*, which defined it as "false, often sensational, information disseminated under the guise of news reporting."[3]

Such words (or un-words) are often invoked as evidence that we are living in a "post-truth" era brought on by autocratic populists like Trump (according to liberals) or by postmodern progressives (according to conservatives). Are we living in a post-truth world of truthiness, fake news, and alternative facts? Have the populists and postmodernists won the day? Is all the political, economic, and social progress we have achieved over the past several centuries—the abolition of slavery and torture; the decline of homicide, crime, and violence; the cessation of European Great Powers wars; and the expansion of the moral sphere to include civil rights, women's rights, children's rights, worker's rights, and LGBTQ rights for more people in more places more of the time—being reversed? Are we lurching backward to the Middle Ages, when bigots lighted faggots to torch women as witches?

No. Here's why.

What Is Post-Truth?

For the fall 2019 issue of *Skeptic* magazine, I commissioned a cover story from the Harvard psychologist Steven Pinker, which we titled "Why We Are Not Living in a Post-Truth Era."[4] We had originally planned to pose it in the form of a question, "Are We Living in a Post-Truth Era?," in order to invoke (Ian) Betteridge's law of headlines, which states, "Any headline that ends in a question mark can be answered by the word *no*,"[5] but ultimately decided on the more definitive declarative statement and instead opened the essay with this question: Is the statement "We are living in a post-truth era" true?

If it is, then it isn't! In other words, if you argue that the statement is true, then you are making an argument, which means you are committed to determining whether the statement is true or false, which further means we have not passed into a post-truth world, whether populist or postmodern. Similarly, is the statement "humans are irrational" rational? If it is, then it can't be, because, as Pinker asks rhetorically, "If humans were truly irrational, who specified the benchmark of rationality against which humans don't measure up?"[6] As Pinker noted in his 2018 book *Enlightenment Now*, "Mendacity, truth-shading, conspiracy theories, extraordinary popular delusions, and the madness of crowds are as old as our species, but so is the conviction that some ideas are right and others are wrong."[7]

In the subsequent issue of *Skeptic*, the philosopher of science Lee McIntyre, author of the book *Post-Truth*,[8] challenged Pinker, starting with his own definition of post-truth as the "political subordination of reality," which he ascertains to be "a tactic in the authoritarian toolbox."[9] McIntyre's definition of post-truth is much narrower than the way Pinker and I use the term, confining it as he does to political propaganda and power, which he says "is not meant to convince you, but to show you who's boss."[10] McIntyre references Jason Stanley's book *How Propaganda Works*[11] to explain that the post-truth message is "I am so powerful that I can dominate your reality, and there is nothing you can do about it." To reinforce the political nature of post-truth, McIntyre also invokes the noted historian of fascism Tim Snyder's observation in his 2017 book *On Tyranny* that "post-truth is pre-fascism,"[12] along with Hannah Arendt's observation that "the ideal subject of totalitarian rule is not the convinced Nazi or the convinced communist, but people for whom the distinction between fact and fiction (i.e., the reality of experience) and the distinction between true and false (i.e., the standards of thought) no longer exist."[13]

Post-truth as political propaganda is certainly one use (or misuse) of truth that neither Pinker nor I discount, but McIntyre then accuses Pinker (and others) of merely knocking down one or more of four post-truth straw men: (1) that truth doesn't matter, (2) that no one really cares about truth anymore, (3) that no one can find the truth, and (4) that if we were actually living in a post-truth era, we should just give up. Instead, to steelman the problem (the opposite of a straw-man argument, steel-manning means to address the strongest form of someone's position), McIntyre asserts that "the claim that we live in a post-truth era is properly based on the idea that truth today is under threat."

Is it? There certainly are people who, *pace* Arendt, cannot seem to distinguish between fact and fiction, true and false, and this shortcoming can lead not only to fascism or communism but also to Holocaust denial, evolution denial, climate change denial, vaccine denial, GMO (genetically modified organism) denial, nuclear power denial, and more. But is it actually the case that people cannot discern reality, or is it that they are motivated to spin the facts to support some other agenda, belief system, or ideology? Holocaust deniers are anti-Semites. Evolution deniers are religious fundamentalists. Climate deniers mistrust big government. Vaccine deniers distrust big pharma. GMO deniers detest Monsanto. Nuclear power deniers are politically motivated environmentalists.

In many cases, it isn't the truth about the facts that is under dispute; rather, the contention comes from an underlying motive properly identified by the cognitive psychologist Keith Stanovich as the *myside bias* in his aptly titled book *The Bias That Divides Us*.[14] "Myside bias occurs across a wide variety of judgment domains. It is displayed by people in all demographic groups, and it is exhibited even by expert reasoners, the highly educated and the highly intelligent," Stanovich observes, noting how it has become a modern driver of cultural divisiveness:

> It has been demonstrated in research studies across a variety of disciplines, including: cognitive psychology, political science, behavioral economics, legal studies, cognitive neuroscience, and in the informal reasoning literature. Myside bias has been found to occur in every stage of information processing. That is, studies have shown a tendency toward biased search for evidence, biased evaluation of evidence, biased assimilation of evidence, biased memory of outcomes, and biased evidence generation.[15]

We tend to characterize those who disagree with us as irrational, unreasonable, uneducated, or even ignorant, but note Stanovich's lumping of expert reasoners who are well educated and highly intelligent with those susceptible to the bias. I would go even further, as I did in my book *Why People Believe Weird Things*, by noting that highly intelligent people are even better at rationalizing beliefs that they hold for non-smart reasons.[16] As Stanovich documents, you might be subject to the myside bias if you do any of these: evaluate acts more favorably when they support your group, apply logical rules better when logical conclusions support your strongly held beliefs, search or select information sources that are likely to support your position, de-emphasize the costs of your moral commitments, distort the perception of risk and reward in the direction of your personal preferences, elevate moral principles amenable to your preferred ethical conclusions, selectively learn facts favorable to your political party, resist evidence when it leads to unwanted social changes, interpret facts favorable to your desired group, and question the scientific status of evidence when it challenges what you have already decided must be true.[17] In other words, if you are human.

■ Postmodernism and Its Discontents, or Why Nature Cannot Be Fooled

At 11:39 a.m. on January 28, 1986, 73 seconds into its flight, the Space Shuttle *Challenger* exploded, killing all seven crew members and leading to a cessation of all shuttle launches until the cause could be determined by a commission appointed by President Ronald Reagan that consisted of, among others, famed astronauts and aviators Neil Armstrong, Sally Ride, and Chuck Yeager, generals Donald Kutyna and William Rogers, and scientists Eugene Covert, Arthur Walker, and Richard Feynman. Known for his heterodox thinking and famed for his rebellious nature, Feynman was something of an outsider in this august group, brought in to ensure that bureaucratic rigidity and political groupthink would not blind the commission to the truth of what really happened.

Less than six months later, on June 9, 1986, the commission issued its conclusive finding of an O-ring failure (due to cold temperatures) in the solid rocket booster that had allowed hot pressurized gases to blow through the seal and ignite the chemicals in the adjacent external fuel tank, which resulted in a catastrophic detonation. Despite commission chairman William Rogers's grumbling that "Feynman is becoming a real pain," the theoretical physicist got to the truth with a simple and direct experiment conducted dramatically before cameras during the commission's press conference:

> I took this stuff that I got out of your seal and I put it in ice water, and I discovered that when you put some pressure on it for a while and then undo it, it does not stretch back. It stays the same dimension. In other words, for a few seconds at least and more seconds than that, there is no resilience in this particular material when it is at a temperature of 32 degrees.[18]

Nevertheless, in full self-denial mode, the commission recommended that "NASA [National Aeronautics and Space Administration] continue to receive the support of the administration and the nation" because it "provides a symbol of national pride and technological leadership."[19]

Feynman would have none of this public-relations obfuscation (figure 1.1). In the closing remarks of his contribution to the Rogers Commission Report, "Personal Observations on the Reliability of the Shuttle," Feynman drilled home in epigrammatic poignancy the commitment to reality, however complicated and obscure, that we all must make: "NASA owes it to the citizens from whom it asks support to be frank, honest, and informative, so that these citizens can make the wisest decisions for the use of their limited resources. For a successful technology, reality must take precedence over public relations, for Nature cannot be fooled."[20]

Call it Feynman's principle: *Reality must take precedence, for nature cannot be fooled.*

Feynman did not live long enough (he died in February 1988) to witness a movement that would complicate our understanding of Nature: postmodernism. My first collision with the movement was in a PhD pro-

Figure 1.1. Richard Feynman, a Nobel physicist and member of the presidential commission investigating the *Challenger* accident, performed a demonstration for reporters on February 11, 1986, at a lunchbreak of the commission's meeting in Washington. He put a piece of the shuttle's O-ring in a cup of ice water for a few seconds. This caused, he said, "no resilience in this particular material" when the temperature reached 32 degrees. Tasked with finding the truth about what really caused the shuttle's destruction, Feynman raised the possibility that cold weather prelaunch might have figured in the failure of the seal. AP photo / Scott Stewart. Reprinted with permission of the Associated Press

gram in the history of science in the late 1980s, which was undergoing its own revolution in overturning an earlier model of science as a progressive march toward a complete understanding of Reality in an asymptotic curve to Truth. That model of science is too Whiggish, but in a paroxysm of postmodern deconstruction, philosophers and historians proffered a view of science as a relativistic game played by European white males in a reductionistic frenzy of hermeneutical hegemony, whose ultimate aim was the suppression of the people beneath the thumb of dialectical scientism and technocracy. Yes, they actually speak like this—one even called Isaac Newton's *Principia* a "rape manual." Seriously. Here is the exact quote from the feminist philosopher Sandra Harding: "Why is it not as illuminating and honest to refer to Newton's laws as 'Newton's rape manual' as it is to call them 'Newton's mechanics'?"[21]

By the mid-1990s, postmodernism had filtered out of humanities departments and wafted into some science departments, so we devoted several articles in *Skeptic* to what became known as the "science wars,"[22] which were being fought over the nature of truth and whether science was the royal road to it. Many thought not, coming to believe that there are no privileged truths, no objective reality to be discovered, and no belief, idea, hypothesis, or theory that is closer to the truth than any other.

In 1996, the New York University physicist and mathematician Alan Sokal put an end to this intellectual masturbation with one of the greatest hoaxes in academic history. Sokal penned a nonsensical article titled "Transgressing the Boundaries: Toward a Transformative Hermeneutics of Quantum Gravity,"[23] which was chockablock full of postmodern phrases and deconstructionist tropes interspersed with scientific jargon, and submitted it to the journal *Social Text*, one of two leading publications frequented by fashionably obtuse academics. Here's a sample sentence:

> It has thus become increasingly apparent that physical "reality," no less than social "reality," is at bottom a social and linguistic construct; that scientific "knowledge," far from being objective, reflects and encodes the dominant ideologies and power relations of the culture that produced it; that the truth claims of science are inherently theory-laden and self-referential; and consequently, that the discourse of the scientific community, for all its undeniable value, cannot assert a privileged

> epistemological status with respect to counter-hegemonic narratives emanating from dissident or marginalized communities.[24]

Sokal's article was accepted for publication as "real" (whatever that means in postmodernism). Upon its release, Sokal revealed it was all a hoax, and he did so, deliciously, in the chief competitor of *Social Text*, the journal *Dissent*. Sokal called it a nonsense parody, but because most of what passes for postmodernism is nonsense and indistinguishable from parody, the editors of *Social Text* could not tell the difference.[25]

This challenge to our understanding of truth led to another Sokal-like hoax by the philosopher Peter Boghossian and mathematician James Lindsay in the form of an article titled "The Conceptual Penis as a Social Construct," published in the peer-reviewed journal *Cogent Social Sciences* in 2017.[26] We exposed the hoax in *Skeptic* in order to reveal "the pretentious nonsense that often passes for scholarship in postmodernism studies." The purpose was not, I explained, to fool journal editors but rather to unveil such literary obfuscation for what it is: "pseudo-profound bullshit." This is the apt descriptor of Gordon Pennycook and James Allan Cheyne, which they take to mean saying something that sounds profound but is nonsense.[27]

Countering Postmodernism

The *Oxford English Dictionary* has tracked the use of the term *post-truth* back to 1992, but by 1994, there was already a critical response to postmodernism in Paul Gross and Norman Levitt's book *Higher Superstitions*.[28] And then there were critics of these critics. The philosopher of science Naomi Oreskes, for example, pointed out that "it is not surprising that when scientists were almost exclusively white men, they developed theories about women and African Americans that were at best incomplete and at times pernicious—theories that have now been rejected. Nor is it surprising that many of the logical and empirical flaws of these early theories were pointed out by women and people of color."[29] One of the debunked theories purported to prove that women should not bother pursuing higher education because menstruation redirects blood from the brain, thereby inhibiting cognition.

Thus, viewpoint diversity is crucial to the scientific process in order to identify the many hidden assumptions that culture envelops science in, especially those that engage our unconscious biases and prejudices. "The greater the diversity and openness of a community and the stronger its protocols for supporting free and open debate," Oreskes advises, "the greater the degree of objectivity it may be able to achieve as individual biases and background assumptions are 'outed,' as it were, by the community."[30] Note the process that exposes these shortcomings of science—more and better science: "Put another way, objectivity is likely to be maximized when there are recognized and robust avenues for criticism, such as peer review, when the community is open, non-defensive, and responsive to criticism, and when the community is sufficiently diverse that a broad range of views can be developed, heard, and appropriately considered."[31]

In 2016, Oxford Dictionaries named *post-truth* its word of the year after it documented a 2,000% spike in usage over the previous year, characterizing it as "relating to or denoting circumstances in which objective facts are less influential in shaping public opinion than appeals to emotion and personal belief."[32] But the response to challenges to objective knowledge is as robust today as it was in the past. As dictionaries track the upswing in post-truth language, and as political pundits pronounce the end of truth, the internet of ideas has responded with tools to combat the illiberalism of unreason: real-time fact-checking. As politicians engaged in the old-time art of spin-doctoring the truth in speeches, fact-checkers at OpenSecrets.org, Snopes.com, FactCheck.org, and PolitiFact.com tallied their errors and lies, the latter cheekily ranking statements as *true*, *mostly true*, *half true*, *mostly false*, and *pants on fire*. As PolitiFact's editor Angie Holan explained, "journalists regularly tell me their media organizations have started highlighting fact-checking in their reporting because so many people click on fact-checking stories after a debate or high-profile news event."[33]

The modern idea of fact-checking reaches back nearly a century to when two young journalists, Briton Hadden and Henry Luce, launched a magazine in response to what they saw as the propaganda (defined at the time by newspaper reporter Ivy Lee as "the effort to propagate ideas") of the muckraking journalism of the 1920s. As the journalist Batya Ungar-Sargon documents this history in her 2021 book *Bad News*,[34] the magazine was initially to be called *Facts*, but marketing interests led them to call their new publication *Time*. The periodical allowed busy readers to snack on a hundred short news items from the previous week, many simply cut-and-pasted from other news sources, sorted by subject, and "accurately chronicled." The goal was accuracy, not objectivity. "Show me a man who thinks he's objective, and I'll show you a man who's deceiving himself,"[35] Luce said. Luce insisted that each article be free of errors of fact, leading to the modern practice of fact-checking, initially conducted by young women who were hired straight out of college. As one reporter recalled, "Charged with verifying every word, they put a dot over each one to signify that they" had done so.[36]

Ungar-Sargon also shows how journalism was originally invented to empower the underprivileged and how the media left the poor behind and now caters almost exclusively to the interests of urban, upper-class liberals. She documents, for example, that the *Wall Street Journal* boasts that four out of five of its readers have a bachelor's degree or higher and half are affluent enough to own liquid assets of $1 million or more, while a *New York Times* media kit brags that their readers are "elite," "affluent," and "influential," with a median household income of $191,000. As such, postmodern identity politics has further divided the rich and the poor. The moral panic around race, for example, which is encouraged by today's elite newsrooms, does little more than consolidate the power of liberal elites and protect their economic interests. And in abandoning the working class by creating a culture war around identity, our national media is undermining American democracy, as Ungar-Sargon explains:

> When you define racism as an omnipresent white-supremacist framework baked into the heart of our nation that can never be solved or extracted, you give people a culture war they can hammer away at forever, a perpetual cudgel against those who disagree with them, even if those who disagree with them are less affluent and less fortunate—the losers of the economic and culture war.[37]

■ How Gullible Are We?

Despite the big hullaballoo around it, the idea that post-truthiness is the result of human gullibility is gainsaid through new research by cognitive psychologists, demonstrating that people are not nearly as credulous as many suspect. That is the thesis of *Not Born Yesterday*, in which cognitive scientist Hugo Mercier presents a mountain of evidence "against the idea that humans are gullible, that they are 'wired not to seek truth' and 'overly deferential to authority,' and that they 'cower before uniform opinion,'" quoting Jason Brennan in his book *Against Democracy*. In fact, Mercier reveals through lab research and real-world examples that "far from being gullible, we are endowed with a suite of cognitive mechanisms that evaluate what we hear or read." And, Mercier notes, rather than believing everything we hear, "by default we veer on the side of being resistant to new ideas. In the absence of the right cues, we reject messages that don't fit with our preconceived views or preexisting plans. To persuade us otherwise takes long-established, carefully maintained trust, clearly demonstrated expertise, and sound arguments."[38]

Mercier notes, for example, that mass persuasion is extremely difficult to pull off, and most attempts at it fail miserably, because the trust cues that are relied on in two-person communication do not scale up accordingly with large audiences. Despite such poignant and tragic examples of cult vulnerability as the mass suicide/murder cases of Jim Jones's Jonestown, Marshall Applewhite's Heaven's Gate, and David Koresh's Branch Davidians, the vast majority of people exposed to the come-ons of cult leaders and their minions do not join, or if they do, they don't give away all their possessions or drink the Kool-Aid. (The now-common idiom "drink the Kool-Aid" is a misnomer, as the Jonestown members imbibed grape Flavor Aid, poisoned with cyanide, among other deadly drugs—figure 1.2.)

Think of the tens of thousands of religious sects, community groups, and self-help movements that never turn cultish; even with the few that do, most members get out before it's too late. Or recall the tens of thou-

Figure 1.2. On November 18, 1978, more than 900 people died in Jonestown, Guyana, many from cyanide poisoning. Some were injected against their will, but many willingly imbibed the grape-flavored deadly concoction. The consequences of belief were never more evidently on display. Wikimedia Commons, file name Jonestown, Guyana bodies.jpg

sands of cons and frauds thrust upon us since the rise of the internet, such as Nigerian spam scams, car warranty scams, holiday scams, disaster scams, IRS scams, identity scams, real estate scams, gift card scams, catphishing scams, kidnapped grandchild scams, credit scams, and emails that promise untold riches for some personal information. They all depend on the law of large numbers in which even a tiny fraction of suckers generates a sizable payoff if hundreds of millions of people are targeted.[39] Most preachers, prophets, and demagogues fail, but because of the availability bias, we only remember the biggest names in the genre, such as Jesus and Hitler.

Even these two prominent examples fail upon further inspection. In his own time, Jesus was a disappointment at starting a new religion (which might not have been his mission in any case), and the apostle Paul barely got Christianity rolling. It wasn't until the fourth century that the number of Christians reached the millions, which sounds impressive until we consider the power of compound interest, in which a small but steady growth can yield an enormous figure given enough time. Invest one dollar at a constant yearly interest rate of 1% in year 0; if the dividends are reinvested, by the year 2020, the investment would be worth over $2.4 billion. Mercier cites statistics compiled by the sociologist of religion Rodney Stark, who estimates Christianity's growth rate at 3.5% over the centuries. If each Christian only saves a few souls in a lifetime, the religion could compile tens of millions of members in a matter of a few centuries and over two billion by today.

As for Hitler, I have spent much of my career trying to understand how a nation of educated, enlightened, and cultured people could be brainwashed into becoming goose-stepping Nazis in a matter of a few years. Compelling evidence shows that most Germans, in fact, *did not fully accept Nazi ideology* or many of the planks in the regime's platform, especially its militarist and exterminationist policies. We now know that most of Hitler's military leaders did not want war in 1939 and warned their führer that they would be unprepared if other nations fought back ferociously. The euthanasia of the disabled in the 1930s was resisted by most Germans and got so much bad press that the Nazis made the program secret and issued orders to never speak of it, a policy carried through the Final Solution and the Holocaust, which was shrouded in secrecy and mostly carried out in Poland, far from the prying eyes of German citizens, the church, and what little media remained. Hitler's anti-communism appealed to right-leaning Germans but was rejected among industrial workers. By 1942, most citizens did not believe the declarations of victory issued by the propaganda minister Joseph Goebbels, instead relying on secreted BBC reports of how the war was really going for Germany (not well). As the Nazi intelligence agency Sicherheitsdienst reported: "Our propaganda encounters rejection everywhere among the population because it is regarded as wrong and lying."[40]

The entire Nazi regime—not unlike the Soviet Union and North Korea—was held aloft by a psychological concept called *pluralistic ignorance*, in which most individual members of a group don't believe something but assume that the majority of others in the group do. When no one speaks up—or when people are prevented from speaking up through everything from cancel culture to state-sponsored censorship and imprisonment—a *spiral of silence* is produced that can transmogrify into witch hunts, purges, pogroms, and repressive political regimes.[41] Figure 1.3 captures the phenomenon visually in the form of a Nazi rally that was carefully orchestrated to produce mass compliance.

Pluralistic ignorance explains European witch hunts, for example, which degenerated into preemptive accusations of guilt lest one be thought guilty first, so no one dared to come to the defense of the defenseless. Oppressive dictatorships are often maintained through enforced—and even self-enforced—silence, as in this account from Aleksandr Solzhenitsyn's *The Gulag Archipelago* in which a district party conference was underway in Moscow, at the conclusion of which "a tribute to Comrade Stalin was called for," leading everyone to leap to their feet as they had done "during the conference at every mention of his name." Here's what happened next:

> For three minutes, four minutes, five minutes, the "stormy applause, rising to an ovation," continued. But palms were getting sore and

Figure 1.3. "Reich Party Rally of Unity and Strength." Roll call of the SA and SS, paramilitary organizations, with Adolf Hitler, Viktor Lutze, and Heinrich Himmler, September 5–10, 1934, in Nuremberg, Germany. Such scenes well represent the type specimen of belief conformity. Wikimedia Commons, Bundesarchiv, Bild 102-04062A / Georg Pahl / CC-BY-SA 3.0

> raised arms were already aching. And the older people were panting from exhaustion. It was becoming insufferably silly even to those who really adored Stalin. However, who would dare be the first to stop? The secretary of the District Party Committee could have done it. He was standing on the platform, and it was he who had just called for the ovation. But he was a newcomer. He had taken the place of a man who'd been arrested. He was afraid! After all, NKVD [Narodnyy Komissariat Vnutrennikh Del] men were standing in the hall applauding and watching to see who quit first! . . . the applause went on—six, seven, eight minutes! . . . The director of the local paper factory, an independent and strong-minded man, stood with the presidium. Aware of all the falsity and all the impossibility of the situation, he still kept on applauding! Nine minutes! Ten! . . . With make-believe enthusiasm on their faces, looking at each other with faint hope, the district leaders were just going to go on and on applauding till they fell where they stood, till they were carried out of the hall on stretchers! . . . Then, after eleven minutes, the director of the paper factory assumed a businesslike expression and sat down in his seat.[42]

That man was subsequently arrested and sent to the gulag for a decade.

To break a spiral of ignorance, two elements are necessary: knowledge and communication. This is why totalitarian and theocratic regimes restrict speech, press, trade, and travel and why the route to breaking the bonds of such repressive governments and ideologies is the spread of liberal democracy, open borders, and free speech, press, trade, and travel. In this context, Pinker agrees with Mercier when he notes that it won't do "to write off humans as hopelessly irrational." Why?

> Just as our foraging ancestors lived by their wits in unforgiving ecosystems, today's conspiracy theorists and miracle-believers pass the demanding tests of their own worlds: they hold down jobs, bring up kids, and keep a roof over their heads and food in the fridge. . . . To understand popular delusions and the madness of crowds, we have to

> examine cognitive faculties that work well in some environments and for some purposes but that go awry when applied at scale, in novel circumstances, or in the service of other goals.[43]

Here, Pinker draws a distinction between what he calls "the reality mindset" and "the mythology mindset." The former consists of the physical objects around us, people in our lives, our memories of our interactions with others, and so forth. People are reasonably rational in this zone, Pinker says, because "that's the only way to keep gas in the car, money in the bank, and the kids clothed and fed." The mythology mindset, however, is beyond the reach of most of us—"the remote past, the unknowable future, faraway peoples and places, remote corridors of power, the microscopic, the cosmic, the counterfactual, the metaphysical." Most of us simply have no way of fact-checking claims made in these realms, "and anyway it makes no discernible difference to their lives. Beliefs in these zones are narratives, which may be entertaining or inspiring or morally edifying. Whether they are 'true' or 'false' is the wrong question. The function of these beliefs is to construct a social reality that binds the tribe or sect and gives it a moral purpose."[44]

I share Pinker's commitment to what he calls *universal realism*—a mindset honored by most scientists, rationalists, and skeptics that the best approach toward understanding the real world and justifying true beliefs about it is to make a commitment to its existence and then apply the methods of science and rationality to understand it. But for the vast sweep of human history, there were no tools for determining the difference between reality and mythology, between empirical truths and mythic truths. So, in accordance with our motivated reasoning toward our myside preferences, we default to believing whatever we *want* to be true and real.

In this sense, the philosopher Daniel DeNicola insists, "you don't have a right to believe whatever you want to."[45] Many beliefs are factive—that is, they are taken to be true—and a great many are morally repugnant, such as those that are racist, sexist, or homophobic. Such beliefs, DeNicola explains, are "often more like states of mind or attitudes than decisive actions" and as such are "not deliberately chosen; they are 'inherited' from parents and 'acquired' from peers, acquired inadvertently, inculcated by institutions and authorities, or assumed from hearsay." Thus, we need not withhold our judgment of the verisimilitude of, say, "the belief that one race is less than fully human" because it "is not only a morally repugnant, racist tenet; it is also thought to be a false claim."[46] This, as I discuss in chapter 7, is an argument for moral realism.

Factiness

In one of my final *Scientific American* columns, I coined my own neologism in the Colbert tradition: *factiness*, or *the quality of something seeming to be factual when it is not*.[47] But how do we know when something is factual and not factiness? We use science and reason. This is why science employs the process of peer review, and while imperfect at catching errors, detecting fraud, and weeding out bad ideas, it is still a self-correcting mechanism that works most of the time. It also motivates scientists to go the extra mile to ensure accuracy and honesty. If you don't catch the flaws in your theory, the slant in your bias, or the distortion in your preferences, someone else will, usually with great glee and in a public forum such as a competing journal. Since they're human, scientists are biased, of course, but science itself, for all its flaws, is still the best system ever devised for understanding how the world works. There is progress in science, and some views really are superior to others, regardless of the color, gender, or country of origin of the scientist holding that view. Despite the fact that scientific data are, in the jargon of postmodernism, "theory laden," science is different from art, music, literature, religion, myth, and other forms of human expression because of the self-correcting machinery built into it.

The post-Enlightenment ideal that beliefs should be tested in the laboratory and marketplace of ideas with the goal of generating objective and disinterested knowledge may seem Sisyphean—we are always in danger of backsliding into truthiness and factiness in which propaganda, superstition, and self-serving sophistry can slow our progress in pushing the boulder of knowledge up the mountain of ignorance—but that is precisely what we've been doing for millennia, and if we continue to do so, there is no telling where it may lead us.

Per aspera ad astra—with difficulty to the stars.

2

What Is Truth, Anyway? Justified True Belief, the Principle of Universal Realism, and Why Extraordinary Claims Require Extraordinary Evidence

Let's begin our journey toward finding truth with a few questions that will give an idea of some of the claims I examine in this book:

- Do you believe global warming is real?
- Do you believe in the germ theory of disease?
- Do you believe face masks work and should be mandated?
- Do you believe Jesus was resurrected?
- Do you believe the Holocaust happened?
- Do you believe there are objective morals and values in life?

As a public intellectual who engages in debates and conversations on a wide range of subjects, I am often asked questions such as these, which I found puzzling until I figured out that my interlocutors were confusing the meaning of beliefs and facts. For example, I don't "believe in" the germ theory of disease. I accept it as factually true, and as we've seen in the recent pandemic, a germ like the SARS-CoV-2 virus is not something to believe in or disbelieve in. It simply is a matter of fact and can cause a deadly disease like COVID-19. Whether or not vaccines and masks slow its spread is also a factual question that science, at least in principle, can answer, although whether vaccines and masks should be mandated by law is a political matter that differs from scientific questions. But asking you if you "believe in" the SARS-CoV-2 virus would be like asking you if you "believe in" gravity. Gravity is just a brute fact of nature. It's not something to believe or disbelieve. As the science fiction author Philip K. Dick famously quipped, "Reality is that which, when you stop believing in it, doesn't go away."[1]

■ Objective Truths and Justified True Belief

As the publisher of *Skeptic* magazine, I'm often asked, "What is a skeptic, anyway?"[2] According to the *Oxford English Dictionary*, a *skeptic* is "one who holds that there are no adequate grounds for certainty as to the truth of any proposition whatsoever."[3] This is too nihilistic. There are many propositions for which there is adequate evidence to be justified in believing they are true. I will refer to these as *objective truths* or *external truths*. Here are three examples:

- The Dow Jones Industrial Average closed at 44,544.66 on the final day of January 2025. This is true. I just looked it up.
- Dinosaurs went extinct around 65 million years ago. This is true by verification and replication of radiometric dating techniques for volcanic eruptions above and below dinosaur fossils. Since each layer can be accurately dated (within a narrow error bar window range), we infer that the age of a fossil falls between these two dates. Above the strata dated 65 million years ago, there are no more dinosaurs. Ergo, we can assert with a high degree of confidence that this is an objective fact, and we can be satisfied with the truth of the proposition that dinosaurs went extinct around 65 million years ago, unless and until new data emerge.[4]
- Our universe came into existence at the Big Bang. This is true based on the convergence of evidence of a wide range of phenomena such as the cosmic microwave background, the abundance of light ele-

> ments like hydrogen and helium, the distribution of galaxies and the large-scale structure of the cosmos, the redshift of most galaxies that indicates they are all moving away from one another in a way that resembles a giant explosion, and the expansion of space-time itself that resulted from such a big bang, leading to the accelerating expanding cosmos we see today.[5]

These propositions are "true" in the sense that the evidence is so substantial that it would be unreasonable to withhold our provisional assent. At the same time, it's not impossible, for example, that the dinosaurs went extinct recently, just after the creation of the universe some 10,000 years ago (as young Earth creationists assert). But this proposition is so unlikely, so completely lacking in evidence, and so evidently grounded in a religious truth claim that we need not waste our time considering it any further (the debate about the age of the Earth was resolved over a century ago). Thus we have scientific truth:

> *A scientific truth is a claim for which the evidence is so substantial that it is rational to offer one's provisional assent.*

Provisional is the key word here. Scientific truths are temporary and could change with changing evidence. *Provisional* truths differ from *proofs*, as in mathematics (for example, in Euclidean geometry, the sum of the internal angles of a triangle is always equal to 180 degrees). Nor are scientific truths the same as logical inferences, or *analytic truths*, as in the famous syllogism "All men are mortal. Socrates is a man. Socrates is mortal." Does a proposition have to be proven before we can believe it? Here, if by proof one means an analytic truth claim (such as "Cardiologists are doctors"), then yes, one should believe it—you only need to know what the words mean. If by proof one means a *synthetic truth* claim (such as "Cardiologists are rich"), then income and wealth data would need to be checked to determine if it is true, and the more that the information gathered supports that claim, the more one should believe it (and vice versa).

The late philosopher Daniel Dennett's distinction between analytic truths (those "grounded in meanings independently of matters of fact") and synthetic truths (those "grounded in fact") is instructive. For example, mathematical sentences such as "2 + 2 = 4" are, says Dennett, "*a priori*, necessarily true, and their truth could be determined by an *analysis* of the meanings of the terms in them, without any need to get out of one's armchair and conduct an empirical investigation." By contrast, Dennett continues, "other true sentences, such as 'There is cheese on the plate,' are *a posteriori*, or *synthetic*: you had to look to the world to see if they were true."[6]

The model for my definition of truth comes from the late Harvard paleontologist and historian of science Stephen Jay Gould, who, in a widely cited essay, "Evolution as Fact and Theory," states that "facts and theories are different things, not rungs in a hierarchy of increasing certainty. Facts are the world's data. Theories are structures of ideas that explain and interpret facts." After noting that facts do not cease to exist while scientists debate which theory best explains them ("apples did not suspend themselves in mid-air" while scientists grappled with Einstein's modification of Newton's theory of gravity), Gould adds that scientists "make no claim for perpetual truth" because "in science, 'fact' can only mean '*confirmed to such a degree that it would be perverse to withhold provisional assent.*' I suppose that apples might start to rise tomorrow, but the possibility does not merit equal time in physics classrooms."[7]

What we're after here is *knowledge*, which philosophers traditionally define as *justified true belief*.[8] That is, we want to know what is *actually* true, not just what we *want* to believe is true. But which of the three components of this definition of knowledge is most important—*justified*, *true*, or *belief*—is a contentious issue in epistemology, the branch of philosophy that examines knowledge and how we obtain it. The philosopher Edmund Gettier, for example, in a highly influential 1963 paper, pointed out that people could think they have good reasons for their belief (*justified*), think their belief is correct (*true*), and actually believe it (*belief*) but be right accidentally.[9] For example, mentalists (magicians who appear to read people's minds) tell me that as they're performing their cold reading of strangers (asking a lot of questions and making a lot of statements that are true for most people), they occasionally get accidental hits ("How did you know that my late grandfather gave me a white car for my birthday?"). Thus, the verisimilitude of the *facts* of the knowledge claim matter. Being right by accident does not constitute justified true belief.

Even justification-first epistemology has been challenged by philosophers; for example, Timothy Williamson, in *Knowledge and Its Limits*, replaces it with knowledge-first epistemology, best understood "as a state of mind" that is both reliably constructed and supported by evidence. "A state of a mind is a mental state of a subject," Williamson explains, paradigmatic examples of which "include love, hate, pleasure, and pain. Moreover, they include attitudes to propositions: believing that something is so, conceiving that it is so, hoping or fearing that it is so, wondering whether it is so, intending or desiring it to be so."[10] Okay, but the problem is that our states of mind are often wrong, do not correspond to reality, and are products of misperceptions, misunderstandings, biases, heuristics, deceptions, and self-deceptions.

The larger problem is that none of us are omniscient. If there is an omniscient God (I have my doubts), it's not me, and it's also not you. Or, in the secular equivalent, there is objective reality, but I don't know what it is, and neither do you. In his book *Rationality*, Steven Pinker draws the conclusion from this set of assumptions, starting with the epistemic humility that none of us knows for sure what is true (called *fallibilism*): "Perfect rationality and objective truth are aspirations that no mortal can ever claim to have attained. But the conviction that they are out there licenses us to develop rules we can all abide by that allow us to approach truth collectively in ways that are impossible for any of us individually."[11]

Once we agree that there is objective truth out there to be discovered and that none of us knows for certain what it is, we need to work together through open dialogue in communities of reality-based truth-seekers to figure it out, starting by acknowledging our shortcomings as finite, fallible beings subject to all the cognitive biases that come bundled with our reasoning capacities. As Charles Mackay observed in his 1852 classic book *Extraordinary Popular Delusions and the Madness of Crowds*, "When men wish to construct or support a theory, how they torture facts into their service!"[12]

■ Subjective Truths

In addition to objective truths that can be externally validated, there are *subjective truths* that are internally validated—that is, they are based on personal tastes or preferences and are not subject to external validation. For example, I think that dark chocolate is better than milk chocolate. But maybe you think milk chocolate is better than dark chocolate. Who's right? Neither of us, in any objective truth sense. Or let's say that I think "Stairway to Heaven" is the greatest rock song of all time (typical baby boomer preference, with "Free Bird" a close second), but maybe a Gen Xer would prefer Nirvana's "Smells Like Teen Spirit," a Millennial the Back Street Boys' "Larger Than Life" or Lady Gaga's "Born This Way," or a Gen Zer anything by Adele or Taylor Swift.

There is no right answer here because the "truth" about these assertions is subjective and personal for each of us. There is no way to determine which song—or musical genre for that matter—is "truly" the best. While some music afficionados insist that classical music is objectively better than, say, rock 'n' roll, it is hardly fair to the genius composers and singer-songwriters of the past half century to allocate them to second-class musical citizenship because they didn't happen to be born centuries ago.

■ From Subjective to Objective Truths

Then there are *subjective truths that may become objective truths*. For example, consider the statement "Meditation works for me because it makes me feel better." That's a subjective internal truth. Now consider the proposition "Meditation works." This statement implies more than just "it works for me" or "it works for you." The assertion is that it works for everyone or for some percentage of the population under certain specified conditions. This can be verified through quantitative measures, such as changes in heart rate, blood pressure, stress hormones, or subjective pain levels before and after meditation, and these measurements can then be taken for hundreds or thousands of people with the goal of observing a general effect. If we find evidence that it works—for example, if we can say that "meditation works" for X% of people who use it for Y number of minutes per day, Z days per week—this claim may shift from subjective to objective truth.

By way of example, the consciousness researcher and meditation guru Deepak Chopra has devoted considerable time and resources trying to demonstrate empirically that meditation works in an objective sense. In 2016, for example, Chopra opened his California center to scientists from Harvard Medical School, University of California–San Francisco, and the Icahn School of Medicine at Mount Sinai to run an experiment on the effects of meditation on a number of health measures, including aging biomarkers, stress indicators, and general biological processes, along with self-reports of well-being. At his La Costa Resort and Spa,[13] healthy women aged 30 to 60 were randomly assigned to one of two groups—vacation only (n = 31) and novice meditation (n = 33)—and these were compared to a third group of experienced meditators (n = 30) who were already enrolled for the six-day stay at the facility. Predictably, all three groups "felt greater vitality and decreased distress" (predictably, after six days at a posh five-star resort) and showed immediate impact on molecular networks associated with stress and immune pathways. The research team also examined 20,000 genes to determine which changed before and after the resort stay. *Results*: Both intensive meditation and a relaxing vacation led to beneficial changes in gene networks involved with stress and inflammation, but a week of intense meditation led to additional beneficial changes in gene expression and age-related proteins not observed in the other groups. Compared to the vacationers, novice meditators had beneficial changes in

Alzheimer's-related markers and maintained their lower stress levels a month later.[14]

While there is some debate among scientists about to what extent objective truth claims can be made for the salubrious effects of practices like meditation, the point here is that there are methods to move from subjective to objective truths, and I applaud medical practitioners like Chopra for at least aiming for objectivity in their claims.

■ Sagan's Dragon

The general principle here is that for us to have confidence in the truth value of any claim, there must be a source of *external validation* so that it can be treated as an objective truth. Otherwise, it's just personal taste, opinion, or feeling. Without some form of external validation, knowledge becomes unjustified belief. Here is how my undergraduate philosophy professor Richard Hardison explained the problem:

> The goals of a society that you have valued, and the achievements of the people that you have respected, have depended on objectivity. Even the occasional mystic who impressed you, stepped out of his mysticism when he made the analysis that you read. His very communication, by the nature of communication, was objective. Mystical "truths" by their very nature, must be solely personal. They can have no possible external validation. Nor can they produce any possible communication with those who do not share the particular mysticism. There is a fundamental flaw in all mysticisms: the mystic often seeks external support of his position and in the process, denies his mysticism.[15]

My favorite example of the need for external validation to justify true belief comes from the late astronomer Carl Sagan, in his 1996 book, *The Demon-Haunted World: Science as a Candle in the Dark*.[16] I call it *Sagan's dragon*. It's a thought experiment. Here's how I present it:

Imagine that I tell you that I have a dragon in my garage. Would you like to see it?

Sure you would! Who wouldn't? Dragons are popular in works of fiction, so wouldn't it be exciting if it turned out that dragons are real?

But you need evidence to believe, so you ask to see this dragon.

I eagerly oblige by taking you to my garage and opening the door. You look inside and see some boxes, paint cans, a ladder, a bicycle and other knickknacks, but no dragon. You ask, "Where's the dragon?"

I reply, "Oh, this is an invisible dragon."

An "invisible dragon?" you respond skeptically.

Perhaps there's a way to get around the dragon's invisibility, you suggest, by sprinkling flour on the floor of the garage so that when the invisible dragon walks around, its footprints will become apparent. This would provide empirical evidence in support of a potentially objective truth about the existence of dragons.

"That won't work," I explain, "because this invisible dragon hovers a foot above the ground."

"An invisible hovering dragon?" You raise your eyebrows in doubt. You then suggest that we get one of those portable thermometers everyone has been using during the pandemic and measure the temperature at different places in the garage to detect the dragon's body heat.

"Sorry," I reply, "but this is a cold-blooded dragon. It doesn't give off any heat."

"Let me get this straight," you groan in exasperation. "This dragon of yours is invisible, can levitate, and gives off no heat whatsoever. What about the fire it breathes? Surely our thermometer can detect the hot fire from a fire-breathing dragon?"

"Actually," I say, "this dragon breathes cold-fire, a little-known phenomenon vouchsafed only to this particular species of dragon." By now, you are understandably frustrated and ask me in a challenging voice: "What's the difference between an invisible, levitating, cold-blooded, cold-fire-breathing, undetectable dragon . . . and *no dragon at all?*"

The answer is none. *There is no difference between an invisible, levitating, cold-blooded, cold-fire-breathing, undetectable dragon . . . and no dragon at all.* And that's the point.

We should be skeptical of anyone who claims to believe in something that cannot, even in principle, be tested or for which there is no evidence. When someone tells you a fantastic story or proclaims some (literally) unbelievable truth claim, try asking these questions: What would it take to falsify your claim? How could we test that assertion? What evidence would get you to change your mind? If they don't have a good answer—or if they have no answer at all—then it is reasonable to withhold your provisional assent and assume this is a subjective truth claim, or worse, an outright fabrication. If no evidence whatsoever is on offer, you can invoke what I call *Hitchens's dictum*, after the late journalist and writer Christopher Hitchens:[17]

> *What can be asserted without evidence can also be dismissed without evidence.*

■ The ECREE Principle

In his 1980 television series *Cosmos*, in the episode on the possibility of extraterrestrial intelligence existing somewhere in the galaxy or of aliens having visited Earth, Sagan popularized a principle about proportioning one's beliefs to the evidence when he pronounced that "extraordinary claims require extraordinary evidence."[18] The ECREE principle, now sometimes called *Sagan's standard*, was first articulated in the eighteenth century by the Scottish Enlightenment philosopher David Hume, who wrote in his 1748 *An Enquiry Concerning Human Understanding*: "A wise man proportions his belief to the evidence."[19] Hume's contemporary, Pierre-Simon Laplace, put it this way: "The weight of evidence for an extraordinary claim must be proportioned to its strangeness."[20]

ECREE means that an ordinary claim requires only ordinary evidence, but an extraordinary claim requires extraordinary evidence. Let me provide a quotidian example. I once took a road trip from my home in Southern California to the Esalen Institute on the Pacific Coast Highway in Big Sur in Northern California, home of all things New Age and Self-Empowerment. To get there, I took the 210 Freeway north to the 118 Freeway north to the 101 Freeway north to Santa Barbara, where I picked up Highway 154 to Los Olivos, where I hopped back on the 101 Freeway and continued north to San Luis Obispo, where I exited to Highway 1 and followed the Pacific Coast Highway north through Cambria, San Simeon, and Ragged Point until arriving at the storied home of the 1960s Human Potential Movement. Weirdly, just past Ragged Point, a bright light hovered over my car. Thinking it was a police helicopter, I pulled over to the side of the road, fearful that I had been busted for speeding (which I am wont to do). But it wasn't the cops. It was the aliens, and they abducted me into their mothership and whisked me off to the Pleiades star cluster, where their home planet is located. There, I met extraterrestrial beings who gave me a message to take back to Earth: We must stop global warming and nuclear proliferation . . . or else.

Now, which part of this story triggers your insistence on additional evidence? That's obvious. My claim to have driven on California highways is ordinary and calls for only ordinary evidence (in this case, you can just take my word for it), but my claim to have been abducted by aliens and rocketed off to their Pleiadian home planet is extraordinary, and unless I can provide extraordinary evidence—like an instrument from the dashboard of the alien spaceship or one of the aliens themselves—you should be skeptical.

ECREE also suggests that belief is not an either-or on-off switch. It is not a discrete state of belief or disbelief but a continuum on which you can place confidence in a belief according to the evidence—more evidence, more confidence; less evidence, less confidence (more on this in the next chapter dealing with Bayesian reasoning). Consider the extraordinary claim that another bipedal primate called Big Foot, or Yeti, or Sasquatch survives somewhere on Earth. That would be quite extraordinary, because after centuries of searching for such a creature, none have been found. Before we assent to such a claim, we need extraordinary evidence, in this case a type specimen—what biologists call a *holotype*—in the form of an actual body. Blurry photographs, grainy videos, and stories about spooky things that happen at night when people are out camping do not constitute extraordinary evidence—they are barely even ordinary evidence—so it is reasonable for us to withhold our provisional assent. In the meantime, it is always acceptable to say "I don't know," "I could be wrong," or "I'll change my mind when the evidence changes."

Negative Truths and the Burden of Proof

In addition to objective and subjective truths, there are *negative truths*, or claims for which *the absence of evidence is evidence of absence*—that is, when the nonexistence of something is the truth. For example, I am often asked if I "believe" in aliens or Big Foot. My response is usually along these lines: "Show me the body and I'll believe, otherwise I remain skeptical." At this point, a lot of people will say, "Can you prove Big Foot *doesn't* exist?" or "Can you prove that aliens *aren't* out there somewhere?" Setting aside the philosophical problem of proving a negative, my answer to such questions is no, but the *burden of proof* is not on the skeptic of the claim; it is on the claimant to bring forth evidence in support of the claim. For all I know, Big Foot is stomping around the hinterlands of the Himalayas or aliens are zipping around the Milky Way galaxy even as I write these words. But I'm not the one making the claim, so it's not up to me to disprove it—thus, the *burden of proof principle* applies—and in any case, this couldn't be done unless you searched every square foot of Earth or every star system in the galaxy. Likewise, when dealing with conspiracy theory claims, I cannot prove that 9/11 was *not* an inside job, or that JFK was *not* assassinated by a cabal, or that the government is *not* hiding UFOs and alien bodies at Area 51, but the burden of proof is on conspiracists making positive assertions of such conspiracy theories, not on me to disprove their claims.[21]

Such negative truths can be additionally revealing for claimants considering that if a claim is true, then we should expect certain things to follow. For example, I find it telling that among millions of top-secret government emails, documents, and files leaked through Wikileaks, the declassification of documents, and Freedom of Information Act documents, there is not one mention of a UFO cover-up, aliens at Area 51, a faked moon landing, the CIA's involvement in the assassination of JFK, MLK Jr., or RFK, or 9/11 being an inside job by the Bush administration. Here, the absence of evidence *is evidence of absence*, and so it would be reasonable to either reject the claim outright or at the very least withhold our provisional assent unless and until extraordinary evidence for it emerges.

Impediments to Truth and How to Overcome Them

As with any human trait, there is great variation in reasoning, and there are numerous impediments to the search for truth, including logical fallacies and cognitive biases. Under the rubric of motivated reasoning, there are many biases out there:[22]

> *confirmation bias, hindsight bias, myside bias, self-justification bias, attribution bias, sunk-cost bias, endowment effect, status-quo bias, framing effects, anchoring bias, representative bias, authority bias, bandwagon effect, believability bias, clustering illusion, confabulation bias, consistency bias, expectation bias, false consensus effect, halo effect, herd bias, attentional blindness, and blind-spot bias, in which people can be trained to identify all these biases in other people but can't seem to see the log in their own eye.*

Under the many ways thinking goes wrong, I have warned about these:[23]

> *emotive words and false analogies, ad ignorantiam, ad hominem, tu quoque, hasty generalization, overreliance on authorities, either-or,*

> *circular reasoning, reductio ad absurdum and the slippery slope, post hoc ergo propter hoc and after-the-fact reasoning, why anecdotes are not data, why scientific language by itself does not make a science, why bold statements do not make claims true, why heresy does not equal correctness, why rumors do not equal reality, and why the unexplained is not necessarily the inexplicable.*

With such listicles of cognitive biases and logical fallacies identified by philosophers and psychologists, it's a wonder we can think at all. But we can and do, through experience, education, and instruction in the art and science of thinking. What follows are some of the methods developed by philosophers and psychologists to identify and work around all these impediments to the search for truth.

Practice Active Open-Mindedness

In his research on how people fail to solve problems and determine truth, the psychologist Barry Singer found that when people are given the task of selecting the right answer to a problem by being told whether particular guesses are right or wrong, they:

- Immediately form a hypothesis and look only for examples to confirm it.
- Do not seek evidence to disprove the hypothesis.
- Are very slow to change the hypothesis even when it is obviously wrong.
- If the information is too complex, adopt overly simple hypotheses or strategies for solutions.
- If there is no solution, if the problem is a trick and "right" and "wrong" are given at random, form hypotheses about coincidental relationships they observed. Causality is always found.[24]

In their book *Superforecasting: The Art and Science of Prediction*, Philip Tetlock and Dan Gardner document how bad most people are at making predictions and what skill sets those who are good at it employ.[25] They begin with the results of extensive testing of people's predictions. It's not good. Even most so-called experts were no better than dart-tossing monkeys when their predictions were checked. When asked to make specific predictions—for example, "Will another country exit from the EU in the next two years?" and, presciently, "Will Russia annex additional Ukraine territory in the next three months?"—and their prognosticating feet were held to the empirical fire, most experts, Tetlock and Gardner found, were overconfident (after all, they're *experts*), encouraged by the lack of feedback on their accuracy (if no one reminds you of your misses, you'll only remember the hits—the *confirmation bias*), and are victims of all the cognitive biases and illusions that plague the rest of us.

The worst forecasters were people with big ideas—grand theories about how the world works—such as left-wing pundits predicting class warfare that never came or right-wing commentators prophesizing a socialistic demise of the free enterprise system that never happened. Failed predictions are hand-waved away—"This means nothing!"; "Just you wait!" Superforecasters, by contrast, practice *active open-mindedness*, which Tetlock and Gardner defined quantitatively by asking experts "Do you agree or disagree with the following statements?" Superforecasters were more likely to agree that:

- People should take into consideration evidence that goes against their beliefs.
- It is more useful to pay attention to those who disagree with you than to pay attention to those who agree.
- Even major events like World War II or 9/11 could have turned out very differently.
- Randomness is often a factor in our personal lives.

Superforecasters were more likely to disagree that:

- Changing your mind is a sign of weakness.
- Intuition is the best guide in making decisions.

- It is important to persevere in your beliefs even when evidence is brought to bear against them.
- Everything happens for a reason.
- There are no accidents or coincidences.

The psychologist Gordon Pennycook and his colleagues developed their own instrument of measuring active open-mindedness. They asked people whether they agreed or disagreed with the following statements; the more open-minded answer is indicated in parentheses:[26]

- Beliefs should always be revised in response to new information or evidence. (agree)
- People should always take into consideration evidence that goes against their beliefs. (agree)
- I believe that loyalty to one's ideals and principles is more important than "open-mindedness." (disagree)
- No one can talk me out of something I know is right. (disagree)
- Certain beliefs are just too important to abandon no matter how good a case can be made against them. (disagree)

In additional studies of the process, Pennycook and his colleagues found a strong correlation between active open-mindedness and skepticism of paranormal and supernatural claims, along with higher trust in scientific institutions and consensus science, such as climate change and vaccines.[27] Active open-mindedness is a cogent tool of reason in assessing the truth value of any claim or idea, as is reason itself, of which active open-mindedness is a subset of rational skills that must be cultivated through education and practice.

Valorize Norms of Reason and Rationality

Pinker suggests that in addition to practicing *active open-mindedness* and being willing to change our minds when the evidence changes, we *valorize norms of reason and rationality* and pressure institutions to develop those norms that lead to truth-seeking rather than territory-defending, including and especially academia, with its "stifling left-wing monoculture, with its punishment of students and professors who challenge reigning dogmas on gender, race, culture, genetics, colonialism, and sexual identity and orientation."[28]

The media as well has morphed into partisan politics in which one can toggle between, say, Fox News and MSNBC and note the same story being spun so radically far to the right or the left that one is left wondering how they can possibly be talking about the same subject. Pinker outlines how this valorization could happen:

> But norms can change over time, like the decline of ethnic slurs, littering, and wife jokes, as reflexes of tacit approval and disapproval proliferate through social networks. And so we can each do our part in smiling or frowning on rational and irrational habits. It would be nice to see people earn brownie points for acknowledging uncertainty in their beliefs, questioning the dogmas of their political sect, and changing their minds when the facts change, rather than for being steadfast warriors for the dogmas of their clique. Conversely, it could be a mortifying faux pas to overinterpret anecdotes, confuse correlation with causation, or commit an informal fallacy like guilt by association or the argument from authority.[29]

Avoid Group Polarization and Echo Chambers

Irrational beliefs can be reinforced in echo chambers of like-minded people, a process we are now all familiar with on social media. In his book *Going to Extremes*,[30] Cass Sunstein reports how he and his colleagues explored the problem in a series of experiments in which subjects were divided into two groups—liberals and conservatives—tasked with discussing three issues: climate change, affirmative action, and civil unions for same-sex couples (this was before same-sex marriage became the law of the land in 2015). Participants' opinions were recorded at three stages: (1) at the beginning, privately and anonymously; (2) in the middle, after discussing the issues with each other until they reached a group verdict; (3) after the discussion, privately and anonymously. The findings confirmed the group polarization hypothesis, or what we now call the *echo-chamber* effect:

> On all three issues, both liberals and conservatives became more unified and more extreme after talking only to one another—not merely in their public verdicts but also in their private, anonymous views. Group discussions made conservatives more skeptical of climate change and more hostile to affirmative action and same-sex unions, while liberals showed the opposite pattern. Before discussion, both groups showed far more diversity than they did afterward, and the individuals in the liberal groups were not so very far apart from those in conservative groups. After discussion, the two sets of groups became much more divided.[31]

The solution to the problem is obvious, even if implementing it isn't: On social media, follow people, groups, media sources, and institutions that are not perfectly aligned with your own beliefs and ideologies, talk to people with opinions on hot-button issues that differ from your own, read opinion editorials by authors with whom you disagree, and watch and listen to people voicing positions with which you disagree. In his book *How to Talk to a Science Denier*, the philosopher of science Lee McIntyre elaborated on the echo-chamber problem:

> Once people had been exposed to scientific misinformation, it had some lingering effect. The best possible thing is for people not to be exposed to any misinformation at all. The worst possible thing is for misinformation to be shared and not challenged in any way. Since we live in a world in which scientific misinformation is ubiquitous, it should come as no surprise that further work remains.[32]

McIntyre's follow-up book, *On Disinformation*,[33] has a distinctly liberal-leaning angle that highlights the right as an agent of disinformation more than the left, so on my podcast conversation with him, I pointed out the many ways that liberals—especially progressive leftists—deny science and distort the truth, including and especially on issues related to trans rights, race, abortion, GMOs, nuclear power, and climate doomsdayism.[34] What's good for the goose is good for the gander. Or so I read somewhere. . . .

Develop a Scout Mindset

Julia Galef is one of the researchers who discovered that teaching people how to use the tools of science and reason is not enough to overcome the myriad ways that thinking goes wrong. Learning about cognitive biases, for example, no more improves your judgment than reading about exercise improves your fitness, she analogizes. Instead, Galef argues, we need to cultivate an attitude of truth-seeking through what she calls the *scout mindset*, which involves gathering evidence and using reason to develop a more accurate map of reality; it is "the motivation to see things as they are, not as you wish they were," in her words. The opposite of the scout mindset is the soldier mindset, explained in Galef's martial analogy: "We talk about our beliefs as if they're military positions, or even fortresses, built to resist attack. Beliefs can be *deep-rooted, well-grounded, built on fact*, and *backed up* by arguments. They *rest on solid foundations*. We might hold a *firm* conviction or a *strong* opinion, be *secure* in our convictions or have an *unshakeable* faith in something."[35]

The soldier mindset leads us to defend against people who might "poke holes" in our logic, "shoot down" our beliefs, or confront us with a "knock-down" argument, all of which may result in our beliefs being "undermined," "weakened," or even "destroyed," so we become "entrenched" in them lest we "surrender" to the opposing position.

But what if you're right? Shouldn't you defend truth like a soldier? The problem is that none of us are omniscient, and almost all decision-making happens under uncertainty, so the soldier mindset can easily lead to the defense of erroneous ideas. In seeking truth—that is, an accurate map of reality—we should engage in more open-minded discovery, objectivity, and intellectual honesty in which "I was wrong" and "I change my mind" are virtues instead of vices.

Protect and Defend the Constitution of Knowledge

Objective facts in support of provisional truths about the world are determined by tried-and-true methods developed over the centuries since the Scientific Revolution and the Enlightenment in what are sometimes called *reality-based communities* or *rationality communities*—scholars, scientists, and researchers who collect data, form and test hypotheses, present their findings to colleagues at conferences, publish their papers in peer-reviewed journals and books, and reinforce the norms of truth-telling to their colleagues, their students, and themselves. In his book *The Constitution of Knowledge: A Defense of Truth*, the journalist and civil rights activist Jonathan Rauch outlines and defends the epistemic operating system of Enlightenment liberalism's social rules for attaining reliable knowledge when people cannot agree on what is true.[36] This reality-based community includes:

- Scholars, scientists, and researchers who "gather evidence, form hypotheses, survey the existing literature, engage in critical exchange, conduct peer review, publish findings, compare and replicate findings, credit and cite others' work, populate conferences, edit journals and books, develop methodologies, set and enforce research standards, and train other people to do all of those things."
- Journalists who "gather facts, cultivate sources, organize investigations, sift documents, triangulate viewpoints, develop stories, check stories, edit stories, decide to publish or not publish stories, decide whether to follow or debunk stories published elsewhere, evaluate mistakes and publish corrections, and train other people to do all of those things."
- Government agencies that "gather intelligence, perform research, compile statistics, and develop regulations." These include intelligence communities of people "who develop specialties and exper-

tise, cultivate sources, collect and assess information, weight their confidence in their assessments, evaluate competing assessments, publish their assessments for their clients, conduct post-mortem reviews to understand their errors, and train others to do all of those things."

- Lawyers, judges, and legal scholars comprising the world of law and jurisprudence "who develop specialties and expertise, gather facts, survey case law and precedent, build cases and claims, cite evidence in support of their claims, argue with other professionals, render and justify judgments, publish judgments, hold themselves and each other accountable through layers of appeal, build and respect a cumulating body of precedent, set and enforce professional standards, and train others to do all of those things."[37]

Although these communities differ in the details of what, exactly, should be done to determine justified true belief and reliable knowledge, Rauch suggests several common features of the constitution of knowledge:

- *Fallibilism.* "The ethos that any of us might be wrong."
- *Objectivity.* A commitment to the proposition that there is a reality and we can know it through reason and empiricism.
- *Disconfirmation.* Reality-based individuals "understand that their claims will and must be challenged; they anticipate those challenges and respond; they subject their scholarship to peer review and replication, their journalism to editing and fact-checking, their legal briefs to adversarial lawyers, their intelligence to red-team review."
- *Accountability.* Reality-based community members recognize that "being wrong is undesirable, but it is also inevitable," so we need to hold everyone accountable for their mistakes.
- *Pluralism.* The acceptance of and insistence on viewpoint diversity, along with the "maximum freedom to propose, to critique, to challenge, to defend" any and all ideas.

- *Civility.* Reality-based community members "develop and follow elaborate protocols which encourage them to argue calmly and depersonalize their rhetoric—protocols which it is in their interest to observe."
- *Professionalism.* "Earned credentials count. To develop a track record and reputation, you need to study and practice for years, often decades. . . . As such, you will be accountable to other professionals, and you will share with them a sense of integrity: a deeply instilled understanding that there are right and wrong ways to do things."
- *No bullshitting.* A complete rejection of behaving "without any sincere regard for truth." Liars acknowledge truth when they try to conceal or deny it, whereas bullshitters don't care what reality is or to what extent they accurately express what it is.[38]

To that extent, just as the president of the United States, when sworn into office, must promise to protect and defend the Constitution, we should all pledge to protect and defend the constitution of knowledge. The general idea behind this constitution is the principle of universal realism that underlies this entire book, namely that there is a reality that we can know. The path to it is convoluted, uncertainties abound, and the people on the journey seeking truth don't always agree on what it is or how to get there, so we need mutually approved sets of rules and guidelines to consult when disagreements arise. The most important of these are free speech and open dialogue.

Accentuate Norms of Free Speech and Open Dialogue

Why do we have to listen to people whose opinions we disagree with, don't like, or even hate? In his 1859 classic work, *On Liberty*, John Stuart Mill gave as good an answer as anyone: "If all mankind minus one, were of one opinion, and only one person were of the contrary opinion, mankind would be no more justified in silencing that one person, than he, if he had the power, would be justified in silencing mankind."[39]

The great dissident Rosa Luxemburg put it even more succinctly:

"The freedom of speech is meaningless unless it means the freedom of the person who thinks differently."[40] In my book *Giving the Devil His Due*, I made an impassioned case for free speech fundamentalism and provided a list of reasons why we should defend free speech against censorship and listen to others, including and especially those with whom we disagree:

- Who decides which speech is acceptable and which is unacceptable? You? Me? The majority? The language police?
- What criteria are used to censor certain speech? Ideas that I disagree with? Thoughts that differ from your thoughts? Anything that the majority determines is unacceptable?
- We might be completely right but still learn something new in hearing what someone else has to say.
- We might be partially right and partially wrong, and by listening to other viewpoints, we might stand corrected and refine and improve our beliefs.
- We might be completely wrong, so hearing criticism or counterpoint gives us the opportunity to change our minds and improve our thinking. No one is infallible.
- By listening to the opinions of others whether they are right or wrong, we have the opportunity to develop stronger arguments and build better facts for our positions.
- My freedom to speak and dissent is inextricably tied to your freedom to speak and dissent. If I censor you, why shouldn't you censor me? If you silence me, why shouldn't I silence you?[41]

If you disagree with me, the norms and customs of free speech and open dialogue are what allow you to do so.

■ The Search for Truth Is Dogged as Does It

A final point on overcoming the many impediments to the search for truth came to me in June of 2004, when the University of California–Berkeley historian of science Frank Sulloway and I began a monthlong expedition to the Galapagos Islands, retracing Charles Darwin's footsteps. It turned out to be one of the most physically grueling experiences of my life, granting me new respect for what the young British naturalist was able to accomplish there in 1835 (figure 2.1).

Charles Darwin was not only one sagacious scientist; he was also one tenacious explorer. He was *dogged* in his search for truth. Sulloway outlined five characteristics of Darwin's cognitive style (in my own words):

- Darwin respected others' opinions but was willing to challenge authorities.
- Darwin paid close attention to negative evidence—that is, evidence that went against his theory. In fact, in his revolutionary 1859 work, *On the Origin of Species*, Darwin, after consulting with many of the top scientists of his time, included a chapter ("Difficulties on Theory") in which he asked them to challenge him.
- Darwin generously used and cited the work of others. Remarkably, in the Darwin correspondence project, there are over 14,000 letters, most of which include lengthy discussions and question-and-answer sequences about scientific problems that reveal Darwin's own active open-mindedness.
- Darwin was constantly questioning and always learning and was confident enough to formulate original ideas yet modest enough to recognize his own fallibility.
- Among the many traits that made Charles Darwin one of the greatest minds in science was his doggedness. When facing a daunting problem in biology, Darwin would obstinately chip away at it until its secrets were revealed. His apt description for this disposition came from an 1867 Anthony Trollope novel in which one of the characters opined: "There ain't not a man can't bear if he'll only be dogged. . . . It's dogged as does it."[42]

Figure 2.1. The author (*bottom right*) retracing Charles Darwin's footsteps in the Galapagos Islands, with the historian of science Frank Sulloway, in the volcanic fields of San Cristóbal. The image is a poignant metaphor for the search for truth, which Darwin described as "It's dogged as does it." Photo by Frank Sulloway

Here is how Sulloway summarized Darwin's overall cognitive style: "Usually, it is the scientific community as a whole that displays this essential tension between tradition and change, since most people have a preference for one or the other way of thinking. What is relatively rare in the history of science is to find these contradictory qualities combined in such a successful manner in one individual."[43] Darwin's son Francis recalled his father's temperament thus: "Doggedness expresses his frame of mind almost better than perseverance. Perseverance seems hardly to express his almost fierce desire to force the truth to reveal itself."[44]

The search for truth is dogged as does it.

3

The Truth About Why

Causation, Correlation, Bayesian Reasoning, Signal Detection Theory, and the Determination of Cause and Effect

■ Does drinking coffee cause heart disease? Does smoking cause lung cancer? Does burning fossil fuels cause global warming?

At their core, these questions are about causality. In short, we want to know, does X cause Y? That is, we want to determine the truth about X and Y's relationship so we can determine if they're causally connected. Does drinking coffee (X) cause heart disease (Y)? Does smoking (X) cause lung cancer (Y)? Does burning fossil fuels (X) cause global warming (Y)? That they may seem to be related is what the Enlightenment philosopher David Hume called "a constant conjunction" form of causality.[1] That is, when X is constantly in conjunction with Y, we naturally infer a causal connection. His example was fire and heat. When there is fire (X), there is heat (Y), and we correctly infer that the fire caused the heat. But causal chains are often more than an X and a Y. For example, if you burn yourself with a flame on your stove, it isn't the fire that causes the burn, it is the *heat* from the fire that causes it. So here, we would infer that fire (X) causes heat (Y) that causes burns (Z).

Hume also pointed out that a constant conjunction does not always suffice for understanding causality. A poignant example comes from a story in Geoffrey Chaucer's 1390 *The Canterbury Tales* involving a rooster named Chauntecleer, who believed that his early morning crowing caused the sun to rise. In constant conjunction causality, the rooster crows (X) and the sun rises (Y), yet no one in their right mind (besides Chauntecleer) would infer that a crowing rooster causes the sun to rise. X and Y may be in constant conjunction, but they are not causally connected. So Hume added another definition of causality called *counterfactual causation*—"We may define a cause to be an object followed by another, or, in other words, where, if the first object had not been, the second never had existed."[2] Counterfactual causation offers an alternative world thought experiment to determine causality: If Chauntecleer does not crow and the sun still rises, then we can reasonably infer that the rooster crowing did not cause the sun to rise.

Returning to our opening questions, is there a relationship between drinking coffee (X) and heart disease (Y)? Some researchers thought they were causally connected, until other scientists pointed out that coffee drinkers also smoke more, exercise less, and don't eat as healthily, so coffee was only a proxy for these other factors that cause heart disease. Or, in counterfactual reasoning, if non–coffee drinkers get heart disease (perhaps because they smoke), then we can infer that it wasn't the coffee causing heart disease. The same problem arises in assessing the relationship between smoking and lung cancer or fossil fuels and global warming. How, then, do we determine the truth about causality when there are many factors confounding our understanding?

Determining Causality

For a television show demonstration in 2000, I walked across 1,000-degree burning hot coals barefoot, and I didn't get burned.[3] How can that be? Fire walkers claim it has to do with positive thinking, channeling protective energies, or other such New Age pabulum. But once we think about how to determine causality, a more quotidian explanation emerges. When we diagram a causal chain—fire (X) generates heat (Y) that causes burning (Z)—we can see that *confounding variables* (or *confounders*) break the causal chain. In this case, the hot coals I was walking across barefoot were from burned wood logs, and wood is a poor conductor of heat, especially into the dead skin on the bottom of callused feet. As long as you don't dawdle during the fire walk or stop to take selfies, you likely won't get burned. Some fire walks include a pad of wet grass on either end of the firepit so your feet start off cooler and are quickly cooled again at the end.

An analogy helps us understand the causal chain here: When you bake a cake at 350 degrees in the oven, you can put your hand into the oven without the 350-degree air burning your hand. You can even put your hand on top of the cake and not get burned, even though it, too, is 350 degrees. But if you touch the 350-degree metal cake pan, you will be burned almost instantly. It's not the heat (temperature) X that is the cause of burning Y but the material *conductivity*. Air and cake are poor conductors of heat, whereas metal is an excellent conductor of heat. So here, our causal chain from fire (X) to heat (Y) to burn (Z) is interrupted by the confounding variables of the material being burned, the calluses on your feet, the speed with which you walk, and the cool wet grass.

Consider a more common example of determining causality: Have you ever gone on the same diet as a friend, or one practiced by a great many people through a diet book or weight-loss program, only to find that it didn't work as well for you as it did others? I have, many times, and I could never tell if it was because I didn't do it right or if there were other mitigating factors involved, such as my body type, physiology, genetics, upbringing, amount of exercise, or whatever. As in the fire-walking example, there are many confounding variables in between the simple formula of diet (X) and weight loss (Y).

In such examples, the most we can say initially is that X is *associated* with Y; that is, dieting is associated with weight loss. But determining causality depends on assessing other factors. For example, perhaps people who diet also exercise more, and it is the exercise, not the diet, that causes weight loss. Or maybe losing weight causes people to exercise more because their overall motivation is higher, so the diet was a secondary factor and exercise the primary causal agent (and motivation more primary still). Or maybe it's not the diet per se but the particular type of food (all protein, all carbs, some mix in between) that causes both weight loss and an increase in exercise and motivation. Most effects have multiple causes, so we need a method to tease those variables out so we can assess which are the most important ones. That method is science, which I have defined thusly:

> *Science is a set of methods designed to describe and interpret observed or inferred phenomenon, past or present, aimed at building a testable body of knowledge open to rejection or confirmation.*[4]

Let's unpack this: Science is a *set of methods*—that is, it is something we do, an action, a verb. *Designed to describe and interpret*—this means we describe what we see in the lab or field or world but also interpret what we think we see, because the facts never just speak for themselves but must be interrupted through some model or theory (facts are "theory laden"). *Observed or inferred phenomenon*—we sometimes see things directly but often must infer their presence indirectly; for example, exoplanets are inferred by their effects on their home star, either by the perturbation of the star's motion or by the amount of emitted light that dims when the planet passes in front of it that astronomers can detect. *Past or present*—this is because many sciences are historical in nature, such as cosmology, geology, paleontology, archaeology, and of course history; since past events already happened, we have to infer information about them from indirect sources.

The cardinal clause in this definition is *testable body of knowledge open to rejection or confirmation*. This is the key to science:[5] it must be *testable* so that we can either reject or confirm an idea based on the outcome of the test.[6] As well, for beliefs to be true, they must have a universal element to them[7]—that is, they should be true not just for me, or my culture, or my generation but also for you, or your culture, or your generation. And the discovery of such truths cannot be accidental, as in the Gettier problems we considered in the previous chapter.[8] For example, the cognitive psychologist Andrew Shtulman has discovered that most people who say that they accept the theory of evolution (a true proposition) hold a false understanding of what it is, typically offering the debunked notion of the inheritance of acquired characteristics (Lamarckism) in which, in the holotype case, giraffes stretch their necks to obtain leaves atop tall trees, resulting in offspring with longer necks.[9] So, they are right to believe the theory of evolution but wrong in their reasons to believe. Here's how the Nobel laureate physicist Richard Feynman explained how science works to students in a 1964 lecture: "If it disagrees with experiment, it's wrong. In that simple statement is the key to science. It doesn't make any difference how *beautiful* your guess is, how *smart* you are, *who made* the guess, or *what his name is*. If it disagrees with experiment, it's wrong. That's all there is to it."[10]

In an undergraduate philosophy honors course I took, the professor, Richard Hardison, assigned a short book—*To Know a Fly* by the entomologist and ethologist Vincent Dethier—that so beautifully and passionately described the process of science that it was an early impetus for me to pursue experimental psychology. Here is how Dethier described the process:

> A properly conducted experiment is a beautiful thing. It is an adventure, an expedition, a conquest. It commences with an act of faith, faith that the world is real, that our senses generally can be trusted, that effects have causes, and that we can discover meaning by reason. It continues with an observation and a question. An experiment is a scientist's way of asking nature a question. He alters a condition, observes a result, and draws a conclusion.[11]

The other book that Hardison directed us to read was Lionel Ruby's *The Art of Making Sense*, in which the philosopher explains, "Science, as a method, is loyal not to persons or institutions, but to the process of attaining truth." What kind of truth? *Factual truth*, or when "a statement agrees with, or corresponds with, the facts."[12] This definition maps neatly onto the *correspondence theory of truth*, which holds that the truth or falsity of a claim or statement is best determined by how closely it relates to, conforms to, is in congruence with, or corresponds with the actual state of the world.[13] How do we know if a statement corresponds to the facts? We come to that conclusion through the process of what the philosopher of science Karl Popper called conjectures and refutations. Popper outlined how scientists operate by conjecturing ideas to their colleagues and considering the refutations in response. Since most ideas that scientists propose are wrong (*fallibilism* again), the constant dialogue with one's fellow experts in a field through private communication, public conferences, and especially peer-reviewed papers and books is crucial for determining if one is getting closer to the truth or has gone off the rails.[14]

Distilling the philosophy of science—grounded as it is in *universal realism* (or *metaphysical realism*)—into one short statement renders this:

> *Science is a method to explain the world that is testable and open to change.*

More colloquially, science is a practical tool for helping us move our search for truth from internal subjective truths to external objective truths. As New York Senator Daniel Patrick Moynihan famously quipped: "Everyone is entitled to his own opinion, but not his own facts."[15]

Science and the Null Hypothesis

Science begins with a *null hypothesis*—that is, the nonexistence of something is the truth about it until proven otherwise. Although statisticians mean something very specific about this (having to do with comparing different sets of data), I am using the term *null hypothesis* in its more general sense that X does not cause Y. You claim to have a cure for COVID-19? The US Food and Drug Administration (FDA) will not approve your drug until you demonstrate that it really can eliminate the SARS-CoV-2 virus from bodies and cure the symptoms of the disease; otherwise, they will assume that you have no such remedy. The null hypothesis in this example is that you do not have a cure, and it can only be rejected if you provide substantial evidence of its curative powers. And anecdotes are not helpful here ("I know someone who tried Ivermectin and her COVID symptoms got better"). We need large group comparisons in search of statistically significant differences between the treatment and controlled conditions.

The statistical standards of proof needed to reject the null hypothesis are substantial. Ideally, in a controlled experiment, we would like to be at least 95% to 99% confident that the results are not due to chance before we offer our provisional assent that the effect is real. Everyone is familiar with the process already through news stories about the FDA approving a new drug after extensive clinical trials. The trials to which they refer involve sophisticated methods to test the claim that Drug X (say a statin drug) lowers the risk of Disease Y (say heart disease linked to cholesterol). The null hypothesis states that statins do not decrease the risk of heart disease by lowering cholesterol. Rejecting the null hypothesis means that there is a statistically significant difference in rates of heart disease between the experimental group receiving the statins and the control group that did not.

Here is an entertaining example of how this method of statistical significance works in relation to the null hypothesis to answer this question: Can a psychic using ESP (extrasensory perception) alone determine whether a playing card from a deck is red or black? Psychics often claim that they can do this, but in my experience, what people *say* they can do and what they can *actually* do are not always the same. How can we test this claim? If a psychic was asked to say whether each card we placed face down on the table was red or black, how many correct hits would the psychic need in order for us to conclude that the card color determinations were not due to chance? In this scenario, the null hypothesis is that the psychic will do no better than chance, and thus to reject the null hypothesis, we must establish a figure for the number of correct hits needed in each round. By chance, we would expect the psychic to get about half correct. In a deck of 52 cards, half of which are red and half of which are black, random guessing or flipping a coin will produce, on average, 26 correct hits.

Of course, as anyone who has flipped coins for fun knows, 10 flips do not necessarily always result in 5 heads and 5 tails. There are streaks and deviations from symmetry—6 heads and 4 tails, or 3 heads and 7 tails—all within the realm of chance. Or, as anyone who has gambled at a roulette wheel knows, sometimes red comes up more than black, or vice versa, without any violations of chance and randomness. In fact, we count on such asymmetrical streaks in our betting schemes and hope that we're disciplined enough to walk away from the table during a temporary deviation from chance in our favor before it swings the other way.

So, we can't just test our psychic on one short series of card guesses, because the psychic may be expected to get a series of hits by chance alone. We need to run multiple trials, and some rounds may have below-chance results (say, 22, 23, 24, or 25 hits), while others may have above-chance results (say, 27, 28, 29, or 30 hits). The variation may be even greater than this and still be due to nothing but chance. What we need to determine is the number by which we can confidently reject the null hypothesis. In this example, that number is 35. The psychic would need to get 35 correct hits out of a 52-card deck in order for us to reject the null hypothesis at the 99% confidence level. The statistical method by which this figure is derived need not concern us here.[16] The point is that even though 35 out of 52 doesn't sound like it would be that hard to obtain, in fact, by chance alone, it would be so unusual that we could confidently state ("at the 99% confidence level") that something else besides chance was going on here.

What might that something else be? It could be ESP. But it could be other factors. Perhaps our controls were not tight enough. Maybe the psychic was getting the red/black information by some other normal (as opposed to paranormal) means of which we're not aware (such as the reflection of the card face on the table surface). Possibly the psychic was cheating, and we don't know the method. I've seen the magician James "the Amazing" Randi do this very experiment with an entire deck of cards, resulting in two perfect piles of all red and all black cards.[17] The magician Lennart Green shuffles and scrambles a deck of cards, fumbles with them for a while as if he's all thumbs, clumsily pushes them back together, then proceeds to deal out four winning poker hands or an entire sequence of a suit in order, all while blindfolded.[18] But Randi and Green are magicians, and these are magic tricks. That I do not know how these tricks are done does not make them real (paranormal) magic, and the fact that most scientists do not know how they are done means we need to be even more vigilant in our controls when testing psychics, perhaps even attaching a magician to our research team. The argument from personal incredulity—if I can't explain it, then it must be true—does not hold water in science.

Even with all these controls in place, certainty still eludes science. Rejecting the null hypothesis is not a warranty on truth, yet failure to reject the null hypothesis does not make the claim false. We must keep an open mind, but not so open that our brains fall out, as the popular idiom cautions. Provisional truths are the best we can do.

Correlation and Causation

Is a college degree worth the tuition price?

This is another causality question, one being asked by many tuition-paying parents and grandparents of late as the academy experiences its biggest crisis since the campus protests of the late 1960s. The answer very much depends on what criteria of "worth" are being applied. In 2020, the cumulative federal student loan debt hit a staggering figure of $1.5 trillion, double that of 2010 and primarily caused by the rapid rise in tuition for both private and public colleges and universities. In response, administrators and professors alike—and I am one of the latter—talk up the value of a college degree, not only to enhance one's personal growth through the liberal arts and sciences but also to increase one's personal income and lifetime earnings. To wit, a bachelor's degree is worth around $1 million dollars more in lifetime earnings compared to only a high-school diploma, and a graduate degree is worth about $1.5 million dollars more (different studies vary on the amount of the benefit, but few dissent from the general conclusion).[19] Thus, we academics like to argue that earning a college degree is worth it despite the exorbitant costs.

Is that causality assertion true? It looks simple enough: Just compare tuition costs incurred versus lifetime earnings. If the latter exceeds the former, bingo! Not so fast. Determining causality with such complex variables as education and income is tricky. There is certainly a positive *association* between these two variables—as one goes up (education), the other one goes up (income). The two variables are co-related, and, as the name implies, a *correlation* means that for each unit, the value of one variable depends on or is related to the value of the other variable.[20] Correlations are usually graphed as a scattershot of data points with a line through them that is the closest fit to the center average for all the points (figure 3.1). For example, height and weight are strongly positively correlated. As height goes up, weight goes up, although because of normal human variation, the dots on

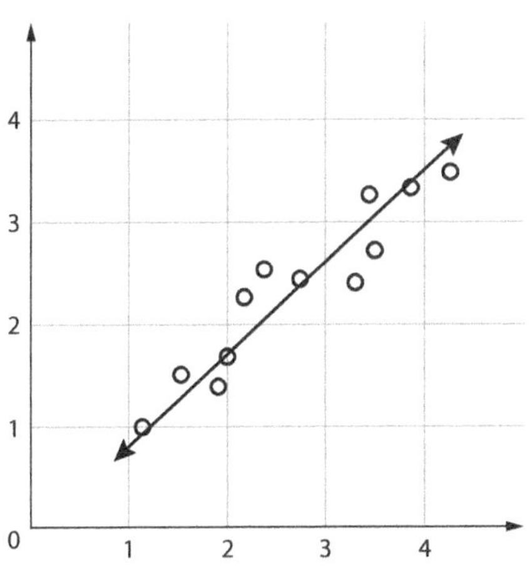

Figure 3.1. Correlations are usually graphed as a scatterplot of data points with a line through them that is the closest fit to the central average for all the points. Author-generated graphic

the graph do not all perfectly fit onto the straight line, since some people who are taller than average are skinny and weigh less than other tall people who are huskier and weigh more. And, on the other end, some people who are shorter than average who are stocky and muscular weigh more than short people who are svelte and ectomorphic in body type. Clearly, there are other factors at work—those complicating *confounding variables.*

The correlation coefficient is one of the most common statistics used by social scientists, and it is represented by the lowercase letter r, which has a range from −1.0 to 0.0 to +1.0—from a perfect negative correlation (−1.0, as one variable goes up the other variable goes down) to no correlation (0.0) to a perfect positive correlation (+1.0). Correlations of real phenomena typically range from 0.01 to 0.99 (or −0.01 to −0.99), with most falling somewhere in between. For example, the correlation between height and weight is $r = 0.70$. In most correlations of human variables, this is extremely high. Even so, it is still 0.30 below a perfect 1.0 correlation, so obviously other things cause the correlation to depart from a perfect fit line, such as genetics, diet and nutrition, exercise, lifestyle, upbringing, and so on.

If you square a correlation, it produces what is called the *coefficient of determination*, or the proportion of the variation in the dependent variable that is predictable from the independent variable(s).[21] In this case, height is the independent variable and weight is the dependent variable (inasmuch as it *depends* on height). In the case of the height and weight correlation of 0.70, you square 0.70—that is, multiply 0.70 x 0.70 to get $r^2 = 0.49$. That is, 49% of the variation in weight between people of the same height is roughly half. This means that the other half of the variation between people's weights is caused by something other than height.

In most social science research, correlations often fall below $r = 0.50$, even in studies with identical twins. For example, the correlation of religious interests between identical twins reared apart is $r = 0.49$, a very significant figure that indicates a strong genetic component to religiosity.[22] And yet, this correlation yields an $r^2 = 0.24$, meaning only 24% of the variation between people on their religiosity can be accounted for by their genes. The rest of the variation—a full 75%—is accounted for by the environment, in this case the religiosity of one's parents, grandparents, peers, teachers, and mentors, the culture at large, where and when you happened to have been born in different societies with their various religious preferences, and the unique life history of the individual. Even one's relationship with one's parents makes a difference. In a study I conducted with my University of California–Berkeley psychologist colleague Frank Sulloway, we found that people who had *low conflict* with parents tended to show a higher correlation with their parents' levels of religiosity—either high or low—and people who reported having *high conflict* with parents tended to go in the opposite direction of their parents' levels of religiosity: If their parents were not very religious, they became more religious; if their parents were very religious, they became less religious.[23]

With these basics in mind, let's return to the correlation between education and income and the larger question about the value of a college education. There are many confounding variables in between education and income that complicate the relationship between the two. For example, smarter parents are more likely to send their kids to college, and we know that intelligence is highly heritable and that there's a positive correlation between intelligence and income, so maybe it was the genetic inheritance of a high IQ that led to greater lifetime earnings for these students and not the education.[24]

As well, parental income is a predictor of offspring income,[25] so maybe it isn't IQ or education but some other factor that leads to the children having higher incomes, like guidance on investing, or connections to good investors, or parental loans, or family inheritance. We also know that healthier people earn more money in a lifetime,[26] so maybe some combination of genetics and environment that makes some people healthier also makes them wealthier, such that education, IQ, parental guidance, or parental income may not be what matters so much. In all likelihood, *all of these factors*—and many more besides, not the least of which is luck—factor in one's lifetime earnings.

So, to return to our original question, does a college education make you richer over your lifetime? Sure it does. But why? That's hard to say, exactly, but of course there are other values of an education besides making money, such as learning how to think critically, to appreciate literature, art, music, science, and culture, and to more deeply understand the richness of the world and its varied cultures and peoples. To diagram an analysis like this, we might say that

> *A (income) is correlated with B (education), but it is also correlated with C (IQ), D (health), E (parental income), F (parental upbringing), as well as with G (neighborhood), (H) culture, (I) lifestyle, (J) nutrition, (K) connections, (L) luck, and so on.*

To determine the relative influence of each of these variables, scientists employ sophisticated research methods such as case-control studies, cohort studies, randomization, matching, and stratification and statistical methods like multivariate regression,[27] a detour that would take us too far afield here.

Let's consider another important issue in life, namely how long yours will last. I presume that you would like to live a long and healthy life. If you're a baby boomer like me, you will likely be happy with making it into your 80s relatively healthy. If you're a Gen Xer or Millennial, you are probably thinking of stretching things out into your 90s. Gen Zers could very well make it into their 100s, on average. Whatever your aspirations, a causal question arises: What should you do to bring about that salubrious outcome?

For starters, we can look at the literature on health and longevity and see what researchers have discovered. There, you will find a lot of correlational studies, but, as in the example of the correlation between education and income, there are a lot of *confounders* that complicate matters and are best controlled through *randomized controlled trials* (RCTs).[28] You're probably familiar with RCTs in media stories about studies on medications and disease in which people are randomly assigned to the experimental treatment group that receives the drug, the placebo group that receives an inert drug, and the control group that receives no drug. The results are then compared, controlling for confounding variables like preexisting conditions (comorbidities), socioeconomic status, race, sex, weight, and age.

The problem with RCTs is that they can't be done for a lot of issues we care about. For example, we can't conduct an RCT in which we force some people to smoke and others not to smoke and then measure their health outcomes. Instead, we study what are called "natural experiments"—experiments that happen naturally, as it were, without scientists doing anything other than measuring the effects after the fact.[29] For example, there are millions of smokers, so we can separate them from nonsmokers and compare their health outcomes. This has been done in thousands of correlational studies since the 1950s, and the conclusion is clear: Smoking is bad for you and will shorten your life. Yes, there are some people who smoke like a chimney and live to be 100 and others who lead a perfectly healthy smoke-free life and drop dead at age 35, so we're talking about averages here.[30]

Another example of natural experiments are the "Blue Zones" of longevity. That is, you look around the world and find the longest-living people and then conduct a study to see what it is they're doing or what it is about where they live, or how they live, or what they eat, or whatever. Blue Zones include certain geographic regions, such as Okinawa (Japan), Sardinia (Italy), Nicoya (Costa Rica), and Icaria (Greece), and the people who live long lives there tend to do a lot of things differently from people in other zones who don't live as long. To wit, Blue Zone people tend to walk a lot and exercise, have rich family and social lives, get plenty of sleep, drink moderate amounts of wine, eat a lot of plant-based foods, keep stress at a minimum, and have a sense of purpose.[31] Although, as these things go in science, there are now good reasons to doubt these studies, challenged as they are by skeptics who doubt the purported ages of the peoples studied, along with their self-reported diets, activities, and lifestyle choices.[32]

One of the most interesting natural experiments in all of science involves identical twins reared apart. These are twins separated at birth and raised in different environments. Behavior geneticists compared identical twins raised apart to identical twins raised together, biological siblings reared together, biological siblings reared apart, and adoptees reared together,[33] measuring hundreds of characteristics, including height and weight, health and longevity, personality and personal preferences, spouse and career choices, religious and political preferences, and many others. What they found is that identical twins reared apart are far more alike than biological siblings and adoptees reared together. Most of these measured variables show high correlations, with r^2 in the 0.50 range.[34] In other words, heredity plays an outsized role in how lives turn out.

The point of this chapter, however, is not how lives turn out but rather how we can *figure out* how lives turn out; even though it is very difficult to determine causality from correlation, it is strongly suggestive of the types of factors we should control for and study more.

Bayesian Reasoning Toward the Truth

Another weapon in our arsenal to combat misinformation, misunderstanding, self-deception, lies, and bullshit is Bayesian reasoning—or Bayes's rule—invented in the eighteenth century by the Reverend Thomas Bayes. Roughly speaking, Bayesian reasoning has to do with the strength of evidence for a claim, and the rule involves how much we should revise our estimation of the probability of the claim being true based on that evidence. And when the evidence changes, we should change our probability estimates accordingly.[35] (Or, more colloquially, follow the advice of the economist John Maynard Keynes—or whoever actually said it[36]—when he opined, "When the facts change, I change my mind. What do you do, sir?")

These estimations of probabilities based on prior knowledge of conditions are called *priors*, or our *initial degree of belief* before new evidence is gathered. The probability of something being true determines the *credence* of belief, or the *credibility* or strength of one's confidence that the claim is true. Think of credence as the probability of something being true as a percentage. For example, you should believe with 50% credence that a randomly chosen card from a deck of cards will be red or black. Or, if a box contains nine black stones and one white stone, and you withdraw one stone at random, then you should believe with 90% credence that the random stone will be black and 10% credence that it will be white.

In essence, to phrase it in a slightly different way, Bayesian reasoning has to do with the probability governing the strength of evidence and when we should change our minds when the evidence changes or revise our probabilities when we learn new facts or observe new evidence.[37] In his 2021 book *Mental Immunity*, the philosopher Andy Norman describes Bayes's rule as "reason's fulcrum."[38] Picture a playground seesaw in which the fulcrum is in the middle of the beam and the competing hypotheses or theories or ideas are positioned on either end of the perfectly balanced beam. This would represent a 50% credence, as in the example of randomly choosing a red or black card from a deck of cards. In the example of withdrawing a stone at random from a box with nine black stones and one white stone, the fulcrum would be 90% of the way toward one end of the beam, representing 90% credence that the stone will be black. Figure 3.2 is a visual demonstration of the principle, developed by Ed Gibney and

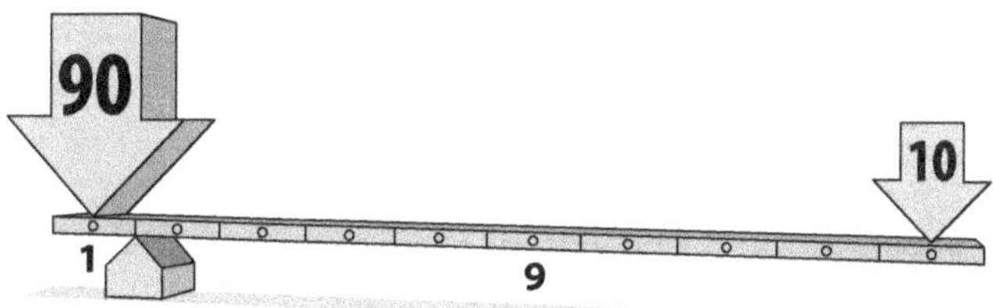

Figure 3.2. Ratio of 90:10 for people Without:With a condition. A 10% chance of having the condition gives a beam ratio of 1:9. This illustrates Bayesian reasoning in the probability of something being true (having the condition) versus false (not having the condition). Illustrations by Jim W. W. Smith. Reprinted with permission of *Skeptic* magazine

Zafir Ivanov, of "how Bayesian reasoning can set us free from the search for absolute truth." Here is their translation of the seesaw analogy for Bayesian reasoning: "The position of the fulcrum in Reason's Fulcrum is the balancing point of the likelihood of observing the available evidence for two competing claims. This position is called our *credence*. As we become aware of new evidence, our credence must move to restore a balanced position."[39]

The problem with this analogy, as Gibney and Ivanov note, is that many claims to knowledge do not come packaged with precise false-positive and false-negative percentages. They use Bigfoot sightings as an example: "If ten drunken campers over the course of a few decades each swear they saw something that looked like Bigfoot in the woods, we would treat that body of evidence differently than we would if it were nine drunken campers plus the pictures from one BBC high-definition camera trap set by a team of professional documentarians."[40] The power (and shortcomings) of Bayesian reasoning are on display in a classic medical diagnostic problem presented to both medical practitioners and the general public:

> *A patient is diagnosed with cancer that has a 1% prevalence rate (that is, it happens to 1 out of 100 people). The test sensitivity for this type of cancer is 90%, that is, the test will be right 90% of the time. The false-positive rate of the test is 9%, that is, the test will be wrong 9% of the time. What is the percent likelihood that the patient has cancer?*[41]

When people are presented with this problem, the most common answer given is between 80% and 90%. The correct answer is 9%. In a sample size of 1,000 people, 10 have cancer—the base rate of 1%. Of these 10 people, 9 will test positive—the 90% sensitivity of the test. Of the 990 people without cancer, 89 will test positive—the 9% false-positive rate. A person tests positive. Does this person have cancer or not? Here is how to compute the answer: Out of 1,000 people tested for cancer, 98 of them test positive in all (9 + 89), 9 of them have cancer (9 ÷ by 98 = 0.091 or ~9%).

Why do most people—including physicians—get this problem wrong? The answer is threefold: (1) *base rate neglect*, that is, the rate of the phenomenon happening is ignored or discounted[42]—in this case, a low 1% base rate means the cancer is rare (in Bayesian language, the prior probability was low), and the rate of false positives applied to the entire sample size is ignored; (2) *probabilities are counterintuitive*, that is, they apply to *populations of people*, not to *one person*, but our minds are tuned to thinking of a person having cancer or not, and not some incoherent notion of 80% cancer;[43] (3) *cognitive heuristics*, that is, we're not naturally Bayesian in our reasoning and instead we use cognitive shortcuts or rules of thumb.[44] Here's an example to illustrate the problem. Imagine that you are looking to hire someone for your company and you are considering for employment the following candidate:

> *Linda is 31 years old, single, outspoken, and very bright. She majored in philosophy. As a student, she was deeply concerned with issues of discrimination and social justice and also participated in antinuclear demonstrations.*

Which is more likely? (1) Linda is a bank teller or (2) Linda is a bank teller and is active in the feminist movement. When this scenario was presented to subjects, 85% chose the second option of Linda as both a bank teller and a feminist.[45] Mathematically speaking, this is the wrong choice, because the probability of two independent events occurring together (in "conjunction") will always be less than or equal to the probability of either one occurring alone. Here, it is far more likely that Linda is a bank teller than that she is *both* a bank teller *and* active in the feminist movement. Here is how the calculation might be done, assigning to Linda a low probability of being a bank teller and a high probability of being a feminist:

- Probability of Linda being a bank teller = P (Linda is a bank teller) = 0.05
- Probability that Linda is a feminist = P (Linda is a feminist) = 0.95

- Probability that Linda is both = P (bank teller *and* feminist) = 0.05 × 0.95 or 0.0475
- This is lower than P (Linda is a bank teller) = 0.05.

The cognitive psychologists Daniel Kahneman and Amos Tversky call this the *representative fallacy*, meaning "an event is judged probable to the extent that it represents the essential features of its parent population or generating process." And, more generally, "when faced with the difficult task of judging probability or frequency, people employ a limited number of heuristics which reduce these judgments to simpler ones."[46]

The reason the representative fallacy is so general is that we are good at telling stories about people and gleaning from these narratives bits of information that we then use to make snap decisions about them, but we are lousy at computing probabilities from large numbers and thinking in terms of the chances of something happening, on average, to a group.[47] The reason is that in the world in which our brains evolved, what counted most were anecdotes about other people, so the modern world of statistics, probabilities, data sets, averages, and percentages is not intuitive and does not come easily without familiarity and/or training and practice.[48]

A final medical example illuminates the problem. Let's say you have a bull's-eye rash on your arm. Do you have Lyme disease? Well, Lyme disease has been on the increase and is not at all uncommon, so it has a high prior. The bull's-eye rash doesn't occur 100% of the time, but it is a very common symptom of Lyme disease. And bull's-eye rashes are uncommon otherwise. So our credence that you have Lyme disease given that symptom is high. As medical students are taught: "If you hear hoofbeats, think horse, not zebra." Of course, if you live near a zoo that has zebras, or near a zebra ranch, you might update your priors and change your credence, but otherwise, zebras are rarer than horses, and to think otherwise is base rate neglect. "A blindness to base rates also leads to public demands for the impossible," Steven Pinker notes:

Why can't we predict who will attempt suicide? Why don't we have an early-warning system for school shooters? Why can't we profile terrorists or rampage shooters and detain them preventively? The answer comes out of Bayes's rule: a less-than-perfect test for a rare trait will mainly turn out false positives. The heart of the problem is that only a tiny proportion of the population are thieves, suicides, terrorists, or rampage shooters (the base rate). Until the day that social scientists can predict misbehavior as accurately as astronomers predict eclipses, their best tests would mostly finger the innocent and harmless.[49]

Signal Detection Theory

For a documentary film on cursed horror films—that is, horror films in which bad things seemed to happen on the set or to the actors—I was tasked with explaining such spooky events as the following:

- Months after the release of *Poltergeist*, its 22-year-old star, Dominique Dunne, was murdered by her abusive ex-boyfriend.
- Julian Beck, who played the "beast" in *Poltergeist*, died of stomach cancer before the film's release.
- Twelve-year-old Heather O'Rourke died months before the release of what would be her last starring role in *Poltergeist III*.
- During the filming of *The Exorcist*, its young star, Linda Blair, injured her back when she was thrown from her bed when a piece of rigging broke.
- Ellen Burstyn was injured on *The Exorcist* set when flung to the ground, and that take was included in the film.
- *The Exorcist* actors Jack MacGowran and Vasiliki Maliaros both died while the film was in postproduction (their characters died in the film).
- *The Omen* star Gregory Peck was on his way to London for the filming when his plane was struck by lightning, as was producer

Mace Neufeld's plane a few weeks later; Peck avoided a later aerial disaster when he cancelled another flight at the last moment and that plane crashed, killing everyone on board.
- Two weeks after the filming of *The Omen*, an animal handler who worked on the set was eaten alive by a lion.
- *The Crow* star Brandon Lee was accidentally shot to death by a stage gun that should have held blanks, and he was the son of Bruce Lee, who also died mysteriously at a young age.
- While filming *Twilight Zone: The Movie*, star Vic Morrow was decapitated by a helicopter.

For many people, these eerie coincidences suggest evil supernatural forces at work. But such a conclusion is not warranted. As I explained on camera, picture a 2 × 2 grid with four cells (table 3.1).

- Cell 1 contains Cursed Horror Movies (*Poltergeist*, *The Exorcist*, *The Omen*, *The Crow*, *Twilight Zone: The Movie*).
- Cell 2 contains Cursed Non-Horror Movies (*Superman*, *Wizard of Oz*, *Rebel Without a Cause*, *Apocalypse Now*).
- Cell 3 contains Non-Cursed Horror Movies (*It*, *The Ring*, *Sixth Sense*, *The Shining*).
- Cell 4 contains Non-Cursed Non-Horror Movies (*The Godfather*, *Star Wars*, *Casablanca*, *Citizen Kane*).

When put into this perspective, it is clear that those seeing supernatural intervention are remembering only the horror movies that seemed cursed (the hits) and forgetting all the other possibilities (the misses).

Call it the *fallacy of excluded exceptions*, or instances that do not support the generalization. In Cell 1, for example, *Halloween* is not included because there are no "curse" stories associated with it; in fact, its star, Jamie Lee Curtis, went on to a successful motion picture career, and the film launched a film franchise. In Cell 2, no one attributes evil forces at work on the California highway where James Dean lost his life after making *Rebel*

Table 3.1. Cursed Horror Films

Horror Films Cursed	**Horror Films Not Cursed**
Poltergeist and *Poltergeist III* *The Exorcist* *The Omen* *The Crow* *Twilight Zone: The Movie*	*It* *It II* *The Ring* *The Sixth Sense* *The Shining*
Non-Horror Films Cursed	**Non-Horror Films Not Cursed**
Superman *The Wizard of Oz* *Rebel Without a Cause* *Apocalypse Now*	*The Godfather* *Star Wars* *Casablanca* *Citizen Kane*

Without a Cause. In Cell 3, spine-chilling films like *The Shining* should be haunted by curses, but this movie is instead the subject of conspiracy theories about Stanley Kubrick filming the faked moon landing and tipping us off through clues, such as little Danny wearing an Apollo 11 jumper, jars of Tang visible in the pantry, and room 237 referencing the 237,000 miles from the Earth to the moon (the actual distance varies between 225,623 miles and 252,088 miles, for an average of 238,855 miles, so the conspiracy theory isn't even factual).

The psychology behind the *fallacy of excluded exceptions* is the *confirmation bias*, where, once one commits to a belief, the tendency is to look for and find only confirming examples and ignore the disconfirming. For example, in other paranormal claims, what about all the psychic or astrologer predictions that did not come true or the major events that were not predicted by psychics and astrologers? In the faith realm, cancers that go into remission after intercessory prayer are often considered religious miracles, but what about the cancers that disappeared without faith-based intervention or prayed-for cancer patients who died? Divine providence is often adduced when a few faithful people survive a disaster, but all the religious folks who died (or atheists who lived) are expediently ignored.

Signal detection theory is a tool for deciding what to do or how to act given what one believes to be the truth about assertions when the problem of uncertainty and excluded exceptions is rampant.[50] Medical cure claims associated with this or that medicinal plant or alternative treatment modality typically include only testimonials and anecdotes from Cell 1 and exclude in their reports cases from the other cells—for example, where treated patients were not cured or were cured but possibly due to other causes. Crime waves are often linked to economic downturns (Cell 1), but this hypothesis is gainsaid by counter examples, such as the relatively low crime rates during the 1930s depression era and the 2008–2010 recession or cases where crime rates are high during economic booms (other cells).

Excluded exceptions test the rule in *counterfactual causation* reasoning. Without them, science reverts to selective speculation from just one of the cells in the 2 × 2 grid. The social psychologist Carol Tavris employed the 2 × 2 grid concept in a 2017 *Skeptic* article on the "cycles of abuse" hypothesis that contends abused children grow up to become abusive parents. "If you created a fourfold table ('abused as a child? yes/no'; and 'abusive as a parent? yes/no'), most people pay attention to only two cells: the abused children (yes) who become abusive parents (yes)," Tavris explained. "They don't attend to the many people in the invisible cells: abused children who do not become cruel parents (yes/no), and the nonabused children who do (no/yes)."[51] Table 3.2 presents the 2 × 2 grid for applying signal detection theory to this problem.

Tavris then applies this heuristic to the #metoo movement to inquire about the missing voices in this necessary national dialogue: "women who thoroughly enjoyed their years of sexual freedom and experimentation; who slept with professors and bosses and coworkers for pleasure and excitement, and whose careers were not ruined thereby"; "women who had some awful encounters, or boring ones, or regrettably stupid ones, but

Table 3.2. Abusive Parents

Abusive parents who were abused as children	Abusive parents who were not abused as children
Abused children who grow up to be abusive	Abused children who do not grow up to be abusive

would never blame, let alone sue, their partners on the grounds that they were at least 50% of the people in the bed"; "shy men and boys who have felt pressured or even coerced by women, whether the women were their employers or dates"; "men who would not dream of having sex with a woman who is blotto drunk, unconscious, or unwilling."[52]

Life is a series of signal detection problems that include, in the jargon of the signal detection theory, *hits*, *misses*, *false alarms*, and *correct rejections*. The medical diagnosis example is a signal detection problem (table 3.3): You really have cancer and you conclude you do (*hit*); you really have cancer but you conclude you don't (*miss*); you don't have cancer but you conclude you do (*false alarm*); and you don't have cancer and you conclude you don't (*correct rejection*).

Table 3.3. Cancer

You have cancer Diagnosis of cancer **Hit**	You have cancer Diagnosis no cancer **Miss**
You do not have cancer Diagnosis of cancer **False Alarm**	You do not have cancer Diagnosis no cancer **Correct Rejection**

Table 3.4. Criminal Justice

Defendant is guilty Jury convicts **Hit**	Defendant is guilty Jury acquits **Miss**
Defendant is innocent Jury convicts **False Alarm**	Defendant is innocent Jury acquits **Correct Rejection**

Criminal justice is another signal detection problem (table 3.4). The defendant is guilty and the jury convicts (*hit*); the defendant is guilty and the jury acquits (*miss*); the defendant is innocent and the jury convicts (*false alarm*); the defendant is innocent and the jury acquits (*correct rejection*).

In this case, most juries agree with the renowned jurist William Blackstone's signal detection ratio of 10:1 (what has become known as Blackstone's ratio). He wrote: "It is better that ten guilty persons escape than that one innocent suffer."[53]

The COVID-19 pandemic was a signal detection problem we can examine through the 2 × 2 grid (table 3.5): The disease is extremely deadly, and we mandate masks and vaccines and close schools and businesses and

Table 3.5. COVID-19 Lockdowns

COVID very deadly Masks / social isolation **Hit**	COVID very deadly Business as usual **Miss**
COVID not very deadly Masks / social isolation **False Alarm**	COVID not very deadly Business as usual **Correct Rejection**

save lives (*hit*); the disease is extremely deadly, and we carry on business as usual (*miss*); the disease is no more deadly than the flu, and we mandate masks and vaccines and close schools and businesses (*false alarm*); the disease is no more deadly than the flu, and we carry on business as usual (*correct rejection*).

The problem we faced in the spring of 2020 is that we did not have sufficient information to make a proper response criteria of "yes" or "no" to the available options, and while COVID-19 was certainly deadlier than the common flu, it was not deadly enough to justify the extreme measures of school and business closures that caused deep hurt to the economy and the education of students that many commentators think was known by the fall of 2020.[54]

Even the search for true love in dating with a goal of marriage is a signal detection problem (table 3.6): The person you are dating is the perfect spouse for you, and you propose or accept a proposal for marriage (*hit*); the person you are dating is the perfect spouse for you, and you decline to propose or accept a proposal for marriage (*miss*); the person you are dating is not the right person for you, but you marry anyway (*false alarm*); the person you are dating is not the right person for you, and you decline to propose or reject a proposal for marriage (*correct rejection*).

Where you set your response criteria—that is, at what point you declare "yes" or "no" to whether the evidence is sufficient to correctly determine *hits* and *correct rejections* or incorrectly conclude a *false alarm* or a *miss*—very

Table 3.6. Marriage

Date is perfect spouse Marriage **Hit**	Date is perfect spouse No marriage **Miss**
Date is not a good fit Marriage **False Alarm**	Date is not a good fit No marriage **Correct Rejection**

much depends on the particular example under study and the evidence for it. More evidence means we should increase our credence in the likelihood of the claim being true; less evidence means we should withhold our assent that the assertion is true. And, again, Bayesian reasoning helps us determine what is likely true or false, while signal detection theory helps us decide what we should do given our beliefs about what is true or false.

■ Why? The Ultimate Causality Question

The goal of science is to understand the cause of things, which is why the computer scientist and leading scholar of all things causality, Judea Pearl, titled his magnum opus (coauthored with Dana Mackenzie) *The Book of Why: The New Science of Cause and Effect.* In the book, Pearl outlined his three-tiered "Ladder of Causation," which includes (from lower- to higher-rung causality):

1. Association
   a. *Activity*: Seeing, Observing.
   b. *Questions*: What if I see . . . ? (How are the variables related? How would seeing X change my belief in Y?)
   c. *Examples*: What does a symptom tell me about a disease? What does a survey tell us about the election results?
2. Intervention
   a. *Activity*: Doing, Intervening.
   b. *Questions*: What if I do . . . ? How? (What would Y be if I do X? How can I make Y happen?)
   c. *Examples*: If I take aspirin, will my headache be cured? What if we ban cigarettes?
3. Counterfactuals
   a. *Activity*: Imagining, Retrospection, Understanding.
   b. *Questions*: What if I had done . . . ? Why? (Was it X that caused Y? What if X had not occurred? What if I had acted differently?)

c. *Examples*: Was it the aspirin that stopped my headache? Would Kennedy be alive if Oswald had not killed him? What if I had not smoked for the last two years?[55]

Following Hume's reasoning about counterfactual causality, Pearl takes it even further to argue that counterfactual reasoning is the most sophisticated of the three causality rungs and may even constitute a turning point in the evolution of human consciousness—namely, the ability to not only learn from the past but to imagine a different future as a result of our actions: "Every philosophical theory, scientific discovery, and technological innovation, from microscopes to airplanes to computers," Pearl conjectures, "had to take shape in someone's imagination before it was realized in the physical world."[56]

While rungs one and two on the causality ladder involve things that are seen, counterfactual causality requires minds that can imagine what cannot be seen or that even contradict what is seen. It is from this cognitive capacity that we developed not only science and technology but architecture, art, music, literature, religion, morality, customs, norms, laws, government, economics, and most of what constitutes culture. Thus, understanding the truths of science and reason is arguably the most important thing humans have ever done or will ever do. As the physicist David Deutsch suggests, we may very well be only now at the beginning of infinity.[57] How so? In Deutsch's view—which closely parallels my own philosophy—science is about offering explanations for the world, statements "about what is there, what it does, and how and why," and as such, there are good and bad explanations. Good explanations start with the recognition that they could be wrong (fallibilism) and thus must always be open to revision (Popper's *conjecture and refutation* model of science): "The real source of our theories is conjecture, and the real source of our knowledge is conjecture alternating with criticism. We create theories by rearranging, combining, altering and adding to existing ideas with the intention of improving upon them."[58]

Since none of us are omniscient, all knowledge is provisional. Nevertheless, if we apply the tools of science and reason, our explanations can get closer to the truth. Deutsch asserts that "everything that is not forbidden by laws of nature is achievable, given the right knowledge."[59] The implications for the future of humanity with the right knowledge, Deutsch imagines in poetic imagery, are almost unimaginably ennobling:

> Like an explosive awaiting a spark, unimaginably numerous environments in the universe are waiting out there, for aeons on end, doing nothing at all or blindly generating evidence and storing it up or pouring it out into space. Almost any of them would, if the right knowledge ever reached it, instantly and irrevocably burst into a radically different type of physical activity: intense knowledge-creation, displaying all the various kinds of complexity, universality and reach that are inherent in the laws of nature, and transforming that environment from what is typical today into what could become typical in the future. If we want to, we could be that spark.[60]

Let's be that spark. Unleash the power of science and reason.

4

The Truth About Coincidences and Miracles

How to Think About Highly Unlikely Events

■ An automobile I once purchased had the license plate 6NWL485. What are the chances that I would get that particular configuration? *Before* I knew what license plate I would get, the odds of receiving this particular configuration of numbers and letters would have been 1 in 175,760,000 (the total number of letters to the power of the number of letters on the plate, or 26^3, times the total number of digits, 10, to the power of the number of digits on the plate, 4, or $26^3 \times 10^4$).[1] *After the fact*, however, the probability is 1.

This is what the economist Gary Smith calls the *survivor bias*, which he highlights as one of many statistically related cognitive biases in his book *Standard Deviations*.[2] Smith illustrates the effect with a playing-card hand of three of clubs, eight of clubs, eight of diamonds, queen of hearts, and ace of spades. The odds of that particular configuration are about three million to one, says Smith, but "after I look at the cards, the probability of having these five cards is 1."[3]

The conclusion seems obvious once you think about it, but most of us are regularly fooled by randomness. This is one of many obstacles to our search for truth that can be overcome through understanding how to think about highly unlikely events, from the coincidental to the miraculous.

How to Think About Coincidences

Imagine a series of five rolls of a die. Which sequence seems more likely, 2-6-5-3-4 or 6-6-6-6-6? Intuitively, most of us feel like the first sequence is more likely than the second because we equate randomness with an equal distribution of the numbers, yet they are both equally likely. Something similar happens when subjects are asked to make up a random-looking sequence of coin tosses:[4] Most propose a sequence of heads and tails close to 50/50, whereas real world coin-flip models produce sequences with long streaks of heads and tails.[5]

There's an oft-told story about what happened when Apple computer company first introduced the iPod's "random" music shuffle feature: People complained that it wasn't random, because some songs came up more often than others, which to most people doesn't feel random. Customers complained to Apple, leading Steve Jobs to have the iPod feature reprogrammed through "Smart Shuffle," which enabled users to determine the likelihood of hearing the same songs in a set. As Jobs said, "We're making it less random, to make it feel more random."[6]

In fact, that's what randomness is: clusters of events. Many "cancer clusters" that send public health officials and politicians into a search for some causal agent like a chemical plant or toxic waste dump are, in fact, just a random assortment of cases (there are also "cancer fortresses" where there are *no* cases of cancer in a geographical area, but no one looks for the protective forces at work within). Likewise, if you toss a handful of coins into the air and watch where they land on the ground, they will not be perfectly spaced on the ground. If they were, it would mean there is some force determining their perfectly even distribution. Or consider the random scattering of stars in the sky. When you look up at the night sky, you see that the stars do not appear random. They look like, well, constellations of familiar figures, like eagles, rams, fish, lions, bears, chariots, and dippers—big and little. The two scatterplots of dots, in figure 4.1, where one is random and the other not, demonstrate how deceptive randomness

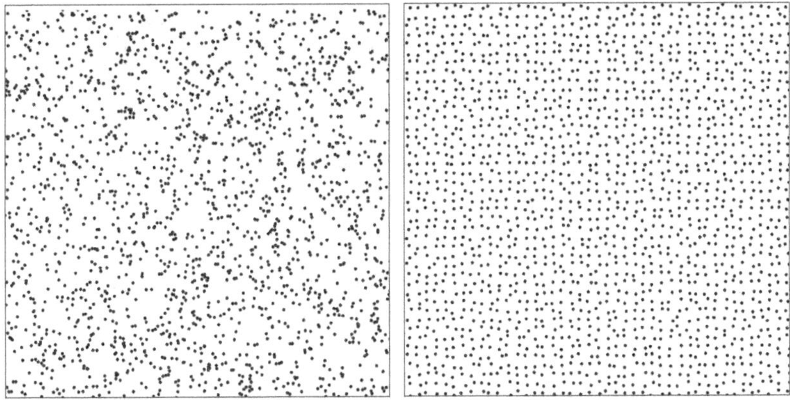

Figure 4.1. Two scatterplots of dots, one random and one not random, illustrate that the appearance of randomness can be deceiving. Many choose the *right* scatterplot as the random one, even though its dots were purposely dispersed. The *left* scatterplot, with its clumps and imaginable patterns, is the random one. Author-generated graphic

can be. People often choose the spaced-out configuration of dots in the right scatterplot as the random one, whereas it is the left one, with its clusters, that is random.[7]

Stephen Jay Gould made this point in noting the distribution of glowworms on the grotto ceiling of Waitomo Cave on the North Island of New Zealand as he glided silently by boat beneath the assembly of lights:

> I was dazzled by the effect because I found it so unlike the heavens. Stars are arrayed in the sky at random with respect to the earth's position. Hence, we view them as clumped into constellations. This may sound paradoxical, but my statement reflects a proper and unappreciated aspect of random distributions. Evenly spaced dots are well ordered for cause. Random arrays always include some clumping, just as we will flip several heads in a row quite often so long as we can make enough tosses—and our sky is not wanting for stars. The glowworms,

on the other hand, are spaced more evenly because larvae compete with, and even eat, each other—and each constructs an exclusive territory. The glowworm grotto is an ordered heaven.[8]

Another example of misunderstanding coincidences and randomness comes from the world of business book publishing. Gary Smith analyzed two of the bestsellers in the genre. In the 2001 book *Good to Great* (over four million copies sold), the author Jim Collins culled 11 companies out of 1,435 whose stock beat the market average over a 40-year time span and then searched for shared characteristics among them that he believed accounted for their success. What he should have done, says Smith, is start with a list of companies at the *beginning* of the test period, then "use plausible criteria to select eleven companies predicted to do better than the rest. These criteria must be applied in an objective way, without peeking at how the companies did over the next forty years. It is not fair or meaningful to predict which companies will do well after looking at which companies did well! Those are not predictions, just history."[9] In fact, Smith notes, from 2001 through 2012, the stock of 6 of Collins's 11 "great" companies did *worse* than the overall stock market, meaning that this system of post hoc analysis is fundamentally flawed.

Smith found a similar problem with the 1982 book *In Search of Excellence* (over three million copies sold), in which Tom Peters and Robert Waterman identified 8 common attributes of 43 "excellent" companies. Since then, says Smith, of the 35 companies with publicly traded stocks, 20 did worse than the market average. Given these facts, Smith advised thusly: "If we think we know any secrets for success, a valid way to test our theory would be to identify businesses or people with these traits and see how they do over the next ten or twenty or fifty years. Otherwise, we are just staring at the past instead of predicting the future."[10]

The survivor bias was evident in the reception of Walter Isaacson's best-selling biography of Steve Jobs, as readers (including me) scrambled to understand what made the mercurial genius so successful. I called it the *biography bias*, a variant of the survivor bias.[11] Want to be the next Steve Jobs, create the next Apple, and become the next billionaire? Attend an elite liberal arts college, drop out before graduation, move back in with your parents, and start a business with your buddy in the garage. How many people have followed the Jobs model and failed? Who knows? No one writes biographies about them and their failed companies. But venture capitalists (VCs) have data on the probability of a garage start-up becoming the Next Big Thing, and here, the survivor bias is of a different sort. David Cowan, a VC at Bessemer Venture Partners in Menlo Park, California, explained it to me:

> For garage-dwelling entrepreneurs to crack the 1% wealth threshold in America, their path almost always involves raising venture capital and then getting their startup to an initial public offering (IPO) or a large acquisition by another company. If their garage is situated in Silicon Valley they might get to pitch as many as 15 VCs, but VCs hear 200 pitches for every one we fund, so perhaps 1 in 13 startups get VC, and still they face long odds from there. According to figures that the National Venture Capital Association diligently collects through primary research and publishes on their web site, last year was somewhat typical in that 1,334 startups got funded but only 13% as many achieved an IPO (81 last year) or an acquisition large enough to warrant a public disclosure of the price (95 last year). So for every wealthy startup founder, there are 100 other entrepreneurs who end up with only a cluttered garage.[12]

Surviving those statistical odds is rare indeed.

The Sum of All Coincidences Equals Certainty

The statistician David Hand makes a related point in his book *The Improbability Principle*, aptly subtitled *Why Coincidences, Miracles, and Rare Events Happen Every Day*.[13] Hand begins with a definition of *coincidence* by the statisticians Persi Diaconis and Frederick Mosteller as "a surprising concurrence of events, perceived as meaningfully related, with no apparent causal connection."[14] Here is an example from the skeptic and science writer Martin Gardner: One day, Martin was perusing a used bookstore when he came across a familiar title. His father had given him a copy of that book when he was a child, but he had lost it during a move many years prior. As he considered purchasing this replacement copy, Gardner flipped through the pages and found his own handwritten notes in the margins. It was the *very book* Gardner had lost.[15]

An even spookier coincidence happened to the actor Anthony Hopkins, who, in 1972, was signed to star in the film adaptation of George Feifer's novel *The Girl from Petrovka*. Hopkins went to several London booksellers to purchase a copy, but none had it in stock. Heading for home, he chanced upon a book on a bench at the Leicester Square tube station. Unbelievably, it was *The Girl from Petrovka*. Two years later, when Hopkins met Feifer and mentioned the coincidence to him, the author noted that he had lent his last copy to a friend with handwritten edits in it for the American edition, changing "labour" to "labor," for example. When Hopkins flipped open his copy, he saw Feifer's annotations—it was *the very same book!*[16]

Given the human propensity to find meaningful patterns in both meaningful and meaningless noise (what I call *patternicity*) and to infuse those patterns with intentional agents (what I call *agenticity*),[17] many people see in such concurrences the hand of the divine or some mysterious force, like Carl Jung's "synchronicity" or Rupert Sheldrake's "morphic resonance," that somehow connects things based on their meaning. These propensities lead us away from the truth about how the universe works, which is namely that it is not saturated with design and purpose like our minds think it is. Attempts at a scientific explanation often include quantum mechanics, with its mysterious "spooky action at a distance" (in Albert Einstein's famous characterization of it). But just because quantum physics is spooky and weird—and many coincidences seem spooky and weird—does not mean there is a causal connection.

In fact, says Hand, such paranormal or supernatural explanations are unnecessary. Hand recounts Hopkins's book story—plus dozens of equally unlikely events—to illustrate why, in a world as vast as ours and with so many possible events in the offing, "the extraordinarily unlikely *must* happen; events of vanishingly small probability *will* occur."[18] As Diaconis said, "The really unusual day would be one where nothing unusual happens."[19]

There are several laws of probability at work here, says Hand, starting with the "law of inevitability," which states that "if you make a complete list of all possible outcomes then one of them must occur." Then, the "law of truly large numbers" means that "with a large enough number of opportunities, any outrageous thing is likely to happen." Evelyn Marie Adams, for example, won the New Jersey Lottery in 1985 and again in 1986. The odds of this occurrence were about one in a trillion. But, Hand notes, *someone* had to win the lottery, and "when we look at the number of lotteries there are around the world, the number of people who play, the number of tickets they buy, and the number of weeks that they play, we rapidly approach a truly large number." In fact, Hand cites three more people who have won lotteries twice and many more still who have won second prizes in lotteries multiple times in what he calls the "law of near enough," in which "events which are sufficiently similar are regarded as identical."[20]

Finally, Hand's "law of selection" means that we notice coincidences *after the fact*. This would be like an archer drawing a series of concentric circles around the arrow he just shot and embedded in a barn door and then declaring it to be a bull's-eye—the Texas sharpshooter fallacy. No one else but Gardner or Hopkins would have thought anything about finding those particular books, for example, and no one asks why Hopkins did not find a copy of *The Silence of the Lambs* on a subway when he landed that role. No one keeps track of such noncoincidences.

Here's a back-of-the-envelope calculation I did: According to Google Books, there are about 130 million book titles in the world. If the average print run was around 5,000 copies each, that totals 650 billion books. With a world literacy rate of 84.1%, that means around 5.9 billion people are reading some of those 650 billion books. It would be miraculous if someone somewhere sometime did not find a surprising connection of some sort with one of those books.

The principle here is this: *The sum of all coincidences equals certainty.*

Here's another example of this principle at work. Have you ever gone to the phone to call a friend, only to hear the phone ring first and find your friend on the line? What are the odds of that? Not high, to be sure, but to say it another way, *the sum of all probabilities equals one*. Think of all the other things that also could have happened but didn't at that particular time. For example, how many times did you phone your friend without him or her calling you at that moment? How many times did your friend phone you when you weren't thinking of him or her? Multiply that by a couple hundred million people in the United States alone making dozens of calls a day, and it becomes almost inevitable that this seemingly synchronous connection—which many people attribute to synchronicity or Karma or coincidence—is fully explained by the *law of inevitability*, the *law of very large numbers*, and the *law of selection*.

■ Monty Hall's Mathematical Misunderstanding

A final (and famous) example of our innumeracy comes straight out of the classic television game show *Let's Make a Deal*. It's called the Monty Hall problem, after the name of the longtime game show host. Here's the setup. You are chosen out of an audience to be the contestant and tasked with selecting one of three doors on stage. Behind one of the doors is a brand-new car. Behind the other two doors are goats. Let's say you choose door number one. Monty Hall, who knows what is behind all three doors and will only show you a goat, shows you what's behind door number two (a goat) and then inquires: Would you like to keep the door you chose or switch?

Most people figure that at the start of the game you had a one-third chance of being right, but now that Monty has revealed one of the goat doors, the probability shifts from one-third to one-half, so it doesn't matter whether you switch or not. But in this case, you—along with almost everyone presented with the problem—would be wrong. Amusingly, in a real-life example of the innumeracy of even statisticians and mathematicians, when the Monty Hall problem was presented by Marilyn vos Savant in her weekly *Parade* magazine column—a magazine read by tens of millions of people each week—most people, including the math mavens, upbraided her in no uncertain terms for the ignorance of her ways. One Scott Smith, PhD, from the University of Florida, for example, explained in exasperated tones:

> You blew it, and you blew it big! Since you seem to have difficulty grasping the basic principle at work here, I'll explain. After the host reveals a goat, you now have a one-in-two chance of being correct. Whether you change your selection or not, the odds are the same. There is enough mathematical illiteracy in this country, and we don't need the world's highest IQ propagating more. Shame![21]

W. Robert Smith, PhD, from Georgia State, admonished vos Savant: "I am sure you will receive many letters on this topic from high school and college students. Perhaps you should keep a few addresses for help with future columns." Don Edwards, from Sunriver, Oregon, mansplained to the world's smartest person: "Maybe women look at math problems differently than men."[22]

The column received over 10,000 letters, 1,000 of which included signature lines with a PhD after the correspondents' names. They were all wrong. Here's why: At the start of the game, you had a one-third chance of picking the car and a two-thirds chance of picking a goat. Switching doors is bad only if you first chose the car, which happens only one-third of the time. Switching doors is good if you first chose a goat, which happens two-thirds of the time. Thus, the probability of winning by switching is two-thirds, or double the odds of not switching. Another way to think about it is that there are three possibilities for the three doors: (1) *good bad bad*;

(2) *bad good bad*; (3) *bad bad good*. In possibility (1), you lose by switching. In possibilities (2) and (3), you can win by switching. Still not convinced? Imagine that there are 100 doors; you choose door number 1 and Monty shows you door numbers 2 through 99, all goats. Now would you switch? Of course you would, because your chances of winning increase from 1/10 to 99/100![23]

If this still feels counterintuitive, you can actually play the three-door game at https://montyhall.io/, and on other websites, you can find computer programs that have run hundreds of thousands of simulations of the game and prove that in the long run, it is better to switch doors.

A proximate explanation for why this problem trips up so many people was provided by Steven Pinker, who invoked Daniel Kahneman's distinction between System 1 cognition (rapid and intuitive) and System 2 cognition (slow and reflective) in noting that such brain teasers are designed to "bring out the stupid in our System 1." Yet, even our more reflective System 2 often gets such problems wrong. Why? "A clue comes from the overconfident justifications that the know-it-alls offered for their blunders, sometimes thoughtlessly carried over from other probability puzzles," Pinker suggests. "Many people insist that each of the unknown alternatives (in this case, the unopened doors) must have an equal probability. That is true of symmetrical gambling toys like the faces of a coin or sides of a die, and it is a reasonable starting point when you know absolutely nothing about the alternatives."[24]

An ultimate explanation for this fallacy, as well as those seen in the law of small numbers and the law of large numbers, has to do with our evolved psychology of anecdotal thinking that developed in a land midway between short and long, small and large, slow and fast, young and old. Call it *Middle Land*. In the Middle Land of space, our senses evolved for perceiving objects of middling size—between, say, grains of sand and mountain ranges. We are not equipped to perceive atoms and germs, on one end of the scale, or galaxies and expanding universes, on the other end. In the Middle Land of speed, we can detect objects moving at a walking or running pace, but the glacially slow movement of continents (and glaciers) and the mind-bogglingly fast speed of light are imperceptible. Our Middle Land time scales range from the psychological "now" of three seconds in duration to the few decades of a human lifetime, far too short to witness evolution, continental drift, or long-term environmental changes. Our Middle Land folk numeracy leads us to pay attention to and remember short-term trends, meaningful coincidences, and personal anecdotes. Artificial tasks, such as playing card games in gambling casinos, trading stocks on Wall Street, or participating in television game shows, are unnatural and counterintuitive. Thinking in terms of probabilities is not natural; thinking in terms of stories with personal meaning is.

Amusingly, when I wrote about the Monty Hall problem in *Scientific American*, referencing vos Savant's *Parade* column, its numerous letters, and why her PhD interlocutors were wrong, I too received hundreds of letters, mostly critical; some even suggested that for making such egregious blunders in basic probability theory, I had no place writing in such an august publication. In a subsequent response, I noted the explanations discussed earlier and added that one of my correspondents ran his own simulation of more than 10,000 trials and concluded that "switching doors yields a two thirds success rate while running without switching doors yields a one third success rate."[25]

■ Hot Hands and Gambler's Fallacies

A related statistical effect and popular issue for sports fans is the notion of "hot hands" in basketball. As both fans and players know, when you're hot, you're hot, and when you're not, you're not, and you can see it on any given night on the court. To test the hypothesis, cognitive psychologists Robert Vallone, Thomas Gilovich, and Amos Tversky analyzed every shot taken by the Philadelphia 76ers basketball team for the entire 1985 season, only to discover that the probability of a player hitting a second shot did not increase following an initial successful basket beyond what one would expect by chance and the average shooting percentage of the player. That is, the number of successful baskets in sequence did not exceed the predictions of a statistical coin-flip model.[26] This was a controversial finding, especially among professional basketball players and their avid fans, with none other than superstar Stephen Curry—the all-time greatest three-point shooter in basketball—proclaiming:

> They don't know what they're talking about at all. It's literally a tangible, physical sensation of "all I need to do is get this ball off my fingertips, and it's gonna go in. . . ." There are times you catch the ball, and you've maybe made one or two in a row—and . . . the rim feels like the ocean. And it's one of the most rewarding feelings.[27]

One reason to trust Steph Curry's intuitions about his own abilities over that of the statisticians is that, unlike the flip of a coin, the roll of the dice, or the spin of a roulette wheel—whose events are independent of one another (the coin, die, and roulette wheel have no memory of what came before the current flip, roll, or spin, so individual events cannot be influenced by what came before)—athletic performance can be influenced by emotions, confidences, worries, distractions, and the like, so basketball shots are not independent of one another.

Nevertheless, are such dependent events in fact streaky beyond what one would predict statistically? A 2021 study of a dozen NBA (National Basketball Association) seasons (2004–2016) by Robert Lantis and Erik Nesson that looked at free throws (more controlled) and field goal attempts (less controlled) found "a small hot hand effect for free throws, which more than doubles for longer streaks of consecutively made free throws. However, if a player makes a field goal, he is no more or less likely to make his next field goal attempt, and longer streaks of consecutively made field goals reduce the probability that a player makes his next field goal attempt."[28] A 2022 study by Konstantinos Pelechrinis and Wayne Winston analyzed over 400,000 shot sequences across all NBA players over two seasons (2013–2014, 2014–2015) and found a slight hot hand effect, with qualifications: "Considering in-game basketball game situations, our analysis provides statistical evidence that individual players do indeed exhibit the hot hand in varying degrees, that is, individual players can consistently get in a streak of successful shots beyond random chance. However, as a whole, the average player exhibits shooting regression, that is, after consecutive makes he tends to perform below expectations."[29]

One complication in such analyses was identified by the economists Joshua Miller and Adam Sanjurjo, namely that when the researcher chooses to start and end a streak in a long run of data—which may be arbitrary—can lead to a bias that can support or refute the hot hand hypothesis (referencing the original 1985 study):

> The magnitude of this streak selection bias generally decreases as the sequence gets longer, but increases in streak length, and remains substantial for a range of sequence lengths often used in empirical work. We observe that the canonical study in the influential hot hand fallacy literature, along with replications, are vulnerable to the bias. Upon correcting for the bias we find that the long-standing conclusions of the canonical study are reversed.[30]

In other words, there are good reasons to believe Steph Curry over the math mavens because (1) athletic performance streaks contain individual events that may be dependent on one another (subjective confidence or lack thereof can make one hot or not), and (2) gambling and game streaks seen in coin tosses, die rolls, and roulette wheel spins contain individual events that are independent of one another. Our intuitive evaluations of streaky things in life tend to confuse the dependent or independent nature of the individual elements of the streak.[31]

An illustrative example of these effects was provided by Richard Hardison in his book *Upon the Shoulders of Giants*, in the aptly titled chapter "Dice Have No Memories"—a computer tournament involving 1,165 "subjects" playing roulette for a total of 208,680 spins of the wheel, in which bets of one dollar were placed for each spin. The overall loss for all 1,165 subjects was a staggering $33 million. Nevertheless, 24 of the "subjects" beat the computer and finished in the green. In the real world of professional gambling, these are the people celebrated by casinos, which know that most people will remember the winners and forget the losers. "This may help to explain how we may know of individual people who are ahead after quite a number of trips to Las Vegas or to the horse races, even though the average loss is both predictable and large," Hardison explains.[32] Here, we are justified in saying that the 24 gamblers were lucky, but only in a statistical sense, not in any cosmic synchronicity. Luck is a description of past events, not a portend of the future. "Anyone who believes that one player has a better chance of winning because he is 'luckier,'" noted the gambling expert and card shark John Scarne, "is no smarter than the customers of the sorcerers and witches of the Middle Ages."[33]

If any such people did exist, casinos around the world—from Las Vegas and Atlantic City to Monte Carlo and Venice—would know about them and implement countermeasures before they were bankrupted by the cosmically lucky. That hasn't happened for a reason—that type of luck does not exist. Instead, casinos depend on the law of large numbers, namely that lots of gamblers play lots of games over long stretches of time, such that even small percentages of the "take" accumulate into massive profits in the long run. American roulette wheels, for example, in addition to 18 red slots and 18 black slots, have 2 green slots, giving the house a 5.26% advantage. Straight bets in craps generate a 1.4% profit for the casino. In blackjack, if a player follows the dealer's strategy of play—"stay" on 17 or above, otherwise "hit" for another card—the house take is 5.5%. Slot machines are the worst for players, averaging around 10% for the house (depending on the casino and slot machine algorithms). The point is that if you play long enough, you will lose, which is why casinos are designed to keep customers seated for as long as possible, with no windows or clocks to keep track of time, confusing mazes of pathways out of the casino to the exits or hotel room elevators, cheap buffet food, and even free drinks (mine was a White Russian while playing blackjack).

Another form of gambling in which loss aversion applies (in which losses hurt twice as much as gains feel good) is the casino known as Wall Street. If you invest in the stock market, for example, you should be careful not to be overly sensitive to short-term losses, as studies show that despite the sawtooth curve of daily ups and downs, in the long run, the overall saw blade is angled upward. Gilovich cites a study showing that from 1963 to 1993, the stock market averaged an annual return of almost 12%. An investment of $10,000 in 1963 that remained fully invested the entire time would net you $233,000. But if you panicked during the countless downturns in the market and missed the 40 best-performing days, that 1963 investment of $10,000 would only earn you about $80,000. Loss aversion is not just disconcerting, it is expensive.[34]

■ Miracles as Highly Improbable Events

Do you believe in miracles?

That was the question asked by the ABC television sports commentator Al Michaels when the US Olympic hockey team defeated the supposedly unbeatable Russians, 4–3, in what became known as "the miracle on ice" in the 1980 Olympics. To many hockey fans, at least those in the United States, it was a seemingly miraculous event, although as you can imagine, the Russians did not think of this as a miracle at all.

We toss that word around a lot—*miracle*. When someone wins the lottery or recovers from an apparently deadly disease, they will often describe it as "miraculous." People who survive deadly car crashes consider their good fortune to be the product of divine intervention, although they rarely have an explanation for why other people in the car died. After 9/11, many survivors close to or inside the World Trade Center buildings attributed their good fortune to a miracle, but what about the 3,000 people who died? One person exits via the left stairwell and lives to talk about their miraculous survival, while another person uses the right stairwell and is trapped in a fiery inferno or leaps to their death. It is not satisfying to say "God works in mysterious ways," as that's a hand-waving nonfalsifiable explanation. Such events as these—and many more in the genre—are the product of probabilities and natural forces, not supernatural divine intervention (or lack thereof).

Earlier, we saw how many people think of coincidences and synchronicities as small miracles, inasmuch as they seem to be highly improbable events—so improbable that they intuitively feel miraculous. But feelings and intuitions are not reliable methods of determining whether or not miracles are true events in the world. We need to examine miracles with a skeptical eye, because, as we just saw in considering coincidences and randomness, we are not well equipped to grasp the truth about probabilities and the statistics of natural events.

To examine miracles from a scientific perspective, we must begin by defining what we're talking about. Since most people think of miracles as highly improbable events, let's stipulate for the following thought experiment that a miracle is an event with million-to-one odds of occurring—that seems unlikely enough to count as miraculous. Then, let's apply some back-of-the-envelope calculations along the lines of apparently miraculous events in daily life.[35] Assuming we are awake and alert for 12 hours a day and that, say, 1 bit per second of information flows into our brains through our senses, we are left with 43,200 bits of data per day, or 1,296,000 per month. Even assuming that 99.999% of these bits are totally meaningless (and so we filter them out or forget them entirely), at million-to-one odds, that still leaves 1.3 "miracles" per month, or 15.5 miracles per year. That is, even things with million-to-one odds of happening will happen fairly often, given enough time and events, and our propensity to remember the hits and forget the misses ensures that we will notice them.

I also conducted a similar back-of-the-envelope calculation to explain death premonition dreams—the type where someone has a dream about a loved one dying and finds out the next day that the person passed away in the middle of the night, maybe even around the time of the dream.[36] How unusual is that? Well, let's put some numbers on it. The average person has about five dreams per night, or 1,825 dreams per year. If we remember only 1/10 of our dreams, then we recall 182.5 dreams per year. Let's say that there are 300 million adult Americans who thus produce 54.7 billion remembered dreams per year. Sociologists tell us that each of us knows about 150 people fairly well (the so-called *Dunbar number*, named after Robin Dunbar, who discovered this in his research on human social networking), thus producing a network social grid of 45 billion personal relationship connections. With an average annual death rate of 2.4 million Americans per year (all causes, all ages), it is inevitable that some of those 54.7 billion remembered dreams will be about some of these 2.4 million deaths among the 300 million Americans and their 45 billion relationship connections. In fact, it would be a *miracle* if some death premonition dreams did *not* come true!

Here's an announcement you'll never hear on television:

> *Next up on the show, we'll introduce a woman who has had numerous death premonition dreams, not one of which has come true yet . . . but stay tuned because you won't want to miss her incredible story.*

In this sense, nonmiracles are non-news stories, so we never hear about the billions of things that *could have happened by chance but didn't.*

The late physicist Freeman Dyson made a similar calculation in a *New York Review of Books* article titled "Littlewood's Law of Miracles" (John Edensor Littlewood was a Cambridge University mathematician):

> In the course of any normal person's life, miracles happen at a rate of roughly one per month. During the time that we are awake and actively engaged in living our lives, roughly for eight hours each day, we see and hear things happening at a rate of about one per second. So the total number of events that happen to us is about thirty thousand per day, or about a million per month. With few exceptions, these events are not miracles because they are insignificant. The chance of a

> miracle is about one per million events. Therefore we should expect about one miracle to happen, on the average, every month.[37]

Nevertheless, and as an example of how none of us—even supremely smart people—are immune from magical thinking, Dyson concludes his analysis with a "tenable" hypothesis that "paranormal phenomena may really exist," because "I am not a reductionist," he says; "that paranormal phenomena are real but lie outside the limits of science is supported by a great mass of evidence." That evidence is entirely anecdotal, he admits, but because his grandmother was a faith healer and his cousin edits the *Journal of the Society for Psychical Research* ("They may have been deluded, but neither of them was a fool"), and because anecdotes gathered by the Society for Psychical Research and other organizations suggest that under certain conditions (e.g., stress) some people sometimes apparently exhibit some paranormal powers (unless experimental controls are employed, at which point the powers disappear), Dyson concludes:

> I claim that paranormal phenomena may really exist but may not be accessible to scientific investigation. . . . The hypothesis that paranormal phenomena are real but lie outside the limits of science is supported by a great mass of evidence. . . . I am suggesting that paranormal mental abilities and scientific method may be complementary. . . . The classic example of complementarity is the dual nature of light. . . . I find it plausible that a world of mental phenomena should exist, too fluid and evanescent to be grasped with the cumbersome tools of science.[38]

Dyson was one of the greatest minds of our time, and I admired him immensely. But even a genius of this magnitude cannot override the cognitive biases that favor anecdotal thinking over data, the intuitive sense that highly improbable events cannot just be due to chance and coincidence and that spooky quantum physics experiments with light must somehow be connected to spooky paranormal claims. The only way to find out if anecdotes represent real phenomena is with controlled experiments that account for probabilities and chance through statistical tests. Either people can read other people's minds (or ESP cards), or they can't. Science has unequivocally demonstrated that they can't. And being a holist instead of a reductionist, being related to psychics, reading about weird things that befall people, and analyzing eerie physics experiments do not change this fact. The truth of the matter is that purported miracles are misunderstandings of how the world works.

Miracles as Divine Events

So, highly improbable and statistically unusual events cannot be miracles because they are still in the realm of natural possibilities that brook no need for divine intervention. That brings us to the understanding of miracles shared by most Christians, theologians, and religious apologists—divine intervention to alter the laws of nature to bring about a favorable outcome. By this definition of *miracle*, believers mean something divine has happened, and to make this case, Christian apologists go deep into the weeds of philosophy and theology (and sometimes even science) to make their case.

A typical work in this genre is the evangelical writer Lee Strobel's book *The Case for Miracles*, which includes a chapter on my own journey from embracing religious belief and accepting miracles (I was once a born-again Christian) to adopting scientific skepticism and rejecting miracles.[39] In response, the former evangelical and now skeptic John W. Loftus compiled a comprehensive analysis (titled, appropriately, *The Case Against Miracles*[40]) of such arguments, including the philosophical arguments of Christian apologists, biblical miracles from the Old Testament to the New, the miracle of creation, the miracle of life, the miracle of Noah's Flood, the miracle of the virgin birth of Jesus, the miracle of Jesus turning water into wine and raising the dead, and, of course, the greatest miracle of them all (for Christians anyway), Jesus's resurrection from the dead and ascendency into heaven.

Let's drill down deeper into the concept of "miracle" historically. In prescientific periods, the religious definition of miracles as "signs and wonders" applied to just about everything that happened in the world, from the ordinary to the extraordinary—from normal births to virgin births, from rain to deluges, from illness to pandemics, and from famines to feasts. Clearly, this will not suffice for an analysis of miracles—if everything is a miracle, then the term is meaningless. As science developed over the centuries, more and more of these signs and wonders were explained by natural forces, laws, and events, leaving fewer and fewer divine miracles, and thus less for a deity to do.

Enter the Enlightenment philosopher David Hume, whom we met before in discussing the proportionality principle of evidence. In his 1758 *An Enquiry Concerning Human Understanding*, Hume defined a miracle simply as "a violation of a law of nature" and more specifically as "a transgression of a law of nature by a particular volition of the Deity or . . . some invisible agent."[41] In fact, his Section X, titled "Of Miracles," provides a generalized, when-all-else-fails analysis of miraculous claims. That is, when one is confronted by a true believer whose apparently supernatural or paranormal claim has no immediately evident natural or normal explanation, Hume recommended using an argument that even he thought was so important that he placed his own words in quotes and called it a maxim (Hume was not a modest man). Let's honor Hume and call it *Hume's maxim*. Here is what Hume wrote:

> The plain consequence is (and it is a general maxim worthy of our attention), "That no testimony is sufficient to establish a miracle, unless the testimony be of such a kind, that its falsehood would be more miraculous than the fact which it endeavours to establish." When anyone tells me that he saw a dead man restored to life, I immediately consider with myself whether it be more probable, that this person should either deceive or be deceived, or that the fact, which he relates, should really have happened. I weigh the one miracle against the

> other; and according to the superiority, which I discover, I pronounce my decision, and always reject the greater miracle. If the falsehood of his testimony would be more miraculous than the event which he relates; then, and not till then, can he pretend to command my belief or opinion.[42]

In the two and a half centuries since Hume wrote this passage, we have learned much about deception and self-deception—especially the plethora of cognitive biases that distort our picture of reality—from the study of human perception, memory, and cognition, so *Hume's maxim* is even more supported today than it was in his time. People are routinely self-deceived and deceived by others, misunderstand what others tell them, misremember and confabulate memories, exaggerate and embellish stories about what they think happened, and misperceive how the world works. When a person tells us of a miracle they witnessed or that was described to them by someone else, it is far more likely that they *are either deceiving or have been deceived than the miracle really occurred.*

When we are thinking about miracles, as with anything else that happens in the world, what we are after is a causal explanation, and here, the insights of the philosopher David Kyle Johnson are instructive toward understanding what is signified by the word *miracle*. To wit, in Johnson's definition, "A miracle is simply an event caused by God." As Johnson explains, modifying Hume further, "For any given event, if we knew that God took special care to cause it, we would (and should) call that event a miracle—regardless of whether it involved the violation of natural law."[43] (One can imagine, for example, God curing someone's cancer by directing the body's immune system to target cancerous cells, which can happen naturally so is not a violation of natural law.) It is important to distinguish this from something that only *appears* to be divinely caused but was, in fact, simply a highly improbable natural occurrence, along the lines of my million-to-one odds calculation. We want to distinguish between a natural and a supernatural event when considering miracle claims. Here is Johnson again:

> Not only can't testimony justify belief that a miracle occurred, but not even seeing such an event for yourself would justify belief that a miracle occurred. It would still be more likely that your senses had led you astray. And even if you could confirm your observation with well-controlled experiments successfully repeated by the scientific community, it would be more likely that you were mistaken about what the laws were. Belief in miracles, it seems, will always be a matter of faith.[44]

I concur, and this is why I agree with Loftus's definition: "A miracle is a supernaturally caused extraordinary event of the highest kind, one that's unexplainable and even impossible by means of natural processes alone."[45]

Recall our discussion in chapter 3 of the "null hypothesis" in science. When a claim is made, a hypothesis proposed, a theory proffered, we assume it is *not true* (null) until proven otherwise. Scientists would say that your claim of a miracle is not true until you rule out all possible natural and probabilistic explanations. And, notably, the *burden of proof* is on the miracle claimant, not the skeptic or scientist, to disprove the miracle claim, which would be difficult in any case. For example, Jesus purportedly turned water into wine and walked on water. If true, these would be miraculous feats because they would require some sort of supernatural intervention. And yet, I have witnessed the magicians Penn and Teller do both. A specially prepared glass exchanges water for wine, and a clear plastic platform sunk just beneath the surface of a calm body of water allows the person on it to appear to walk on water.

Of course, believers in miracles could always reply, "Those are magic tricks! Jesus did it through divine power." But since none of us were there to witness Jesus's miracles, we can't determine how he did it, and as we shall see in the next chapter, followers of many prominent religious leaders make similar proclamations about miracles they claim to have seen before their very eyes or heard about from people they trust. Consider the Indian spiritual guru and saint who many millions of people believe to be the incarnation of God; he was performing miracles in another part of the globe from where Jesus performed his that were witnessed by and attested to by many people. These miracles included his alleged ability to levitate, read minds, perform exorcisms, cure the dying, and even raise the dead. His name was Shirdi Sai Baba, and many millions of Hindu and Muslim followers believe the fakir is the incarnation of Lord Shiva.[46] People attest to Sai Baba's divinity and his ability to perform miracles with powerful anecdotes as emotive as those told by Christians. So why don't most Christians believe such miracles? For the same reason I don't believe their miracle stories.

Also consider the 1917 "cosmic miracle of the sun" that happened in Fátima, Portugal, purportedly witnessed by some 70,000 people on October 13, during which the sun began to spin wildly and tumble down to Earth, radiating indescribably beautiful colors (figure 4.2). A 10-year-old girl named Lucia yelled "The sun!" As the crowd's collective gaze turned upward, they "saw that a silvery disc had emerged from behind clouds, they experienced what is known [as] a 'sun miracle,'" in which "the sun seemed to tear itself from the heavens and come crashing down upon the horrified multitude. . . . Just when it seemed that the ball of fire would fall upon and destroy them, the miracle ceased, and the sun resumed its normal place in the sky, shining forth as peacefully as ever."[47]

Accounts diverge about what really happened. As the journalist and science writer Benjamin Radford explains:

> Not everyone reported the same thing. Some present claimed they saw the sun dance around the heavens; others said the sun zoomed toward Earth in a zigzag motion that caused them to fear that it might collide with our planet (or, more likely, burn it up). Some people reported seeing brilliant colors spin out of the sun in a psychedelic, pinwheel pattern, and thousands of others present didn't see anything unusual at all.[48]

Here we face two possibilities: (1) The sun really did move about the sky and then came crashing down toward the crowd; (2) 70,000 witnesses were

O MILAGRE DE FÁTIMA

Varios aspectos do povo ajoelhado e orando no momento de descobrir o sol e de se dar o fenomeno que tanto impressionou a multidão.

(Carta a alguem que pede um testemunho insuspeito).

Quebrando um silencio de mais de vinte anos e com a invocação dos longinquos e saudosos tempos em que convivemos n'uma fraternal camaradagem, iluminada então pela fé comum e fortalecida por identicos propositos, escreves-me para que te diga, sincera e minuciosamente, o que vi e ouvi na charneca de Fátima, quando a fama de celestes aparições congregou n'aquele desolado ermo dezenas de milhares de pessoas mais sedentas, segundo creio, de sobrenatural do que impelidas por mera curiosidade ou receosas de um logro... Estão os catolicos em desacordo sobre a importancia e a significação do que presencearam. Uns convenceram-se de que se tinham cumprido prometimentos do Alto; outros acham-se ainda longe de acreditar na incontroversa realidade de um milagre. Foste um crente na tua juventude e deixaste de sel-o. Pessoas de familia arrastaram-te a Fátima, no vagalhão colossal d'aquele povo que ali se juntou a 13 de outubro. O teu racionalismo sofreu um formidavel embate e queres estabelecer uma opinião segura socorrendo-te de depoimentos insuspeitos como o meu, pois que estive lá apenas no desempenho de uma missão bem dificil, tal a de relatar imparcialmente para um grande diario, *O Seculo*, os factos que diante de mim se desenrolassem e tudo quanto de curioso e de elucidativo a eles se prendesse. Não ficará por satisfazer o teu desejo, mas decerto que os nossos olhos e os nossos ouvidos não viram nem ouviram coisas diversas, e que raros foram os que ficaram insensiveis á grandeza de semelhante espectaculo, unico entre nós e de todo o ponto digno de meditação e de estudo ..

* * *

O que ouvi e me levou a Fátima? Que a Virgem Maria, depois da festa da Ascenção, aparecera a tres crianças que apascentavam gado, duas mocinhas e um zagalete, recomendando-lhes que orassem e prometendo-lhes aparecer ali, sobre uma azinheira, no dia 13 de cada mez, até que em outubro lhes daria qualquer sinal do poder de Deus e faria revelações. Espalhou-se a nova por muitas leguas em redondeza; voou, de terra em terra, até os confins de Portugal, e a roma-

Figure 4.2. Page from *Ilustração Portuguesa*, October 29, 1917, showing people looking at the sun during the Fátima apparitions attributed to the Virgin Mary, supernatural events that supposedly took place on October 13, 1917. Wikimedia Commons, file name Newspaper fatima 353.jpg

mistaken, or deceived, or misperceived, or their accounts were misrepresented. Which one is more likely? As impressive as it is that 70,000 people witnessed something this miraculous, in a Humean sense, it is an even greater miracle that the sun would stop—that is, that the Earth would stop moving. If it had, everyone on Earth would have experienced it, and there would have been catastrophic consequences, such as massive sloshing of lakes and oceans and the wiping out of coastal cities around the globe. And yet, there are no reports of any such events happening anywhere on Earth.

What really happened at Fátima? Radford suggests that the crowd experienced an optical illusion possibly triggered by a *sundog*—an optical effect in which an atmospheric halo of ice crystals surrounding the sun results in bright lights on either side of the sun:

> Thousands of people looking up at the sky, hoping, expecting, and even praying for some sign from God. It is of course dangerous to stare directly at the sun, and to avoid permanently damaging their eyesight, those at Fátima that day were looking up in the sky around the sun, which, if you do it long enough, can give the illusion of the sun moving as the eye muscles tire.[49]

The Fátima sun miracle was attributed to the Virgin Mary, who also allegedly made an appearance in 1984, when 1,000 people, including doctors, lawyers, psychologists, and psychiatrists, were said to have seen her apparition near a waterfall in Betania, Venezuela. Such visions and apparitions, in fact, are not uncommon: One study of 15,000 people found 7.8% of men and 12% of women reported having had at least one vivid hallucinatory experience in their lives. A 1991 study of 18,000 people found 13% claimed to have had at least one vision. Bereavement visions are also common, especially when the experiencers are physically and emotionally exhausted, the deceased person was loved by the experiencer, and the death was unexpected or tragic.[50]

In terms of our search for truth and the importance of falsification and experimentation in the aspirational goal of moving from subjective truths to objective truths, this question comes to mind: What criteria can be applied to tell the difference between true accounts of Christian miracles performed by Yahweh or Jesus and false accounts of such miracles as those performed by Shirdi Sai Baba or witnessed at Fátima or Betania? It is understandable why Christians would believe Jesus was the one true miracle worker and all the others are false (or mistaken) prophets, but then each of the other religions has followers who said and believed the same. Some Christians argue that Jesus's disciples and other eyewitnesses went to their deaths believing Jesus performed such miracles, and this level of commitment purportedly should adjust our skeptical priors into giving the miracles credence. But would not that same logic apply to Jim Jones (Jonestown), David Koresh (Branch Davidians), Charles Manson (and his murderous family cult), Shoko Asahara (Aum Shinrikyo cult), Marshall Applewhite (Heaven's Gate cult), or Joseph Di Mambro (Solar Temple cult)?

Christians often counter my challenge by noting that 2.6 billion people believe Jesus was a miracle worker, whereas these examples of false prophets had comparatively few adherents. But there are today around two billion Muslims in the world who believe Muhammad's miracles just as strongly as Christians believe in the miracles of Jesus. To wit, Muslims believe that Muhammad split the moon; caused blindness to Qurashite warriors assembled at his door to assassinate him; caused a horse of an enemy pursuing him to sink into the mud; accurately predicted where enemy chiefs would be killed before the Battle of Badr; quenched the thirst of thousands of his soldiers; caused two trees to move at his command; caused a barren ewe to produce milk; caused it to rain during a drought in Medina; could understand the language of animals; did not cast a shadow; could hear the voices of the dead in their graves; could heal the sick and cure the blind by only touching the patient; and, most famously, flew on a winged horse from Mecca to Jerusalem to Heaven. And as for going to their deaths believing in such miracles, one need only note what Muhammad Atta and his fellow Muslim hijackers did on 9/11, declaring "Allahu

Akbar!"—"God is most great!"—as they went to their martyred deaths in anticipation of a glorious afterlife.

Most Muslims believe these miracles really happened, whereas most Christians are skeptical. If there is no test for the validity of a miracle claim, then the default position should be skepticism—the null hypothesis—that is, assume that no miracles are real unless and until an unmistakable miracle can be performed and attested to by objective outsiders or experts not of the same religious persuasion. An example popular among atheists is this: growing a limb on an amputee. If God can cure cancer, as many Christians believe in their intercessory prayers, surely an omnipotent deity could grow a limb on a sufficiently devout amputee; even salamanders can do that. So the null hypothesis here is that a claim of a miracle is not true until proven otherwise, and remember the ECREE principle: *extraordinary claims require extraordinary evidence.*

In the next chapter, I discuss the most extraordinary religious miracle claim in history, namely the resurrection from the dead of a certain carpenter from Nazareth, and why this account is better thought of not as an empirical truth but as a religious or mythic truth.

PART II

KNOWN UNKNOWNS

■ Reason and experiment have been indulged, and error has fled before them. It is error alone which needs the support of government. Truth can stand by itself.

—**Thomas Jefferson**, *Notes on the State of Virginia*

5

Religious and Mythic Truths How to Think About the Resurrection and Other Myths

■ About 2,000 years ago, a remarkable man was born in a remote part of the Roman Empire. His mother was said to have been informed by a divine being that the child she was about to conceive would be not a mere mortal but a deity, and she gave birth to him in a miraculous way. When this child became a young man, he left home and went on an itinerant preaching ministry, urging his listeners to live not for the material things of this world but for the spiritual. He collected disciples around him who came to believe that he was the Son of God, and he performed miracles as evidence of his divinity—he healed the sick, cast out demons, and even raised the dead. As a result, he was persecuted by the Roman authorities, and at the end of his life, he ascended to heaven. Sometime later, his followers told stories about him and recounted his supernatural powers.

I am speaking here not of Jesus of Nazareth but of Apollonius of Tyana, a Greek philosopher contemporaneous to Jesus and widely known in his own day.[1] We know about the life of Apollonius from the writings of his later follower Philostratus, who based his account, he tells us, on earlier eyewitness reports.[2] Subsequently, there were debates between the followers of Jesus and the followers of Apollonius over who was the true Son of God.[3]

These were, in fact, not the only miracle-working sons of God in the ancient world. There were a number of them, enough so that the idea of a divine human being was widely known throughout antiquity. The early church father Justin Martyr (100–165 CE) said this to his fellow Romans when defending what he believed about Jesus:

> When we say that the Word, who is our teacher, Jesus Christ the first-born of God, was produced without sexual union, and that he was crucified and died, and rose again, and ascended to heaven, we propound *nothing new or different from what you believe* regarding those whom you consider sons of Jupiter (supreme Roman deity).[4]

So the divine nature of Jesus was not unique. Nor was his virgin birth. Among those alleged to have been conceived without the usual assistance from the male lineage were: Dionysus, Perseus, Buddha, Attis, Krishna, Horus, Mercury, Romulus, and, of course, Jesus. Consider the parallels between Dionysus, the ancient Greek god of wine, and Jesus of Nazareth. Both were said to have been born from a virgin mother who was a mortal woman but were fathered by the king of heaven; both allegedly returned from the dead, transformed water into wine, introduced the idea of eating and drinking the flesh and blood of the creator, and were liberators of their people.[5]

Even the miracle of the resurrection is not unique to Christianity. Osiris is the Egyptian god of life, death, and fertility and is one of the oldest gods for whom records have survived.[6] Osiris first appears in the pyramid texts around 2400 BC, by which time his following was already well established. Widely worshipped until the compulsory repression of pagan religions in the early Christian era, Osiris was not only the redeemer and merciful judge of the dead in the afterlife; he was also linked to fertility, most notably (and appropriately for the geography) the flooding of the Nile and growth of crops. The kings of Egypt themselves were inextricably connected with Osiris in death, such that when Osiris rose from the dead, so would they in union with him. By the time of the New Kingdom, not only pharaohs but mortal men believed that they could be resurrected by and with Osiris at death if, of course, they practiced the correct religious rituals. Sound familiar? Osiris predates the Jesus messiah story by at least two and a half millennia.

Miraculous flood myths were also not uncommon in the ancient world. Predating the biblical Noahian flood story by centuries, the *Epic of Gilgamesh* was written around 1800 BC. Warned by the Babylonian Earth-god Ea that other gods were about to destroy all life by a flood, Utnapishtim was instructed to build an ark in the form of a cube that was 120 cubits (180 feet) in length, breadth, and depth, with seven floors, each divided into nine compartments, and to take aboard one pair of each living creature.[7] In point of fact, most cultures located on large bodies of water that flood have similar flood myths.[8]

Religious Beliefs as Mythic Truths

In considering religious truths, we must begin with religion itself, which I have defined as "a social institution that evolved as an integral mechanism of human culture to create and promote myths, to encourage altruism and reciprocal altruism, and to reveal the level of commitment to cooperate and reciprocate among members of the community."[9] That is, there are two primary purposes of religion:

1. The creation of stories and myths that address the deepest questions we can ask ourselves: Where did we come from? Why are we here? What does our ultimate future hold?
2. The production of moral systems to provide social cohesion for the most social of all the social primates. God figures prominently in both these modes as the ultimate subject of mythmaking and the final arbiter of moral dilemmas and enforcer of ethical precepts.[10]

In chapter 7, I deal with the second purpose of religion—morality. Here, I focus on myths and their truth value. What is a myth? Scientists and skeptics tend to use the term to mean a falsehood of some sort, as in "the Genesis story is just a myth" or "the Noah flood story is just a myth." This is partially correct. The *Oxford English Dictionary* defines it as "a purely fictitious narrative usually involving supernatural persons, actions, or events, and embodying some popular idea concerning natural or historical phenomena."[11] The original Greek meaning of *mythos* is "word," as in a final authoritative pronouncement, though one that is not necessarily true or false in an empirical sense (which avoids authoritative pronouncements, or at least ought to). In considering religious beliefs as *mythic truths*, I argue that whether a story or account or narrative is true or false is secondary—or even beside the point—to the deeper meaning of what it represents about the world that itself is true.

In this sense, to ask if the characters and events in a narrative are real is to miss the point of the story. Were there really Karamazov brothers in nineteenth-century Russia about whom the Russian author Fyodor Dostoevsky wrote in his 1880 work, *The Brothers Karamazov*? What a ridiculous question! It's a philosophical novel that probes the depths of human morality, volition, patricide, hierarchy, jealousy, power, and God in the context of a modernizing Russia. To ask if there really existed Karamazov brothers Fyodor, Dmitri, Ivan, and Alexei is no more relevant than wondering if there really is a Middle Earth, as in J. R. R. Tolkien's fantasy work *The Lord of the Rings*, or if there exists in reality a King's Cross Platform 9¾ visible only to non-Muggles as they begin their journey to Hogwarts, as narrated by J. K. Rowling in her *Harry Potter* books.

In this sense, myths are a form of art, like literature, poetry, and drama. One of the purposes of the arts is to tell stories about the human condition from which we learn truths about ourselves. That is the power of art. Shakespeare's *The Merchant of Venice* shows us how the hatred of Jews comes from stereotypes that people hold about Jews as rich, stingy, conniving, manipulative, and so on. Through his fictional story, Shakespeare is pointing out how ridiculous this is and that Jews are ordinary human beings like the rest of us, as the character Shylock declares (act III, scene 1):

> I am a Jew. Hath not a Jew eyes? Hath not a Jew hands, organs, dimensions, senses, affections, passions; fed with the same food, hurt with the same weapons, subject to the same diseases, healed by the same means, warmed and cooled by the same winter and summer as a Christian is? If you prick us do we not bleed? If you tickle us do we not laugh? If you poison us do we not die? And if you wrong us shall we not revenge? If we are like you in the rest, we will resemble you in that.[12]

Shakespeare is telling us a truth about the nature of human prejudice through a completely fictional story.

Literary truths are more like imaginary beliefs than empirical truths, and in his book *Religion as Make-Believe*, the cognitive neuroscientist Neil Van Leeuwen argues that in order to understand the nature of religious belief, we must look at how our minds process the world of imagination as reflected in such literature. The problem scientists have faced in trying to understand religious beliefs, he argues, is that we often assume that they are no different in kind from ordinary factual beliefs; for example, we may think that "believing that May comes before June" is in the same epistemological and ontological category as "believing in the existence of God or of supernatural entities that hear our prayers." As he shows through empirical research, however, our brains do not process religious beliefs like they do beliefs concerning mundane reality; instead, religious beliefs function more like make-believe literary truths with an additional aim of reinforcing group identity.[13]

By way of example, believing that *the church building has a parking lot* is not at all the same as believing that God *is three persons in one*. When Christians profess such religious beliefs as the Trinity, Van Leeuwen contends, they do so to signal group solidarity, as when Church authorities say, "*God is three persons in one*." Inasmuch as the concept of the Trinity violates Aristotle's fundamental Law of Identity (A is A, A cannot be non-A)—and Christian scholars have been arguing for centuries how to get around this fundamental fact of logic—for the average religious believer, the verisimilitude of the Trinity belief is beside the point. It is what their faith holds to be true, and that's all followers need to know.

The problem of confusing mythical truths for empirical truths sometimes plagues religious skeptics. At *Skeptic*, for example, we periodically receive articles submitted for publication purporting to provide natural explanations for apparently supernatural phenomena. The parting of the Red Sea was caused by a tsunami. Noah's flood was the result of a massive volcanic eruption on the Greek island of Thera. The plagues of locusts, flies, frogs, and the like are the results of fluctuating ecological and climatic changes. Earthquakes and meteor impacts are invoked as explanations for biblical miracles. A number of medical explanations have been offered to suggest Jesus didn't actually die on the cross but instead had slumped into a coma, was taken down from the cross and put into a cool chamber (the tomb), woke up after three days, and, if you want to go full Dan Brown, was whisked off to southern France, where he and Mary Magdalene married and had a child together, whose lineage continues to this day.

This latter account of what "really" happened to Jesus is an actual hypothesis by Michael Baigent, Richard Leigh, and Henry Lincoln in their surprise 1982 nonfiction bestseller *Holy Blood, Holy Grail*, reconfigured by Dan Brown in his 2003 novel *The Da Vinci Code*.[14] Emblematic of this confusion of facts and fiction, in 2005, Baigent and Leigh sued Brown's publisher for plagiarism and copyright infringement. The judge ruled against the plaintiffs on the grounds that works of fiction like Brown's novel could not infringe on the copyright of a work of nonfiction. In other words, a work of nonfiction is a claimed empirical truth, whereas a novel, however "inspired by true events," is a mythic truth. Let's explore these themes deeper.

In his 1949 book, *The Hero with a Thousand Faces*,[15] the comparative mythology scholar Joseph Campbell includes such figures as examples of individuals who shared similar hero stories (at least a thousand!), whose lives and adventures in narrative accounts that we call myths have played a central role in human history and culture. What they mean, exactly, very much depends on how they are perceived and applied by believers in and adherents to them. "The various judgments are determined by the viewpoints of the judges," Campbell reflects. "For when scrutinized in terms not of what it is but how it functions, of how it has served mankind in the past, or how it may serve today, mythology shows itself to be as amendable as life itself to the obsessions and requirements of the individual, the race, the age."[16] In his follow-up 1972 classic, *Myths to Live By*,[17] Campbell outlines four functions of myth:

1. *Mystical:* "Serves to awaken and maintain the individual sense of awe and gratitude in relation to the mystery dimension of the universe, not so that one lives in fear of it, but so that he recognizes that he participates in it."
2. *Cosmological/explanatory:* "An image of the universe which will be in accord with the knowledge of the time, the sciences and the fields of action of the folk to whom the mythology is addressed."
3. *Sociological/normative*: "Validate, support, and imprint the norms of a given, specific moral order that, namely, of the society in which the individual is to live."
4. *Pedagogical/guidance*: "To guide him, stage by stage, in health, strength and harmony of spirit, through the whole foreseeable course of a useful life."[18]

These are proximate or immediate explanations for the role of myths in our lives. In *How We Believe*, I proposed an ultimate or deeper explanation of myths as "a form of symbolic communication that invests stories not only with ordinary people and events but also with gods, supernatural beings, and extraordinary happenings, often unfolding in a place or time different from that of ordinary human experience." As such, myths cover a wide swath of life, including *origins* (cosmogony and creation), *time and eternity* (ages of humanity, periods of history), *providence and destiny* (mastery over fate), *memory and forgetting* (previous lives, collective unconscious), *higher beings* (gods), *heroes* (humans with special powers and experiences), *founders of religions, nations, and peoples* (Abraham, Moses, Buddha, Romulus and Remus), *transformation* (coming of age), *rebirth and renewal* (seasons and ages and life transformations), *eschatology* (end times and destruction), and *messianic and millenarian* (resurrections, second comings, and new world orders).[19]

An ultimate evolutionary case for myths finds support in their universality—that all cultures have them and that while the particular myths vary across cultures, certain universal themes appear time and time again. Why? Because myths represent deep truths about human nature and society, human relationships and conflicts, good and evil, right and wrong, forgiveness and revenge, love and jealousy, truth-telling and lying, who can be trusted and who cannot, who has power and who does not, and especially how individuals can navigate the complexities of the social world, from when we lived in small bands and tribes to the modern world of states and nations.

The anthropologist Donald E. Brown has compiled a comprehensive catalogue of human universals, to which he attributes human nature—and thus evolution—for their ultimate origin.[20] Human universals, he explains, "comprise those features of culture, society, language, behavior, and psyche for which there are no known exceptions to their existence in all ethnographically or historically recorded human societies."[21] Of his list of 373 human universals, 202 (54%) related to religion and morality were included in my own content analysis reported in my book *The Science of Good and Evil*.[22]

Again, while the specific expression of such universals may vary across cultures, that there should be such universals at all hints at their deeper evolutionary origin. As such, we can presume that there is a genetic predisposition for these traits to be expressed within their respective cultures and that these cultures, despite their considerable diversity, nurture these genetically predisposed natures in a consistent fashion that, in this context, are reflected in common themes of myths that represent these deeper truths.[23]

Myths are a collective explanation for why things happen as they do. We continue constructing and communicating myths today because it is in our nature to do so. Why? An ultimate explanation may be found in the epigenetic rules for mythmaking that still reside in our nature. By way of example, consider myths of monsters and beasts. From the earliest cave paintings of our Paleolithic ancestors to today, monsters and beasts lurk at the interstices between the natural world and the made world. They appear on the margins of our perception (perhaps this is why Bigfoot and the Loch Ness Monster images always appear as grainy or blurry), dwell in dangerous lands remote from human habitation (most of us cannot travel to the hinterlands of the Himalayas in search of Yeti), and come out at night or in our nightmares—fear of the dark is a universal human trait that evolved in the environment of our Paleolithic past in which nightmares may have served as early-warning signals for potential dangers.

Consider snakes. Our brains have changed since our evolutionary past, but we have retained an epigenetic rule for fear of snakes that generates narratives in the form of snake myths in cultures worldwide. Why? There's a game-theoretic logic behind such fears grounded in signal detection theory (see chapter 3). For millions of years, primates in general and hominins in particular evolved alongside millions of other species in a rich zoological world. The correct identification of possibly dangerous creatures would include Type 1 Hits and Type II Correct Rejections, but because of our fallible brains, it is inevitable that Type 1 False Positive and Type II False Negative errors will creep into our cognition. Better to err on the side of caution by assuming the worst—just in case.

Imagine you are a hominin living on the plains of Africa hundreds of thousands of years ago and you hear a rustle in the grass; is it a dangerous predator or just the wind? Your "yes" or "no" response sets up our 2 × 2 matrix. If you assume the rustle in the grass is a dangerous predator and it is, that's a hit, and you (hopefully) escape with your life. If you assume it is not a dangerous predator and it is, that's a costly miss that could take you out of the gene pool early. Thus, it is better to assume the rustle in the grass is a dangerous predator and not just the wind, because being cautious when it is unnecessary to do so is a less costly error to make. Why couldn't our ancestors delay their signal detection decision until they had more information? Because predators don't wait around for their prey to detect them; that's why they're camouflaged, stealthy, and sneak up on their potential prey.

The environment of our evolutionary ancestry was full of such signal detection problems, and we are the descendants of not only the most successful game-theoretic calculators at getting it right but also those who were less likely to get it wrong. And telling stories and constructing myths about animals have obvious survival significance to humans living in a Paleolithic environment as a pedagogical tool of information transfer about the local flora and fauna. Myths codify this information into the permanent record of a culture's storehouse of wisdom by which its members can best survive and thrive. The anthropologist Melvin Konner described this ultimate function of myths for the !Kung San people of Africa, whose knowledge covered "everything from the location of food sources to the behavior of predators to the movements of migratory game. Not only stories, but great stores of knowledge are exchanged around the fire among the !Kung and the dramatizations—perhaps best of all—bear knowledge critical to survival. A way of life that is difficult enough would, without such knowledge, become simply impossible."[24]

Dragons are a type specimen in mythmaking epigenetics. They are usually portrayed as a hybrid of a serpent and some other creature and composed of any number of mix-and-match parts, such as the wings or head of a bird, the scales of a fish, the ears of an ox, the head of a lion, the feet of a tiger, the claws of an eagle, or the horns of a deer. In ancient myths, dragons were winged lizards or serpents considered to be dangerous to humans and were thwarted or defeated by the gods or heroes of the mythmaking culture. Dragons are nearly universal myths, worshipped as gods, endowed with both beneficent and malevolent attributes, treated as dangerous monsters, or assumed to have supernatural powers.

The Bible alone mentions dragons no fewer than 31 times, starting with what is arguably the most famous dragon-like creature in all Western culture: the mythical serpent who tempted Adam and Eve in the Garden of Eden. In other cultures, dragons are associated with bodies of water like lakes (think Loch Ness Monster) or dwell in caves. In medieval myths, the dragon was believed to have caused droughts, famines, and other natural disasters. And many of the most famous heroes of mythology are dragon slayers: Marduk, Heracles, Apollo, St. Michael, St. George, Beowulf, and King Arthur. Some mythologists have speculated that the male dragon slayer is an archetype representing the shift from egalitarian to patriarchal societies.

Now, does anyone think the existence of dragons should be treated as a purely empirical scientific question? Of course not! Dragons are obviously mythic or literary creatures representing other truths about ourselves and our societies. (If there is any basis in truth to the dragon myth, it is likely to be related to serpents, frilled lizards, or reptiles that spit toxic venom.[25]) When I queried him about the ultimate function of myths, the evolutionary biologist E. O. Wilson explained the role of such stories: "Storytelling may be central in language because, in simulating real experience, they bring into play all of the cognitive and emotional circuitry evolved to deal with real experience. In other words, narrative is the best mnemonic procedure; it maximized rate of learning and understanding."[26] From this analysis, here is my general evolutionary explanation for myths and my defense of the value of mythic truths:

> Some individuals inherited an epigenetic rule for mythmaking, in this case, myths related to animals, that enabled them to survive and reproduce better in the surrounding environment and culture than individuals who lacked these rules, thus spreading the rules. As part of gene-culture coevolution, myth culture was reconstructed by each generation collectively in the minds of individuals. When oral myths were supplemented by written myths, the culture of myth grew indef-

initely large, but the fundamental influence of the epigenetic rules for myths remained constant. Since some myths survived and reproduced better than competing myths, this caused mythic culture to evolve in a track parallel to, and faster than, genetic evolution. This quicker pace of mythic culture evolution loosened the connection between genes and culture, although the connection was never completely broken. Thus, we witness the plethora of modern myths and our fascination with them.[27]

■ Oppression-Redemption Myths

On New Year's Day in 1889, a total solar eclipse passed over the plains of North America, during which a Paiute Indian named Wovoka, in a fever-induced hallucination, received a vision from God "with all the people who had died long ago engaged in their old-time sports and occupations, all happy and forever young. It was a pleasant land and full of game."[28] Wovoka's followers believed that in order to resurrect their ancestors, bring back the buffalo, and drive the white man out of Indian lands, they needed to perform a ceremonial dance that went on for hours and days at a time. This Ghost Dance (figure 5.1), as it came to be called, united the oppressed Indians but alarmed the oppressive government agents, and this tension led to the massacre at Wounded Knee.[29]

Naturally, modern readers do not accept the account of the resurrection of dead Native American ancestors as a literal truth, but what if it was never intended to be treated as such? Consider this interpretation of the Ghost Dance by the anthropologist James Mooney, who was sent by the Smithsonian Institution to study the phenomena and recorded what he found in his 1896 book, *The Ghost-Dance Religion and the Sioux Outbreak of 1890*:

> And when the race lies crushed and groaning beneath an alien yoke, how natural is the dream of a redeemer, an Arthur, who shall return from exile or awake from some long sleep to drive out the usurper and

Figure 5.1. The Ghost Dance by the Oglala Lakota at Pine Ridge Agency, drawn by Frederic Remington from sketches taken on the spot and published in *Harper's Weekly*, December 6, 1890. The long oppressed Native Americans believed that the Ghost Dance would bring them redemption. Library of Congress, LCCN 90707734

> win back for his people what they have lost. The hope becomes a faith and the faith becomes the creed of priests and prophets, until the hero is a god and the dream a religion, looking to some great miracle of nature for its culmination and accomplishment. The doctrines of the Hindu avatar, the Hebrew Messiah, the Christian millennium, and the Hesunanin of the Indian Ghost dance are essentially the same, and have their origin in a hope and longing common to all humanity.[30]

These are what I call *oppression-redemption myths*—classic tales of cheating death, overcoming adversity, and throwing off the chains of bondage—and there are many such cases.[31] The anthropologist Weston La Barre, for example, notes that during the colonial domination of parts of

Africa by the English, a South Xhosa girl encountered spirit entities while obtaining water at a nearby stream.[32] She told her uncle, who in turn spoke to the deities and was informed that they would help the Xhosa drive the English from the country. In this version, the ritual ceremony that would trigger the English departure was the slaughter of cattle. The girl's uncle, Umhlakaza, ordered his tribesmen to destroy all of their herds as well as the granaries of corn. If this ritual was carried out properly, the Xhosa came to believe, the dead would be resurrected, the old would become young again, illnesses would disappear, herds of fattened cattle would rise from the Earth, and ready-for-harvest millet fields would suddenly appear. Tragically, what actually happened is that after the mass butchering of some 2,000 head of cattle, a famine decimated the Xhosa tribe, nearly driving it into extinction. *Oppression-redemption.*

A similar story unfolded in a Maori village in New Zealand at the end of August 1934, when a visionary member of the tribe had a dream in which an angel told him that a Holy Ghost would deliver his people from the whites and return their confiscated lands to them. For days following the dream, the Maori fasted, chanted, danced, and waited for the day of deliverance. Then, as members of some end-of-the-world cults today have done, Maori villagers gave away their belongings. White administrators got wind of the ceremonies and came to investigate. Finding starving children and sleep-deprived and emotionally crazed adults, they declared the visionary insane and shipped him off to a mental hospital.[33] *Oppression-redemption.*

The Cargo Cults of the South Pacific provide additional examples of the oppression-redemption myth. Most people are familiar with those that arose during and after World War II, but according to the anthropologist Marvin Harris, Cargo Cults began centuries ago with Pacific Islanders scanning the horizon for phantom canoes delivering goods. As centuries and technologies changed, so too did the delivery vessels. In the eighteenth century, the Polynesians watched for the sails of ships. In the nineteenth century, they scanned the horizons for the smoke from steamships. And in the twentieth century, they sought the telltale signs of airplanes. The cargo also evolved—first it was matches and steel tools; then shoes, knives, rifles, ammunition, and foodstuffs like canned meat; and finally it morphed into radios, appliances, and modern tools. The Ghost Dance leitmotif intertwined with the Cargo Cults in places like Papua New Guinea, where the indigenous peoples built a thatch-roofed hangar, a bamboo beacon tower, an airstrip manned all day by natives wearing simulated uniforms, and even a mock airplane made out of sticks and leaves. Long dominated by whites who seemed to possess the mysterious power to produce such cargo, the natives envisioned the day when their ancestors would return with cargo for them, along with, in Harris's description, "the downfall of the wicked, justice for the poor, the end of misery and suffering, reunion with the dead, and a whole new divine kingdom."[34] *Oppression-redemption.*

The Messiah Myth

With this background in mind, let's reexamine the Jesus crucifixion-resurrection story as a type of oppression-redemption myth. By the first century CE, the Jewish people were engulfed within the Roman empire and feared for their very existence. The regions around and including Nazareth were ruled by King Herod, who responded with violence to numerous Jewish revolts against their oppressors. By the first century BCE, Judea was under direct Roman rule. A youthful Jesus must have been painfully aware of the tensions between his people and their oppressors as well as of the biblical promise of a Messiah who would drive out the Romans and reestablish the Kingdom of God on Earth. By the time of his three-year ministry from CE 27 to 30, after which he was executed by the Romans, Jesus had codified a new theology and eschatology to sustain his followers.[35] The theologian Burton L. Mack identified in this new theology three interconnected ideas that arose following Jesus's death:

1. A perfect society conceptualized as a kingdom. The Jesus people latched onto this idea and acted as if the kingdom they imagined

was a real possibility despite the Romans. They called it the kingdom of God.

2. Any individual, no matter of what extraction, status, or innate capacity, was fit for this kingdom and could act accordingly if only one would.
3. The novel notion that a mixture of people was exactly what the kingdom of God should look like.[36]

Mack concludes that "this was a notion that many groups had used to imagine a better way to live than suffering under the Romans."[37] The British social anthropologist Peter Worsley makes a similar point:

> Christianity itself, of course, as recent interpretations of the Dead Sea scrolls emphasize, originally derived its elan from the millenarist traditions of the Essenes and similar sectaries at the beginning of the Christian era. These people looked for the establishment of an actual earthly Kingdom of the Lord which would free the Jews from Roman oppression. Later this doctrine commended itself as a message of hope to the downtrodden of the Roman Empire.[38]

Oppression-redemption.

Who did Jesus and his followers think he was? In Matthew 16:15–16, Jesus asks his disciples, "Who do men say that I am?" They respond, "Thou art the Christ." *Christos* is Greek for *messias*, from *masiah*, Hebrew for *Messiah*. To many early Christians, the Hebrew Bible spoke to them of a returning Messiah (Jeremiah 23:5): "Behold, the days come, saith the Lord, that I will raise unto David a righteous branch, and a King shall reign and prosper, and shall execute judgment and justice in the earth." Such prophecies must have been especially reassuring to a people under the yoke, as Christianity's founding father, Paul, told the Colossians (1:14): "In whom we have redemption through his blood, even the forgiveness of sins." To the Hebrews, Paul said (9:12): "Neither by the blood of goats and calves, but by his own blood he entered at once into the holy place, having obtained eternal redemption for us." Redemption was not only for individuals but for all of Israel, as Luke notes (24:19–21): "Concerning Jesus of Nazareth, which was a prophet mighty in deed and word before God and all the people. And how the chief priests and our rulers delivered him up to be condemned to death, and have crucified him. But we trusted that it had been he which should have redeemed Israel." *Oppression-redemption.*

Recall that Jesus suggested to his followers that redemption was coming, that the Kingdom "has come upon you" (Luke 11:20). In Luke 17:20–21, Jesus seems to infer that heaven is a state of mind: "And when he was demanded of the Pharisees, when the kingdom of God should come, he answered them and said, The kingdom of God cometh not with observation: Neither shall they say, Lo here! or, lo there! for, behold, the kingdom of God is within you." According to *The Interpreter's Bible*, some scholars contend that a better translation for *within* should be "in the midst of you," but they then add:

> within corresponds to the normal Greek use of the word, and this translation makes Jesus declare that God's rule is a new spiritual principle already operative in the lives of men. In this sense the saying can be compared with the words of Paul in Romans 14:17: "For the kingdom of God does not mean food and drink but righteousness and peace and joy in the Holy Spirit."[39]

Further, they note that *in the midst of* "is a translation that removes the saying from its exceptional category among the kingdom references in the Gospels."[40]

When social and political conditions include the oppression of an entire people, we should not be surprised when the response comes in the form of a belief in a rescuing messiah delivering redemption. Call it the *Messiah myth* (figure 5.2). Like all myths, it may be a fictitious narrative, but it represents something deeply true about human nature and history.

In this sense, what if the greatest religious truth in all of Western Christendom—that if you accept Jesus as your savior, you go to heaven, where you will spend an eternity with God—was never meant to be taken liter-

Figure 5.2. The 1861 masthead of the abolitionist paper *The Liberator* depicted Jesus as the liberator of Black slaves, another historical example of the Oppression-Redemption myth, with Jesus as the type specimen of the genre. Wikimedia Commons, source Digital Commonwealth, Boston Public Library, Rare Books Department, Anti-Slavery Collection

ally? If so, perhaps it illuminates the tantalizing passage in Matthew 16:28 in which Jesus told his disciples, "Verily I say unto you, 'There be some standing here, which shall not taste of death, till they see the Son of man coming in his kingdom.'" Maybe Christians have been misreading passages like this for centuries. Perhaps the "kingdom" to which Jesus refers is the heaven within ourselves or the heavenly communities we build here on Earth. As I wrote in my book *Heavens on Earth*, "Heaven is not a paradisiacal state in the *next world*, but a better life in *this world*. Heaven is not a place to go to but a way to be. Here. Now. Since no one—not even the devoutly religious—knows for certain what happens after we die, Jews, Christians, and Muslims might as well work toward creating Heavens on Earth."[41]

■ Myths as Pragmatic Truths

Mythical truths inhabit a realm different from that of empirical truths and include archetypes representing eternal truths about the human condition. Mythic truths are not to be treated as veridical accounts of actual people and events but as a type of subjective truth in the realm of myth and metaphor, as when US presidential candidate William Jennings Bryan, a deeply religious man, famously pronounced in his 1896 Democratic National Convention "Cross of Gold" speech, "We shall answer their demands for a gold standard by saying to them, you shall not press down upon the brow of labor this crown of thorns. You shall not crucify mankind upon a cross of gold."[42] Or in the story of the resurrection, in which readers might be inspired to "bear" their "own cross" or to be "crucified" in the name of a higher cause or encouraged to become "born again" through good habits and starting life anew—born again.

Many Christians, however, consider the death and resurrection of Jesus as an empirical truth claim—namely, that Jesus was put to death by crucifixion and resurrected from the dead three days later, after which he ascended to heaven, all in order to save humanity that it may be born again in the next life. I will now discuss why this extraordinary claim lacks extraordinary evidence and thus is not in the realm of justified true belief—but what if it was never meant to be that type of truth? What if it was meant to be something like a metaphorical or mythic truth that, in my definitions of truth, would be more like a subjective truth that works for the believer personally but does not rise to the level of objective truth? That is, belief in it has practical benefits for one's life in the same manner as, for example, believing in free will nudges people to be more proactive in improving their habits and choices that lead to greater life satisfaction.[43]

This approach to mythic truths is parallel to the philosophy of pragmatism as developed by Charles Peirce, William James, and Miguel Unamuno and applied in interesting ways by the late Martin Gardner, one of the founders of the modern skeptical movement who nevertheless confessed his belief in God and the afterlife. Gardner called himself a fideist, or a philosophical theist, and here is how he explained it to me in a 1997 interview:

> People think that if you don't believe Uri Geller can bend spoons then you must be an atheist. But I think these are two different things. I

> call myself a philosophical theist in the tradition of Kant, Charles Peirce, William James, and especially Miguel Unamuno, one of my favorite philosophers. As a fideist I don't think there are any arguments that prove the existence of God or the immortality of the soul. Even more than that, I agree with Unamuno that the atheists have the better arguments. So it is a case of quixotic emotional belief that is really against the evidence and against the odds.[44]

In James's *The Will to Believe*, he argued, in essence (in Gardner's rendering), "that if you have strong emotional reasons for a metaphysical belief, and it is not strongly contradicted by science or logical reasons, then you have a right to make a leap of faith if it provides sufficient satisfaction. To me it is entirely an emotional thing."[45] That puts pragmatic beliefs more in the realm of subjective truths, but if so, then couldn't New Age believers make the same argument for astrology, crystal healing, ESP, and other paranormal beliefs? No, says Gardner:

> They could use that argument, except New Agers also have a whole series of beliefs that can be empirically refuted. Like reincarnation—the evidence against that is overwhelming. Most New Agers also accept most of the beliefs of the parapsychologists. They believe in ESP and PK and channeling. We have very strong empirical evidence against these beliefs. So I think there is a big difference between belief in God and belief in the paranormal.[46]

How so?

> In the first place, it has to be a leap of faith about something that has overwhelming importance to an individual. Second, it has to be something for which there isn't any strong empirical evidence or logical argument against it. So there is something radically different about belief in a mind behind the universe and the whole cluster of beliefs that the New Age movement presents.[47]

What about a personal god?

> If you believe in God at all, I think you have to believe in a personal God, in a sense. That is, you have to assign to God something analogous to a human mind because that is the highest type mind we are acquainted with. If God is just another name for nature then I think it is more honest just to say we are humanists.[48]

Indeed, this is why I call myself a humanist, or more specifically an Enlightenment humanist, but this is not what most people believe by "God," which Gardner acknowledged:

> If you do believe in a personal God it is in an analogical sense, so I sometimes like to call myself a theological positivist because I agree completely with [Rudolf] Carnap that metaphysical questions are meaningless—if you can't get at it by logic or by science you really can't say anything at all about the question. If you ask me for details about the nature of God I would have to answer "I don't know." The kind of God I believe in is so completely transcendent and so wholly Other that you really can't say anything about God's nature. To ask, for example, whether God is inside or outside of time, I have no idea what this means or how to reply to it. I can understand arguments saying he is in time, coming from the process theologians; on the other hand I can understand the arguments that place God completely outside of time, in some sort of realm in which time has no meaning. But these are metaphysical arguments and Carnap would say they are meaningless questions, and I would agree to that.[49]

If you are a religious believer in the more traditional sense—that is, if religious truths are also empirical truths—then this approach may prove challenging, as will my assessment of the resurrection of Jesus as an empirical truth to follow.

■ The Resurrection as an Empirical Truth

Literary, mythic, and metaphorical truths play a central role in human culture and learning through the arts, literature, mythology, and religion, but that is not how most Christians think about the resurrection of Jesus. They believe it is literally true. I know because I have debated a number of theologians and biblical scholars on this and related topics, and when they speak of the death and resurrection of Jesus, they are not channeling Joseph Campbell's power of myth, or echoing Jordan Peterson's archetypal truth, or invoking Gardner's pragmatic truth. They accept the Apostle Paul's challenge to the Corinthians that (1 Cor. 15:13–19) "if there is no resurrection of the dead, then Christ is not risen. And if Christ is not risen, then our preaching is empty and your faith is also empty. For if the dead do not rise, then Christ is not risen. And if Christ is not risen, your faith is futile; you are still in your sins!"

The proposition that Jesus was crucified may be true by historical validation, inasmuch as a man named Jesus of Nazareth probably existed, the Romans routinely crucified people for even petty crimes (recall that the two other people crucified with Jesus that day were impenitent thieves), and most biblical scholars—even those who are atheists, such as Bart Ehrman, a renowned professor of religious studies at the University of North Carolina at Chapel Hill—offer their provisional assent to this fact. In between these propositions is Jesus's resurrection, which is not impossible but would be a miracle if it were true. Is it? Like the Apostle Thomas, I have my doubts.

Let's see how the *principle of proportionality*, which demands *extraordinary evidence for extraordinary claims*, cashes out for a miracle like the resurrection and whether or not we should believe it, starting with how extraordinary a claim it is. Demographers estimate that throughout all of human history, approximately 100 billion people have lived and died before the 8 billion people alive today.[50] Not one has returned from the dead, with the possible exception of Jesus of Nazareth. (In *Heavens on Earth*, I show why near-death experiences are not evidence of people who have died and come back to report what it's like on the other side; such experiencers are only *near* death, not *actually dead*.[51]) So the claim that one person out of those 100 billion people who died came back from the dead would be extraordinary indeed. How extraordinary? Well, 100 billion to 1. Is the evidence commensurate with the conviction?

According to the University of Wisconsin–Madison philosopher Larry Shapiro in his 2016 book *The Miracle Myth*, "evidence for the resurrection is nowhere near as complete or convincing as the evidence on which historians rely to justify belief in other historical events such as the destruction of Pompeii." Because miracles are far less probable than ordinary historical occurrences like volcanic eruptions, "the evidence necessary to justify beliefs about them must be many times better than that which would justify our beliefs in run-of-the-mill historical events."[52] But, says Shapiro, it isn't. In fact, it's not even as good as *ordinary* historical events.

What about the eyewitnesses? Maybe, Shapiro suggests, they "were superstitious or credulous" and saw what they wanted to see:

> Maybe they reported only feeling Jesus "in spirit," and over the decades their testimony was altered to suggest that they saw Jesus in the flesh. Maybe accounts of the resurrection never appeared in the original gospels and were added in later centuries. Any of these explanations for the gospel descriptions of Jesus's resurrection are far more likely than the possibility that Jesus actually returned to life after being dead for three days.[53]

As John W. Campbell points out in his book *Cross Examined*, when comparing the account of Jesus's resurrection to claims made in the Book of Mormon, the latter "represents evidence far better than anything supporting the Resurrection of Jesus, and yet no non-Mormon Christian apologist accepts it." Likewise for claims of black magic that led to the Salem witch trials. "Today, these trials are widely considered examples of mass hysteria and a cautionary tale of how false stories can take on lives of their own," yet "the evidence for actual witchcraft at Salem is much stronger than the historical argument for the Resurrection."[54]

The principle of proportionality also means we should prefer the more probable explanation over the less, which these alternatives surely are.

Here, we can think about the resurrection claim in Bayesian terminology, in which the priors of non-Christians are low for their credence that the resurrection really happened, and to date, no new evidence has emerged to change those priors, so our credence in the verisimilitude of the resurrection remains low. In his book *Jesus, Interrupted*, the aforementioned biblical historian Ehrman sounds Bayesian in his analysis of the resurrection:

> Our very first reference to Jesus' tomb being empty is in the Gospel of Mark, written forty years later by someone living in a different country who had heard it was empty. How would he know? Anyhow, suppose that it was empty. How did it get that way? Suppose . . . that Jesus was buried by Joseph of Arimathea in Joseph's own family tomb, and then a couple of Jesus' followers, not among the twelve, decided that night to move the body somewhere more appropriate.
>
> But a couple of Roman legionnaires are passing by, and catch these followers carrying the shrouded corpse through the streets. They suspect foul play and confront the followers, who pull their swords as the disciples did in Gethsemane. The soldiers, expert in swordplay, kill them on the spot. They now have three bodies, and no idea where the first one came from. Not knowing what to do with them, they commandeer a cart and take the corpses out to Gehenna, outside town, and dump them. Within three or four days the bodies have deteriorated beyond recognition. Jesus' original tomb is empty, and no one seems to know why.
>
> Is this scenario likely? Not at all. Am I proposing this is what really happened? Absolutely not. Is it more probable that something like this happened than that a miracle happened and Jesus left the tomb to ascend to heaven? Absolutely! From a purely historical point of view, a highly unlikely event is far more probable than a virtually impossible one.[55]

That Bayesian-like conclusion deserves repetition: *A highly unlikely event is far more probable than a virtually impossible one.*

The number of Gospel inconsistencies and incompatibilities doesn't help the credence of the resurrection either. For example, the Gospels do not agree on how many women came to the tomb (one, two, or three, plus "others"); when they came ("while it was still dark" or "just after sunrise"); why they came ("to look at the tomb" or "to anoint the body with spices"); who they saw (one angel, two angels, a man dressed in white, or Jesus himself); what was said; who said what; who else came (Peter or both Peter and John); who saw the resurrected Jesus first (Peter or Mary Magdalene); or what they did as they left the tomb ("they said nothing to anyone" or "they ran to tell his disciples").[56]

Matthew seems to imply the stone was rolled away in the presence of the women who came to the tomb, while Mark, Luke, and John say the women arrived to discover the stone had already been rolled away. Matthew and Mark have the resurrected Jesus on his way to Galilee by the time the women arrive at the tomb, while Luke and John have the risen Messiah in Jerusalem on the night of the first Easter Sunday. The Q document, thought to be the source for Matthew, does not even mention the resurrection. The Gospel of Thomas, discovered near Nag Hammadi, Egypt, in 1945 and dated to the early second century CE, also does not mention the resurrection (which one would expect given its central importance in Christianity). The earliest reliable written testimony of the resurrection of Jesus is by Paul and the anonymous author of Mark's Gospel. It is important to note, in the context of the propensity of human memory to forget, conflate, confabulate, edit, redact, and falsify events that happened in the past, that the earliest Gospel of Mark was circa 66–70 CE, many decades after the events in question, with the rest of the Gospels written even later.[57]

So, the extraordinary resurrection miracle claim hangs on just two early testimonies, from two ancient authors, neither of whom actually saw Jesus rise from the dead, let alone touched him or sat down with him for a face-to-face conversation. We have nothing written by the Romans—or the Jews for that matter!—about Jesus, the content of his preaching, why he was killed, or what they thought about claims that he had been resurrected. You would think some Roman scribe would have exclaimed "Et tu iterum, Jesus?" or some Jew would have snapped "Oy vey, it's Jesus!" And the accounts from Josephus, Pliny the Elder, and Tacitus that Christians cite in evidentiary support were from the second century, and they reference Christ the Messiah (the prophesized Old Testament redeemer, not Jesus) and also fail to mention the resurrection. What's more, the biblical scholar John W. Loftus notes:

> We have no independent corroboration of the Star of Bethlehem at the birth of Jesus, or that the veil of the temple was torn in two at Jesus' death (Mark 15:38), nor that darkness came "over the whole land" from noon until three in the afternoon (Mark 15:33), or that "the sun stopped shining" (Luke 23:45), nor that there was an earthquake at his death (Matt. 27:51, 54), or another "violent" one the day he arose from the grave (Matt. 28:2).[58]

Could such notable events really have occurred without *anyone noticing* and providing corroborating evidence? Surely, some Roman scrivener would have made a note about a three-hour midday eclipse of the sun, not to mention the other miracles. No such extra-biblical evidence exists. Here, the absence of evidence is *evidence of absence*.

What about the 500 people the Apostle Paul says saw the risen Jesus? Note that we don't have 500 independent eyewitness accounts of seeing Jesus after the crucifixion. We have *one account* saying there were 500 witnesses, and it came from an evangelist who was highly motivated to write a history in support of his newfound religion—recall that Paul was previously Saul and converted to Christianity from traditional Judaism after his vision on the road to Damascus. So who was Jesus, really?

"Jesus was a great spiritual teacher who had a profound effect on many people," writes Lance Grande in his magisterial *The Evolution of Religions*, admitting that "he became what is probably the most influential person in history."[59] But this says nothing about the verisimilitude of the miracle claims made in Jesus's name. In fact, as Grande notes, neither during his own lifetime (~4 BC–30 CE) nor in the earliest writings of the New Testament by Paul were miracle claims made in Jesus's name. Even Paul's mention of the resurrection of Christ was described in 1 Corinthians (15:44) as a *spiritual* event rather than a literal one: "It is sown a natural body; it is raised a spiritual body. There is a natural body, and there is a spiritual body." In Paul's writings about Christ, says Grande, "he speaks of him in a mystical sense, as a spiritual entity of human consciousness." Many contemporary groups, in fact, "saw Christ as a spirit that possessed the man Jesus at his baptism and left him before his death at the crucifixion" (called "separationism"). But since political monarchs in the first century CE were treated as divine, Christian proselytizers began to refer to Jesus as the "King of Kings," and so came to pass the deification of an otherwise mortal man. Here is how Grande recaps the transformation:

> Reports of specific miracles only began to appear several decades after the death of Jesus, in the Gospel of Mark (65–70 CE) and in later gospels (80–100 CE). This suggests that stories of miracles (e.g., controlling the weather, creating loaves and fishes out of nothing, turning water into wine, healing the sick, and raising the physical dead) were layered into the story of Jesus as expressions of an ultimate God experience.[60]

And as is typical of myths in the making, in the retelling across peoples, spaces, and generations, layers of improbability are added as a test of faith:

> Once the stories of miracles began to appear in early Christianity, they were retold repeatedly, until they became ingrained beliefs. More stories were added, such as miracles about singing angels, stars announcing earthly happenings, and even a fetus (that of John the Baptist in his mother Elizabeth's womb) leaping to acknowledge the anticipated power of another fetus (that of Jesus in his mother Mary's womb). These details, many of which probably began as metaphorical lessons, gradually became accepted by many followers as literal his-

toric truths. It is probable that some of these stories were never intended as documents of historical fact.[61]

From metaphorical lessons to historic truths. Perhaps this is what the author of the Gospel of John meant when he wrote (John 20:31): "But these are written, that ye might believe that Jesus is the Christ, the Son of God; and that believing ye might have life through his name."

For Christians who insist that the resurrection be physical and not spiritual, literal and not metaphorical, a challenge I often employ is that Orthodox Jews have never accepted it as real, neither in Jesus's time nor in ours. Think about that: Jews believe in the same God as Christians. They accept the Old Testament of the Bible, as Christians do. They even believe in the Messiah. They just don't think the first-century itinerant preacher was him. The reason Jews don't believe Jesus was the Messiah is that they were expecting a royal monarch descended from King David, a great warrior who would rescue and redeem them from the oppressive Roman rule under which they were subjugated, not the son of an impoverished carpenter from Nazareth. Jewish rabbis, scholars, philosophers, and historians all know the arguments for the resurrection as well as Christian apologists and theologians making the arguments, and yet they still reject them. Why? If the arguments and evidence for the resurrection are so solid, in time, the community most expert in that field would reach a consensus about it. They haven't. Christians believe it. Jews do not. That's revealing.

Finally, it is important to put the resurrection into historical context, which Ehrman does in his book *How Jesus Became God*, where he documents the three models of "divine men" that were common in the ancient world:

1. Sometimes it was understood that gods could and would come down to earth in human form to make a temporary visit for purposes of their own.

2. Sometimes it was understood that a person was born from the sexual union of a god and a mortal; thus, that the person was, in some sense, part divine and part human.
3. Sometimes it was understood that a human was elevated by the gods to their realm, usually after death, and at that point divinized, made into a god.[62]

As Ehrman reveals, there are many stories in ancient myths about gods temporarily assuming human form to meet, speak, and interact with humans, and these stories in many ways are similar to later Christian beliefs about Christ being a preexistent divine being who came to Earth as a human and later returned to the heavenly empyrean.

Given these facts about the ancient world and the reality about the inadequacy of the evidence for the resurrection of Jesus, it would behoove Christians to reframe the proposition as a religious truth and consider the skeptical admonitions of Oliver Cromwell in his letter to the general assembly of the Church of Scotland on August 3, 1650: "Is it therefore infallibly agreeable to the Word of God, all that you say? I beseech you, in the bowels of Christ, think it possible you may be mistaken."[63]

6

Historical Truths

The Noble Dream of Pursuing Objective Truth About the Past

■ In 2019, an editor of the *New York Times Magazine*—the magazine of the purported "newspaper of record" that publishes "all the news that's fit to print"—with no apparent awareness of self-contradiction, declared "there is no such thing as objective history."[1] The declaration appeared in the publication *1619 Project*, which centered on the founding of the United States, not in the revolutionary year of 1776, but in 1619, with the arrival of the first African slaves. After denouncing objective history as something "white historians" do, the editor of the magazine special, journalist Nikole Hannah-Jones, asserted that "anti-black racism runs in the very DNA of this country" and that "one of the primary reasons the colonists decided to declare their independence from Britain was because they wanted to protect the institution of slavery."[2] When five prominent scholars of American history (Victoria Bynum, James McPherson, James Oakes, Sean Wilentz, and Gordon Wood) objected, citing numerous errors that "are matters of verifiable fact" and dismayed at the identity politics in the charge of the "white historians" (as if historical facts are melanin dependent), the editor in chief, Jake Silverstein, responded by explaining that "the project was intended to address the marginalization of African-American history in the telling of our national story and examine the legacy of slavery in contemporary American life." They then admitted, "We are not ourselves historians."[3]

That much was obvious from the beginning, and the *1619 Project* has not fared well among professional historians who care about what actually happened in the past. But it does call forth the deeper epistemological question: Is history what happened in the past, or is it what we *think* happened in the past? Further, can we find some meaning in history, or is it just a meaningless configuration of events? These are some of the most important and pervasive questions considered by philosophers of history, and scholars remain divided on how to answer them. We have not yet discovered any laws or principles governing the unfolding of events in history comparable to those in the physical and biological sciences, for example, but most historians would agree that the past is not just "one damn thing after another."[4] And while we can know something about the past, we cannot know everything about it, so what should we believe is true in history? Here is how the philosopher of science Karl Popper articulated the dilemma in his 1950 book, *The Open Society and Its Enemies*:

> There can be no history of "the past as it actually did happen"; there can only be historical interpretations, and none of them final; and every generation has a right to frame its own. . . . But this does not mean, of course, that all interpretations are of equal merit. First, there are always interpretations which are not really in keeping with the accepted records; secondly, there are some which need a number of more or less plausible auxiliary hypotheses if they are to escape falsification by the records; next, there are some that are unable to connect a number of facts which another interpretation can connect, and in so far "explain." There may accordingly be a considerable amount of progress even within the field of historical interpretation.[5]

■ Toward a Science of History

I am by training a social scientist and a historian, so I operate at the junction of applying the tools of the social sciences and trying to understand the past with some measure of scientific objectivity, to the extent that this is possible for events that already happened and, by definition, cannot be repeated. Much of this chapter recapitulates my many attempts over the decades to see how close we can get to the noble dream of knowing the past as an objective truth, as already practiced in many legitimate historical sciences—cosmology, geology, evolutionary biology, paleontology, and archaeology. Even though these historical sciences do not fit the paradigmatic model of experimental laboratory sciences, hypotheses can nevertheless be tested. Consider biblical archaeology, which goes in search of data to confirm or disconfirm stories in the Bible. Some biblical stories appear to have some basis in fact (e.g., King David); others have not a shred of extra-biblical evidence (e.g., Moses and the exodus to Egypt).

A popular historical theory that has been tested and so far failed all tests is that of the lost civilization of Atlantis, purportedly "found" in numerous locales, including the Mediterranean, the Canaries, the Azores, the Caribbean, Tunisia, West Africa, Sweden, Iceland, and even South America. This story well illustrates the difference between history and myth. Atlantis, in fact, was the creation of the ancient Greek philosopher Plato as a moral homily about what happens to a civilization when it becomes too warlike and corrupt; it was a warning to his fellow Athenians to pull back from the precipice because war and wealth were taking them over. Atlantis is a mythic truth, not an empirical one, for which Plato wove fragments of real history with moral homilies, as he explained: "We may liken the false to the true for the purpose of moral instruction."[6]

How can we tell the difference between mythic history, pseudohistory, and scientific history? As other scientists do, historical scientists form hypotheses and then check them for consistency and accountability with the available evidence, and their conclusions are provisional and continually checked against new evidence. By contrast, *pseudohistory* is the *denial or distortion of the past for present political or ideological reasons* and employs such distorting techniques as:

1. Selective use of evidence, presenting only that which fits the preconceived belief and ignoring that which does not fit (confirmation bias).
2. Highlighting anomalies while ignoring the vast body of non-anomalous evidence (anomaly hunting).
3. Taking evidence out of context with what we already know about the past (decontextualization).
4. Overuse of speculation and conjecture when caution or silence is called for (just asking questions).
5. Assuming that if scientific historians cannot explain everything about a subject, the alternative historian's theory must be right (fallacy of the excluded middle, the argument from ignorance).

A popular focus for pseudohistorians and alternative archaeologists is who preceded Christopher Columbus in peopling the Americas. Among the alternative discoverers of America (besides the Native Americans, of course!) are the Egyptians, Phoenicians, Africans, Trojans, Carthaginians, Romans, Arabs, Irish, Welsh, Germans, Poles, and the always-popular Lost Tribes of Israel, or the Jews. Not to be left out of the discovery process, various Chinese, Japanese, Hindu, Polynesian, and Mongol explorers all purportedly crossed the Pacific and found the American continent before Columbus. Additional errors in thinking that pseudohistorians and alternative archaeologists make that lead them down the path from history to pseudohistory include:

1. Hyper-diffusionism of people beyond their capability or motivation (bad geography).
2. Denial of independent discovery or invention of tools, pottery, art, and masonry (bad anthropology).
3. Assumptions about the similarity of pyramids, statues, and monumental architecture (bad archaeology).
4. Assumptions about the similarity of words, symbols, and language sounds (bad comparative linguistics).

5. Misinterpretation of natural markings on rocks for human inscriptions (patternicity).
6. Acceptance of fakes and hoaxes (gullibility).

The darkest side of pseudohistory I've encountered is that of Holocaust denial, which I began investigating in the early 1990s, when I saw deniers on talk shows. Specifically, Holocaust deniers (they call themselves "revisionists") claim:

1. There was no Nazi policy to exterminate European Jewry. The Final Solution to the "Jewish question" was deportation out of the Reich. Because of early successes in the war, the Reich was confronted with more Jews than it could deport. Because of later failures in the war, the Nazis confined Jews in ghettos and, finally, camps.
2. The main causes of death were disease and starvation and resulted primarily from the Allied destruction of German supply lines and resources at the end of the war. There were shootings and hangings (and maybe even some experimental gassings), and the Germans did overwork Jews in forced labor for the war effort, but all this accounts for a very small percentage of the dead. Gas chambers were used only for delousing clothing and blankets, and the crematoria were used only to dispose of the bodies of people who had died from disease, starvation, overwork, shooting, or natural causes.
3. Between 300,000 and two million Jews died or were killed in ghettos and camps, rather than five to six million.

In our coauthored book, *Denying History*,[7] Alex Grobman and I address these claims and many others in great detail with substantial evidence and documentation. Briefly, here is how a scientific historian answers such pseudohistorical claims:

1. In any historical event, functional outcomes rarely match original intentions, which are in any case difficult to prove, so historians

should focus on contingent outcomes more than intentions. The functional process of carrying out the Final Solution evolved over time, driven by such contingencies as increasing political power, growing confidence in getting away with a variety of persecutions, the unfolding of the war, the inefficiency of transporting Jews out of the Reich, and the infeasibility of eliminating Jews by disease, exhaustion, overwork, and mass shootings. The outcome was around six million murdered, whether extermination of European Jewry was explicitly and officially ordered or just tacitly approved.

2. Physical and documentary evidence corroborate that the gas chambers and crematoria were mechanisms of extermination. Regardless of the mechanism used for murder, however, murder is murder. Gas chambers and crematoria are not required for mass murder, as witnessed in the Rwanda genocide. In occupied Soviet territories, for example, the Nazis killed about 1.5 million Jews by means other than gassing, primarily bullets.
3. Five to six million killed is a general but well-substantiated estimate. The figures are derived by collating the number of Jews reported living in Europe, transported to camps, liberated from camps, killed in Einsatzgruppen actions, and alive after the war. It is simply a matter of population demographics.

Holocaust deniers, like other pseudohistorians, do not play by the rules of historical science. Instead, they make other plays:

1. They concentrate on their opponents' weak points while rarely saying anything definitive about their own position. Deniers emphasize the inconsistencies between eyewitness accounts, for example, but offer no explanation of their own.
2. They exploit errors made by scholars who are making opposing arguments, implying that because a few historians' conclusions were wrong, *all* historians' conclusions must be flawed.

3. They use quotations, usually taken out of context, from prominent figures to buttress their own position.
4. They mistake genuine, honest debates between historians about certain points within a field for a dispute about the validity of the entire field. Deniers take the intentionalist-functionalist debate about the development of the Holocaust as an argument about whether the Holocaust happened or not.
5. They focus on what is not known and ignore what is known, emphasize data that fit, and discount data that do not fit. Deniers concentrate on what we do not know about the gas chambers and disregard all the eyewitness accounts and forensic tests that support that gas chambers were used for mass murder.

In his book *In Defense of History*, the great historian of the Second World War, Richard Evans, after his refutation of Holocaust denier David Irving, offered this succinct definition of his subject: "History is a search for the objective truth about the past."[8]

The Convergence of Evidence Method of Historical Science

Historians know that the Holocaust happened by the *convergence of evidence* method discussed in chapters 2 and 3, or what the nineteenth-century philosopher of science William Whewell called a *consilience of inductions*, by which he meant a "jumping together" of independent lines of evidence.[9] Just as cosmologists, geologists, and paleontologists piece together the history of the universe, the Earth, and life through a convergence of evidence from multiple lines of inquiry, Holocaust historians have reconstructed what happened when the Nazis tried to exterminate European Jewry from independent forms of evidence, including:

Written documents: Hundreds of thousands of letters, memos, blueprints, orders, bills, speeches, articles, memoirs, and confessions.

Eyewitness testimony: Accounts from survivors, Kapos, Sonderkommandos, SS guards, commandants, local townspeople, and even upper-echelon Nazis who did not deny the Holocaust.
Photographs: Official military and press photographs and films, civilian photographs, secret photographs taken by prisoners, aerial photographs, and German and Allied film footage.
Physical evidence: Artifacts found at the sites of concentration camps, work camps, and death camps, many of which are still extant in varying degrees of originality and reconstruction.
Demographics: All those people who the deniers claim survived the Holocaust are missing.

The collection of such evidence began even before the war ended. On April 12, 1945, Generals Dwight D. Eisenhower, Omar Bradley, and George S. Patton inspected an improvised crematory pyre at the newly liberated Ohrdruf concentration camp in Thuringia, Germany (figure 6.1). The next day, Eisenhower visited the Buchenwald concentration camp, because, he wrote:

> I felt it my duty to be in a position from then on to testify at first hand about these things in case there ever grew up at home the belief or assumption that "the stories of Nazi brutality were just propaganda." . . . As soon as I returned to Patton's headquarters that evening, I sent communications to both Washington and London, urging the two governments to send instantly to Germany a random group of newspaper editors and representative groups from the national legislatures. I felt that the evidence should be immediately placed before the American and British publics in a fashion that would leave no room for cynical doubt.[10]

Holocaust deniers, like other pseudohistorians, ignore this convergence of evidence. They pick out what suits their theory and dismiss or avoid the rest. The same thing happened after what came to be known as the Rape of Nanking.

Figure 6.1. Generals Dwight D. Eisenhower, Omar Bradley, and George S. Patton inspect an improvised crematory pyre at the newly liberated Ohrdruf concentration camp in Thuringia, Germany, April 12, 1945. Eisenhower ordered the documentation of the Nazi genocide in anticipation of future Holocaust deniers. Wikimedia Commons, source United States Holocaust Memorial Museum

■ The Rape of History

On December 13, 1937, the Japanese army overran the Chinese city of Nanking, delivering a crushing defeat to Chiang Kai-shek's forces and capturing the prized capital of Nationalist China. The military occupation of the city was followed by brutalities that, in legal terms, came to be described as crimes against humanity. Over the course of seven weeks, somewhere between 260,000 and 350,000 Chinese noncombatants were tortured, raped, and ultimately murdered at the hands of Japanese soldiers. Years before the gas chambers and ovens of Auschwitz were built, tens of thousands of Chinese men served as targets for bayonet practice and decapitation contests; somewhere between 20,000 and 80,000 Chinese women were raped, and many of these were hung, shot, disemboweled, or had their breasts cut off; fathers were forced to rape their daughters in front of their families; men were often castrated; people were burned or buried alive; and German shepherds were encouraged to rip apart people buried in sand to their waists. One Nazi in the city described the massacre as "bestial machinery."[11]

Nanking is only one example of many atrocities committed by the Japanese between 1931 and 1945, in what Iris Chang has called "the forgotten holocaust of World War II," the subtitle of her disturbing book *The Rape of Nanking*.[12] Chang carefully documented the Japanese "Three-all" policy—"loot all, kill all, burn all"—implemented against the Chinese people in Nanking and other cities. "I have received orders from my superior officer that every person in this place must be killed," wrote one Japanese colonel in his diary.[13] As with the Nazi mass murder of the Jews, the total number of Chinese killed varies, ranging from 1,578,000 to 6,325,000, with a midrange moderate estimate of 3,949,000 people exterminated as a direct result of Japanese crimes against humanity (i.e., noncombatants). When total Chinese deaths are calibrated to include Japanese military actions through looting, starvation, bombing, medical experimentation, and battle deaths, historians estimate that the figure may be as high as 19 million.[14]

As is evident from Chang's copious documentation of primary sources and shockingly graphic photographs of decapitations and disembowelments (including heads lying on the ground, a woman strapped to a chair for multiple rapes, and another woman with a bayonet driven deep into her vagina), the Nazis did not hold a monopoly on human cruelty. There seems nothing the Nazis did to Jews that would have shocked their Japanese counterparts (figure 6.2).

The question here is not how these atrocities came about or what drove the perpetrators to such repugnant extremes of evil (I deal with such

Figure 6.2. Chinese to be buried alive by Japanese soldiers during the Nanking massacre, the truth about which was ultimately either ignored or denied by many Japanese politicians and educators until Iris Chang's *The Rape of Nanking* made denial of the truth about this genocide impossible to disappear down a memory hole. Wikimedia Commons, source *A Faithful Record of Atrocity of Japanese Troops* [in Chinese], 1938. Public domain

questions in *The Science of Good and Evil* and *The Moral Arc*) but why so few people know about it. "Sixty years later the Japanese as a nation are still trying to bury the victims of Nanking," writes Chang, "not under the soil, as in 1937, but into historical oblivion."[15] The Rape of Nanking is Japan's Holocaust denial. Officially, the Japanese government has refused to acknowledge most of the crimes against humanity it committed in Nanking and other places, let alone apologize for them. Extremists in Japan accuse the Chinese government and other anti-Japanese forces around the world of exaggerating Chinese losses and fabricating stories of Japanese atrocities that never took place. Even within mainstream Japanese circles, including the media, the academy, and especially the government administration, there are next to no signs of contrition. Whereas Germany has paid tens of billions in reparations to its wartime enemies and Israel, Japan has paid virtually nothing for these crimes.

(One exception is reparations paid to the sex slave victims—the "comfort women," mostly Korean, who were forced into sexual slavery by the Imperial Japanese Armed Forces in occupied countries numbering in the hundreds of thousands—and their families.[16] Even that was not without controversy. While some prime ministers of Japan have offered fragmented and half-hearted apologies for the sexual slavery, preeminent Prime Minister Shinzo Abe in 2007 went so far as to assert there was no evidence that the Japanese military had kept sex slaves at all.[17])

It is noteworthy that the Rape of Nanking was front-page news around the world, not just in the fringe and alternative press but in such august publications as the *New York Times*. Nevertheless, a "second rape" of denial, as Chang calls it, began at the top and worked its way down. The denial of atrocities on the part of the Japanese government has resulted in historical interpretations of the Rape of Nanking ranging from declarations that it involved only the isolated acts of a few out-of-control soldiers to flat-out denial that it happened at all. Such denial, as with the Holocaust, begins with revisionism, and in Japan, this has taken the form of reinterpreting the underlying causes of the Second World War. From this perspective, still found in many Japanese history textbooks, Japan fought to free Asia from the West's exploitative imperialist machinations and ensure its own survival against anti-Japanese sentiments in the geopolitical arena. Ultranationalists in the country not only endorse this view, they "have threatened everything from lawsuits to death, even assassination," says Chang, "to silence opponents who suggest that these textbooks are not telling the next generation the real story."[18]

One leading member of Japan's conservative Liberal Democratic Party, Shintaro Ishihara, for example, told *Playboy* magazine in a 1990 interview: "People say that the Japanese made a holocaust there [in Nanking], but that is not true. It is a story made up by the Chinese. It has tarnished the image of Japan, but it is a lie."[19] The comparison to Holocaust denial was noted by Yoshi Tsurumi in a *New York Times* article in response to Ishihara's *Playboy* comments: "Japan's denial of the rape of Nanking would be politically the same as German denial of the Holocaust." Ishihara fired back with the argument that the International Military Tribunal of the Far East exaggerated the events at Nanking in order to obtain convictions of the charged war criminals and that the *New York Times* correspondent Frank Tillman Durdin, who reported on China in 1937, never witnessed any atrocities. Durdin, aging and retired in San Diego, held a press conference to rebut Ishihara and explained that his reporting predated the massacre. As the rhetoric heated up, Ishihara ratcheted up his revisionism to argue that the Chinese concocted the story about Nanking in order to galvanize the American government into the atomic bombing of Hiroshima and Nagasaki. He concluded by stating that although the German government had acknowledged and apologized for its crimes against the Jews, Japan would never take such actions.[20] And this is why truth matters, so that we can protect ourselves from lies like these.

In a clear example of official denial (one that echoes the techniques and arguments of the Holocaust deniers), the Japanese minister of education, Masayuki Fujio, told *Bungei Shunju* magazine in 1986 that the Rape of Nanking was "just a part of war," the number of those killed had been highly exaggerated, and the Tokyo War Crimes Trial was nothing more than "racial revenge" intended to "rob Japan of her power." In 1988, Seisuke Okuno, then the third most senior member of the cabinet and a former minister of justice and minister of education, told reporters during his visit to a war shrine in Tokyo: "There was no intention of aggression. The white race made Asia into a colony, but only Japan has been blamed. Who was the aggressor country? It was the white race. I don't see why Japanese are called militarists and aggressors."[21] Similar remarks were made in 1994 by General Nagano Shigeto, upon his appointment to the cabinet-level position of minister of justice. Claiming he "was in Nanking immediately afterwards," he told the newspaper *Mainichi Shimbun*, "I think the Nanking Massacre and the rest was a fabrication." Nagano also asserted that the Korean sex slaves were actually "licensed prostitutes" and that Japan entered the war because it was "in danger of being crushed."[22]

The denials made by prominent Japanese politicians were reflected in the textbooks read by Japanese children. All textbooks must be approved by the Japanese Ministry of Education, with social science and history books among the most scrutinized. Throughout the 1960s and 1970s, little to no mention was made that Japan had even been at war with China, with most children just learning that the Americans had firebombed Tokyo and other Japanese cities and were the first to use atomic weapons. The texts included photographs of obliterated Japanese cities.

When textbook authors began introducing the story of the Nanking genocide, the Ministry of Education insisted on revisions to indicate that there were only a few atrocities and that they were committed in the heat of battle and in retaliation against Chinese aggression. Invoking the equivalency argument so favored by Holocaust deniers, Japanese textbooks in the 1970s and 1980s explained that in all wars, atrocities are committed by both sides. Responding specifically to a description of the Rape of Nanking in a textbook, one examiner for the Ministry of Education demanded that it be rewritten because "the violation of women is something that has happened on every battlefield in every era of human history. This is not an issue that needs to be taken up with respect to the Japanese Army in particular."[23]

The textbook debate, however, heated up, and in the early 1980s, Chinese and Korean officials filed formal protests. Eventually, the Japanese government was forced to capitulate somewhat to those who had recognized this to be a classic case of pseudohistory. Yet the debate was not over. "How long must we apologize for the mistakes we have made?" the military historian Noboru Kojima griped in 1991. One answer comes from a Tokyo University professor, Fujioka Nobukatsu, who argued that the number of victims at Nanking has been greatly exaggerated and that those who were killed were Chinese guerrilla soldiers, not noncombatants and women.[24]

The debate on Nanking was not confined to academia or the political arena. When Bernardo Bertolucci's film *The Last Emperor* was released in Japan, it was discovered that the film distributors there had removed a thirty-second scene portraying the Rape of Nanking. Bertolucci was outraged: "Not only did the Japanese distributor cut the whole sequence of the 'Rape of Nanking' without my authorization and against my will, without even informing me, but they also declared to the press that myself and the producer, Jeremy Thomas, had made the original proposition to mutilate the movie. This is absolutely false and revolting."[25] Fumbling for an adequate response, the distributors apologized for the "confusion and misunderstanding," backpedaling behind a defense of ignorance of the larger social issues at hand. One film critic speculated on their motives: "I believe the film's distributors and many theatre owners were afraid these right-wing groups might cause trouble outside the theaters. Some of these people still believe that Japan's actions in China and during the war were part of some sacred crusade."[26]

The similarities between the actions and motives of the Holocaust deniers and those of their right-wing supporters are eerie. In the 1980s, during the *Historikerestreit* ("historians' battle") over whether Hitler's martial actions perhaps represented a preemptive self-defense against Stalin's intended destruction of Germany along with the Jewish "declaration of war" against the Reich, Japanese historians experienced their own *Historikerestreit* starting in 1984, with the publication of Tanaka Masaaki's *The Fabrication of the "Nanking Massacre,"* in which he argued that "you won't find one instance of planned, systematic murder in the entire history of Japan."[27] Further, he contended, such atrocities could not have been committed because the Japanese have "a different sense of values" from Westerners. A battle line was drawn between the "massacre faction" and the "illusion faction." The more liberal "massacre faction" demanded a public apology on the part of the Japanese government, while the more conservative "illusion faction" claimed that any such apology would be an insult to veterans of the war. And like the Holocaust deniers, who are often their own worst enemy in uncovering evidence of Nazi atrocities against Jews (then are forced to rationalize it by the equivalency argument), Nanking deniers demanded eyewitnesses to come forward to present their evidence for the so-called "Rape," only to be presented with multiple lines of evidence that confirmed the massacre.[28]

How do we know that the Rape of Nanking happened? The same way we know that the Holocaust or any other historical event happened—through a convergence of independent lines of evidence, all pointing to the same conclusion. There is simply no other way to explain all the evidence. This kind of convergence underlies all historical sciences. Indeed, Chang's book is an exemplar of first-rate historical detective work, documenting the crimes committed in Nanking with numerous independent sources, including eyewitness accounts from survivors, perpetrators, and bystanders; photographs, newsreels, press reports, orders, memos, diary entries, intelligence reports, and physical remains; and even documents and press statements from the Japanese government, which initially not only did not deny the crimes but actually boasted of them in order to boost slagging public support for the war effort. Only after international condemnation did the Japanese military seal off the city to journalists and the Japanese government start down the path of revising history in a way that would eventually lead to flat-out denial.

The process of piecing together what happened began in March 1944, when the United Nations created the Investigation of War Crimes Committee to collect data on the event, and culminated on May 3, 1946, when the International Military Tribunal for the Far East opened what became known as the Tokyo War Crimes Trial. Two and a half years later (at the end of the longest war crimes trial in history—three times as long as the

Nuremberg trials), a 49,000-page multivolume report was issued that included no less than 779 affidavits and depositions and 4,336 exhibits documenting the crimes against humanity committed by the Japanese.[29]

Nanking denial parallels that of Holocaust denial in methodologies, arguments, and motivations and reflects the larger pseudohistorical trends seen in other claims, such as those made by Putin about Ukraine, Crimea, Chechnya, and other regions targeted by his unquenchable revanchist appetite. Such historical denial is a form of ideologically driven pseudohistory, which adopts techniques designed to undermine historical claims that do not fit with present ideologies and beliefs. Can we extrapolate the lessons we have learned from the Holocaust deniers and the Nanking deniers and apply these to other claims, testing for instances of pseudohistory? And, most important, since historians are in the business of improving (and thus often revising) our understanding of the past and offering new interpretations of history, how can we tell the difference between real revision and dogmatic denial?

■ The Comparative Method of Historical Science

In addition to the convergence of evidence method, there is the *comparative method* of historical science, such as that employed by the University of California, Los Angeles, geographer Jared Diamond in his book *Guns, Germs, and Steel*, in which he explains the differential rates of development between civilizations around the globe over the past 13,000 years.[30] Why, Diamond asks, did Europeans colonize the Americas and Australia, rather than Native Americans and Australian Aborigines colonizing Europe? Diamond rejects the theory that inherited differences in abilities between the races precluded some groups from developing as fast as others. Instead, Diamond proposes a biogeographical theory having to do with the availability of domesticated grains and animals to trigger the development of farming, metallurgy, writing, non-food-producing specialists, large populations, military and government bureaucracies, and other components that gave rise to Western cultures. Without these plants and animals, none of these characteristics of our culture could exist.

How can this historical hypothesis be tested? Through the *comparative method*. Compare, for example, Australia and Europe. Australian Aborigines could not strap a plow to or mount the back of a kangaroo, as Europeans did to the ox and horse. Indigenous wild grains that could be domesticated were few in number and located only in certain regions of the globe—those regions that saw the rise of the first civilizations. The East-West oriented axis of the Euro-Asia continent lent itself to the diffusion of domesticated grains and animals as well as of knowledge and ideas, so Europe was able to benefit much earlier from the domestication process. By comparison, the North-South oriented axis of the Americas, Africa, and the Asia-Malaysia-Australia corridor did not lend itself to such fluid transportation; thus, those areas already not well suited biogeographically for farming could not even benefit from diffusion. In addition, through constant interactions with domesticated animals and other peoples, Euro-Asians developed immunities to numerous diseases that, when brought by them in the form of germs to Australia and the Americas, along with their guns and steel, produced a genocide on a hitherto unseen scale.

An additional comparative test is seen in the fact that modern Australian Aborigines can learn, in less than a generation, to fly planes, operate computers, and do anything that any European inhabitant of Australia can do. Comparatively, when European farmers were transplanted to Greenland, they went extinct when their environment changed, not because their genes prevented success. Thus, Diamond's method is an excellent example of historical science in action.

Natural Experiments of History

Both the convergence of evidence method and the comparative method of historical science are, in part, the result of *natural experiments of history*, numerous examples of which Diamond presents in his 2010 book of that title, including a poignant study comparing Haiti to the Dominican Republic. Both countries inhabit the same island, but because of geopolitical differences, one ended up dirt poor, while the other has flourished.[31] What happened? This is a *natural experiment of borders*. The border that divides the island of Hispaniola is striking: On one side of the border, the land is green and forested, while on the other side, the land is brown and treeless. This border is symbolic of many factors to compare, starting with geography. Rain-loaded weather fronts come from the east and dump their watery load on the eastern Dominican Republic side of the island, leaving the western side drier and with less fertile soils for agricultural productivity. Deforestation of the fewer trees on the Haitian side led to soil erosion, decreased soil fertility, loss of timber for the building industry and wood for charcoal fuel, heavier sediment loads in rivers, and decreased watershed protection, leading to lower hydroelectric power. This set up a negative feedback cycle of environmental degradation for Haiti.

A comparison of the political history of the two sides of the island reveals a second set of factors at work. Columbus's brother Bartolomeo colonized Hispaniola in 1496 for Spain, establishing the capital at Santo Domingo on the egress of the Ozama River on the eastern side of the island. Two centuries later, during tensions between France and Spain, the Treaty of Ryswick in 1697 granted France dominion over the western half of the island, and the border was permanently established by the Treaty of Aranjuez in 1777. Because France was richer than Spain by this time and slavery was an integral part of its economy, it turned western Hispaniola into a center of slave trade, and slaves soon made up 85% of its population, whereas in the eastern half under Spain, 10%–15% were slaves. The raw numbers are staggering: about 500,000 slaves in the western side of the island compared to only 15,000 to 30,000 slaves in the eastern side.

Despite the geographic difference that would have given Haiti a disadvantage, this economic difference resulted in Haiti being richer than the Dominican Republic—but only for a time. This prosperity led to a significantly greater population density, which, when coupled with France's hunger for more timber being imported from Haiti, led to rapid deforestation and subsequent environmental squalor. On top of all this, the Haitian slaves developed their own Creole language spoken by no one else in the world, which further isolated Haiti from the type of economic and cultural exchange that leads to prosperity.

When both the Haitians and Dominicans gained their independence in the nineteenth century, another comparative difference unfolded. Haitian slave revolts were violent, and Napoleon's intervention to try to restore order resulted in the Haitians distrusting Europeans and wanting nothing to do with future trade and investments, imports and exports, and immigration and emigration. This, along with the language barrier, meant that Haiti did not benefit from these and other factors that build prosperity. By contrast, Dominican independence was relatively nonviolent, and the region shuttled back and forth for decades between independence and control by Spain, which, in 1865, decided that it did not want the territory. Throughout this period, the Dominicans spoke Spanish, developed exports, traded with European countries, and attracted European investors and a diverse émigré population of Germans, Italians, Lebanese, and Austrians, who helped build a strong economy. Finally, even when both countries succumbed to the power of evil dictators in the mid-twentieth century, Rafael Trujillo's control of the Dominican Republic involved considerable economic growth because of his desire to personally enrich himself. This led to a vibrant export industry (most of which he owned) along with the importation of scientists and foresters to help preserve the forests for his own personal use and profiteering through his logging companies. By contrast, Haiti's dictator, François "Papa Doc" Duvalier, did none of this and instead further isolated the Haitians from the rest of the world.

Employing the convergence of evidence method and the comparison method with such natural experiments of history is similar to what sociologists and economists do when comparing natural experiments of society today. We cannot intentionally impoverish one group of people and then observe if their health, education, and crime rates change. But we can look around and find pockets of impoverished peoples and then measure various factors for comparison with other socioeconomic classes. The process is as rigorous a scientific methodology as any to be found in the experimental sciences. Once an inferential or historical science is well established through the accumulation of positive evidence, it becomes a testable science.

■ Real Revisionism Versus Dogmatic Denial

In February 1993, the Wellesley College historian and classicist Mary Lefkowitz attended a lecture at her college by Dr. Yosef A. A. ben-Jochannan, known for his strong Afrocentrist focus. Among many controversial claims made in the lecture (including that true Jews are African), one of the more surprising was that Aristotle's ideas, which became the foundation of Western philosophy, were stolen from the library of Alexandria, where Africans had deposited their philosophical works. During the question-and-answer period, Lefkowitz asked ben-Jochannan how this could have happened, since the library was built after Aristotle's death. "Dr. ben-Jochannan was unable to answer the question," she explained, "and said that he resented the tone of the inquiry. Several students came up to me after the lecture and accused me of racism, suggesting that I had been brainwashed by white historians."[32] If this reaction was not disturbing enough, Lefkowitz discovered a "strange silence on the part of many of my faculty colleagues. Several of them were well aware that what Dr. ben-Jochannan was saying was factually wrong. One of them said later that she found the lecture so 'hopeless' that she decided to say nothing." Moreover, Lefkowitz writes,

> When I stated at a faculty meeting that Aristotle could not have stolen his philosophy from the library of Alexandria in Egypt, because that library had not been built until after his death, another colleague responded, "I don't care who stole what from whom." When I went to

> the then dean of the college to explain that there was no factual evidence behind some Afrocentric claims about ancient history, she replied that each of us had a different but equally valid view of history.[33]

Clearly not all views of history are equally valid. When a claim is made that can be refuted by just a cursory look at the historical timeline—such as the one about Aristotle's theft from the library of Alexandria—it suggests some form of ideological denial is at work. Holocaust "revisionism" falls into this category of pseudohistory, whose purpose is *the denial of the past for present political or ideological reasons*. By contrast, real revision—*the modification of history based on new facts or new interpretations of old facts*—is not only a legitimate activity of historians' profession, it is a necessary tool in our continued search for a true and meaningful past. The prevailing viewpoint on any historical topic, including the origins of Western philosophy, can be questioned and plausibly revised when the participating scholars play by the rules of evidence and reason. That is, as long as scholars put their claims forward as testable hypotheses, then those hypotheses can be weighed against the evidence and accepted or rejected in relation to other interpretations.

Cornell University professor Martin Bernal, for example, has presented a revisionist history of the "Afroasiatic influence on classical Western civilization" in his controversial book *Black Athena*.[34] Bernal's revisionist history contrasts the "Aryan Model" of Greek history, which views Greece as essentially Indo-European, with the "Ancient Model," which sees it as Afroasiatic, or Levantine and Egyptian. Bernal suggests replacing the Aryan Model not with the Ancient Model but with what he calls the Revised Ancient Model, which is built on components of both the Ancient and the Aryan models while at the same time replacing them.

This is a good example of a legitimate attempt at revision, of testable historiography, of falsifiable historical hypothesizing. Bernal is not denying anyone's history. Whether his revision is right or not is beside the point. Lefkowitz, for one, believes Bernal is wrong (and makes her case in

Black Athena Revisited), but she has clarified the difference between this type of revision and the denial practiced by extremists:

> We recognize that no historian can write without some amount of bias; that is why history must always be rewritten. But not all bias amounts to distortion or is equivalent to indoctrination. If I am aware that I am likely to be biased for any number of reasons, and try to compensate for my bias, the result should be very different in quality and character from what I would say if I were consciously setting about to achieve a particular political goal.[35]

Bernal presented his revision of history, and it was debated in peer-reviewed publications, with the participants, for the most part, abiding by the rules of evidence.

■ Romanticizing the Past

Differentiating revision from denial and pseudohistory is an ongoing task. A sizable industry of literature deals with claims that the past was not what we think it was. In his book *Frauds, Myths, and Mysteries*, the archaeologist Ken Feder tackles pseudohistory in archaeology and provides a laundry list of the weird and the strange, including the Cardiff giant, the Piltdown hoax, the lost continent of Atlantis, prehistoric extraterrestrials and ancient astronauts, lost civilizations on Mars, psychic archaeology (using ESP to find buried ruins), pyramid builders, the Shroud of Turin, creationism and Noah's Ark, King Tut's curse, and numerous theories about various peoples who allegedly discovered America before Columbus. Why do people distort and deny history? Feder suggests at least five motives, moving from proximate to ultimate:

1. *Money*—from the sale of artifacts, books, lecture tours, and merch like T-shirts, mugs, and the like.

2. *Fame*—by overturning a cherished belief about the past, one may gain considerable attention.
3. *Nationalism*—to show that "we" were first, not "you." The Piltdown hoax was driven by the desire of the British to find an ancient human in Britain. Nazi archaeologists looked for evidence of ancient German settlements in desired territories.
4. *Religion*—to anchor the belief system in a meaningful and significant history of the faith.
5. *Romantic Past*—the belief that the grass is always greener in the other century.[36]

Romanticized pasts proliferate in literature. In her 1987 book, *The Chalice and the Blade*, for example, Riane Eisler takes a "journey into a lost world" in search of the beginnings of civilization.[37] Evidence from Neolithic art and artifacts leads Eisler to this radical conclusion: "In sharp contrast to later art, a theme notable for its absence from Neolithic art is imagery idealizing armed might, cruelty, and violence-based power." In Eisler's reading of the historical record, civilization began peaceably, and for thousands of years, most people lived in relative equanimity with a notable lack of hierarchical domination: "There are here no images of 'noble warriors' or scenes of battles. Nor are there any signs of 'heroic conquerors' dragging captives around in chains or other evidence of slavery." Relying heavily on limited sources, Eisler concludes that there were few gods but plenty of goddesses, whose symbols represented life, water, the sun, plants, animals, rivers, reproduction, agriculture, and the maintenance of good health. "In Neolithic art," she indicates, "neither the Goddess nor her son-consort carry the emblems we have learned to associate with might—spears, swords, or thunderbolts, the symbols of an earthly sovereign and/or deity who exacts obedience by killing and maiming." More important, she says, "the art of this period is strikingly devoid of the ruler-ruled, master-subject imagery so characteristic of dominator societies." Not surprisingly, Eisler finds this dearth of dominator relationships among people to include that of man over woman. In this egalitarian society—symbolized by the chalice—women had an equal partnership with men. When goddesses were in vogue, men and women shared a worldview "in which the primary purpose of art, and of life, was not to conquer, pillage, and loot but to cultivate the earth and provide the material and spiritual wherewithal for a satisfying life."[38]

Eisler infers that a lack of dominator symbols—such as the blade—means a lack of real-world parallels: "If there was here no glorification of wrathful male deities or rulers carrying thunderbolts or arms, or of great conquerors dragging abject slaves about in chains, it is not unreasonable to infer it was because there were no counterparts for those images in real life." For the first several thousand years of civilization, Eisler concludes, society was neither patriarchal nor matriarchal but "remarkably equalitarian."[39] By 7,000 years ago, however, "we begin to find evidence . . . of disruption of the old Neolithic cultures in the Near East." Archaeological evidence, she claims, indicates "invasion, natural catastrophes, and sometimes both, causing large-scale destruction and dislocation." Goddesses were replaced by gods, the chalice by the blade. Males dominated females. Patriarchy became the norm, egalitarianism and matriarchy the exception.[40]

Amazingly, Eisler extrapolates this radical revision of the distant past primarily from a single archaeological dig at Çatalhöyük in Turkey, which, while a remarkable find, is by no means representative of other cultures or other times. Although Eisler claims that Çatalhöyük exemplifies a partnership society at the dawn of civilization, in reality, the culture developed approximately 8,300 years ago. The Paleolithic foundations of civilization were laid between 30,000 and 10,000 years ago, and from the scattered and fragmentary evidence from most sites, it is difficult to say whether they were partnership or dominator cultures.[41]

Here, it seems to me, we begin to unveil a feminist agenda that drives Eisler's research, rather than the reverse. There is only one ideology, she says, to challenge "the principle of human ranking based on violence," and that "is, of course, feminism. For this reason it occupies a unique position both in modern history and in the history of our cultural evolution." As social ills fall away with the collapse of the dominator society, "our drive for justice, equality, and freedom, our thirst for knowledge and spiritual illumination, and our yearning for love and beauty will at last be freed. And after the bloody detour of androcratic history, both women and men will at last find out what being human can mean."[42] Eisler's thesis, while noble in its efforts to correct possible biases in interpretations of ancient history, looks to me like it was strongly influenced by 1980s feminism.

Native American historical revisionists provide another example of the romanticization of the past. The historiographical movement began with the modest and reasonable approach that the written histories of the Americas had been, for the past several centuries, dominated by a distinct Eurocentrism—"how the West was won" and all that. Revising this form of Whiggish history was long in coming and, after initial resistance, eventually found a permanent place in the academy. Vine Deloria Jr.'s classic 1969 book, *Custer Died for Your Sins: An Indian Manifesto*, for example, provided a needed adjustment of the restricted focus and one-sided bias of the anthropology of Native Americans as it had been practiced up to that time. But a few decades later, Deloria changed from scholar to activist, and as a result, his 1995 book, *Red Earth, White Lies*, slides from revisionism into denial.[43] Rejecting all the evidence from genetics, physical anthropology, cultural anthropology, linguistics, and history that converges to link Native Americans to Asian ancestors, Deloria instead bases his theory on Native American myth and lore, suggesting that American Indians had been in the Americas since the time of their creation.

This shift away from scientific evidence dismayed many anthropologists and caused some, like Feder, to scrape "the remnants of our *Custer Died for Your Sins* bumper stickers off of our aging automobiles."[44] They did so not because Deloria's revisionism had gone too far, but because it equated myth with science. As indicated in the subtitle of his book, *Native Americans and the Myth of Scientific Past*, for Deloria, science is no different from other mythologies, including Native American myths, all of which he thinks are equally valid: "Tribal elders did not worry if their version of creation was entirely different from the scenario held by a neighboring tribe. People believed that each tribe had its own special relationship to the superior spiritual forces which governed the universe. . . . Tribal knowledge was not fragmented and was valid within the historical and geographical scope of the people's experience."[45]

This philosophy of history may sound noble, but it is vacuous and impotent, because if all versions of the past are "valid," then none are. If there is no method of discriminating between true and false interpretations of the past, between history and pseudohistory, between revisionism and denial, then there is no point in even having a discipline of history. With this pseudohistory, historiography becomes hagiography, science becomes ideology, history becomes myth, and revision becomes denial. The archaeologist Elizabeth Weiss's recounting of her "battles with Indians, Pretendians, and Woke Warriors"—*On the Warpath*—is an autobiographical account of her opposition to the reburial of Native American skeletal remains, her insistence that indigenous knowledge is not science but myth, and her fight against wokeism and political correctness in academia in general and archaeology in particular, including getting cancelled by the American Anthropological Association for identifying the sex of a skeleton (because, her detractors insist, we don't know what sex ancient peoples identified as).[46]

A more recent example of the romanticization of the past is that of Graham Hancock, an alternative archaeologist and audacious autodidact who believes that tens of thousands of years before ancient Mesopotamia, Babylonia, and Egypt, an even more glorious civilization—he alleges it was Atlantis (figure 6.3)—existed but was so thoroughly wiped out by a comet strike around 12,000 years ago that nearly all evidence of it vanished, other than only the faintest of traces, including a cryptic warning, he thinks, that such a celestial catastrophe could happen to us.

Figure 6.3. Romanticizing the past through Atlantis and its destruction as metaphor for our own civilizational concerns is just one of many ways historical truths are shrouded in the mists of time. *Terror Antiquus*, painted by Leon Bakst, 1908. Wikimedia Commons, source State Russian Museum

I wrote about Hancock in one of my *Scientific American* columns,[47] which led to a debate between me, Hancock, and his colleague Randall Carlson on Joe Rogan's podcast.[48] In preparation for the debate, I put together a list of reasons why alternative archaeologists in general, and Hancock in particular, have failed to convince most archaeologists to abandon the theory about the timeline of the development of civilization over the past 13,000 years and embrace his theory instead, including these:

1. *There isn't just one "alternative" to mainstream archaeology; there are dozens of alternative theories.* For example: claims about the lost tribes of Israel; the Kensington Runestones of Minnesota prove the theory of the Nordic Viking peopling of the Americas centuries before Columbus; Thor Heyerdahl's theory that the peopling of Polynesia was from South America, not Southeast Asia; the theory that South American Olmec statues look African in their features, suggesting that the peopling of the Americas also included voyages from Africa to South America; the theories of Erich von Däniken, Zecharia Sitchin, and other ancient alien theorists.

In response to this litany, Hancock reasonably responded, "What does this have to do with me and my theory?" The answer is "nothing" and "everything." *Nothing*, because to his credit, Hancock is just as skeptical as I am of these alternative theories. *Everything*, because Hancock portrays himself as a lone rogue scholar being unfairly ignored by mainstream archaeologists, whereas in fact there are hundreds of such rogues, all equally convinced of the verisimilitude of their claims and all lacking enough convincing evidence to overturn the accepted theory.

2. *Negative evidence and anomaly hunting.* No matter how devastating an extraterrestrial impact might be, are we to believe that, after centuries of flourishing, every last tool, potshard, article of clothing, and, presumably from an advanced civilization, the writing, metallurgy, and other technologies—not to mention their trash, homes, and bones—were erased? Not likely.
3. *Cherry-picking data, the confirmation bias, and starting with a conclusion and working backward through the evidence to make it fit.* This strongly suggests that if your alternative explanation is based primarily on the cherry-picking of data to fit only your hypothesis,

and if it begins with a conclusion and works backward through the evidence to make it fit what you'd like to be true, you're likely subject to the *confirmation bias*, in which we look for and find confirming evidence for our beliefs and ignore or rationalize disconfirming evidence.

4. *Alternative archaeologists disparage mainstream archaeologists and accuse them of being closed-minded dogmatists in a conspiracy to silence the truth.* Just weeks before Hancock and I collided in Rogan's studio, this calumny was gainsaid by a paper published in the prestigious journal *Nature* in which scientists put forth evidence that they believe indicates early humans (or possibly Neanderthals) inhabited the San Diego area of Southern California some 130,000 years ago, an order of magnitude earlier than mainstream archaeologists' timeline for the peopling of the Americas.[49] The evidence for this conjecture, however, is not as strong as the popular media made it out to be in the considerable press coverage this paper received. The "butchered" mammoth bones may, in fact, have been broken in the excavation of a road recently constructed at the site, and the "stone tools" were nothing at all like the finely crafted Clovis points found all over North America; they might just be broken rocks. That was, in fact, the conclusion in another paper published in a subsequent issue of *Nature*,[50] along with one in the journal *PaleoAmerica*,[51] and is what most mainstream archaeologists now believe about the find. To their credit, Steven Holen and his colleagues responded to these critiques,[52] which is how proper science is done.[53]

On this point, let's return to the *convergence of evidence* argument in contrast with *anomaly hunting*. The vast majority of evidence indicates the peopling of the Americas happened some 20,000 to 25,000 years ago, depending on the accuracy of the dating of these earlier artifacts and the margins of error around the calibrated date. But if people were in the Americas 130,000 years ago, where is all the evidence for their existence between, say, 20,000 years ago and that much older date? Where are their stone tools, their homes, their trash? Surely after living in the Americas for nearly 100,000 years they would have left behind some artifacts. After the *Nature* paper was published and before my debate with Hancock, I queried Jared Diamond, the aforementioned UCLA scholar of human history and prehistory who has for half a century followed the debate over the peopling of the Americas, about his opinion on the matter. He replied with this one-liner: "The latest semi-annual new-paradigm pre-Clovis claim with a credibility half-life of two days."[54]

5. *Falsifiability, conjectures and refutations, and the burden of proof.* During our debate, I asked Hancock several times, "What would it take to refute your hypothesis?" I never received a reply.
6. *The argument from ignorance and positive evidence.* This is the argument that if scientists cannot explain X, then Y is a legitimate theory. The problem here is twofold: (1) scientists *do* have good explanations for Hancock's Xs (e.g., the pyramids, the Sphinx), even if they are not in total agreement; and (2) ultimately one's theory must rest on *positive* evidence in favor of it, not just *negative* evidence against accepted theories.

Although science needs outsiders and mavericks who poke and prod and push accepted theories until they either collapse or are more strongly reinforced, Hancock has not convinced professional archaeologists and historians of the factual nature of his theory, and that's how it often goes in science. Most ideas turn out to be wrong. The standard timeline of how civilizations unfolded over the past 20,000–25,000 years may be one of them, but so far, it has held up fairly well. Hancock's constant refrain on social media that "stuff keeps getting older" and that civilization may be much older than we think it is could turn out to be true, but without compelling positive evidence, it is rational to be skeptical.

Romanticizing the past is appealing, but our aim should be to seek objective truths about history, romantic or not. Peter Novick's search for

That Noble Dream (in his book title[55]) was what the renowned Harvard historian James Kloppenberg echoed in an essay to his fellow historians that is as prescriptive as it is descriptive in its identification of the essential tension between the aspiration of objectivity and the nihilism of relativism:

> Beyond the noble dream of scientific objectivity and the nightmare of complete relativism lies the terrain of pragmatic truth, which provides us with hypotheses, provisional syntheses, imaginative but warranted interpretations, which then provide the basis for continuing inquiry and experimentation. Such historical writing can provide knowledge that is useful even if it must be tentative. It is within that realm that historical truth—like all truth in a world that has moved beyond the discredited dualisms of both positivism and idealism—must be made, questioned, and reinterpreted. As historians, we cannot aspire to more than a pragmatic hermeneutics that relies on the methods of science and the interpretation of meanings. But we should not aspire to less.[56]

7

Moral Truths Science and the Search for Objective Universal Values

■ If there is no God, is murder wrong?

So asks the religious conservative radio talk show host and author Dennis Prager in a PragerU video viewed by millions of people.[1] Prager believes that if divine command theory—God commands it, therefore it is moral, or God forbids it, therefore it is immoral—is not accepted as the basis of morality, only one position is left, namely moral relativism, in which "anything goes." "In a secular world," Prager asserts, "there can only be opinions about morality. Every atheist philosopher I have read or debated on this subject has acknowledged that if there is no God, there is no objective morality."[2]

I challenged Prager on these points in a studio debate on the *Rubin Report*,[3] in which I made the case that this is not an either-or matter and that there can, in fact, be objective moral facts without divine command; indeed, whether or not there is a God, moral values can and should be grounded in secular arguments and evidence. Whether or not there is a God, moral truths exist in the form of objective universal values that can be discovered through observation and inference, just like any other phenomena of the natural and human world.

■ The Naturalism Fallacy Fallacy

The problem with the either-or choice between divine command morality and secular moral relativism is that the former requires belief in a deity, which most professional philosophers and scientists agree is not supported by reason or science (see chapters 5 and 11), and the latter is unsatisfactory for anyone who cares about the origin and nature of moral values—it simply isn't true that "without God anything goes," and no society could prosper if most of its citizens believed that. But even if there was uncontestable evidence of God's existence, that still doesn't produce objective moral values, as we can always ask, "Is what is morally right or wrong commanded by God because it is inherently right or wrong, or is it morally right or wrong only because it is commanded by God?"[4] If murder is wrong because God said it is wrong, what if He said it was right? Would that make murder acceptable? Of course not! If God commanded murder wrong for good reasons, what are those reasons, and why can't we base our proscription against murder on those reasons alone and skip the divine command stage altogether? In other words, if murder is really wrong in the moral universe, then it doesn't matter what God thinks or whether or not there is a god—it's still wrong.

For millennia, philosophers have sought to build reason-based moral systems, a number of which have survived the test of time, most notably Aristotle's virtue ethics, Immanuel Kant's deontological rules-based ethics, David Hume's sentiment ethics, Jeremy Bentham's and John Stuart Mill's consequentialism (or utilitarianism) ethics, and John Rawls's justice theory of fairness behind a veil of ignorance.[5] Now scientists are jumping into the fray, and there are a number of us trying to work out how scientific facts and moral values may overlap. But we are often met with resistance, not only from theists but also from secular philosophers and scientists, who usually reference the philosopher Hume and the *naturalistic fallacy* or the *is-ought problem*, the latter of which holds that there is an unbreachable wall between *descriptive* statements (the way something *is*) and *prescriptive* statements (the way something *ought to be*).[6] It is repeated like a mantra the moment you attempt to apply science and reason to morals and values. "But . . . Hume!" they pronounce.

Before we consider how we can reason our way from *is* to *ought* with an aim toward discovering moral truths, let's distinguish between the scientific study of why people act morally or immorally and what science can tell us about what is, in fact, moral or immoral and how we should live a moral life. In *The Science of Good and Evil*, I argue for the evolutionary origins of the moral sense through kin selection and reciprocal altruism, the neurophysiology of moral emotions through hormones like oxytocin and neurotransmitters like dopamine, and the social circumstances in which people behave morally or immorally, such as in Stanley Milgram's shock experiments and Philip Zimbardo's Stanford Prison Experiment.[7]

These are all important developments in the scientific understanding of why we are moral, but they don't actually tell us what is right or wrong, good or evil. Science might tell us why we feel guilty about hurting other people or breaking our promises, for example, but it supposedly can't tell us when it is acceptable to hurt another person (in self-defense or war, say) or when it's actually moral to break a promise (to lie, for example, when Nazis at your door ask if you're hiding Jews and you are). To be sure, the aforementioned philosophy-based moral systems do not always resolve these issues either, as in conflicts between Kant's categorical imperative that would always and everywhere forbid lying and Bentham's and Mill's utilitarianism that would prescribe lying to murderous Nazis in order to save Jews.

In a subsequent book, *The Moral Arc*,[8] I show how the application of science and reason toward solving problems in the human social world led to the decline of violence and the expansion of the moral sphere to include civil rights, women's rights, gay rights, animal rights, children's rights, and worker's rights and how that naturalism fallacy is itself a fallacy.

There are others, such as the evolutionary ethics of the primatologist Frans de Waal,[9] the group selection theory of the evolutionary biologist David Sloan Wilson,[10] the neuroscience of moral decision-making by Joshua Greene,[11] the social psychological moral foundations theory of Jonathan Haidt,[12] the harm-reduction morality of Kurt Gray,[13] and the well-being moral systems of Sam Harris,[14] Steven Pinker,[15] and me. The latter include the grounding of a moral system in "the well-being of conscious creatures" (Harris in *The Moral Landscape*), "principles that maximize the flourishing of humans" (Pinker in *Enlightenment Now*), and "the survival and flourishing of sentient beings" (my own in *The Moral Arc*).

Critics have pointed out, however, that we are preloading moral values into the scientific facts with which we begin. In their book *Science and the Good*, for example, James Davison Hunter and Paul Nedelisky note, "Shermer's argument must assume at the beginning the values he claims can be demonstrated scientifically." They add that Sam Harris does the same thing in his analogy between physical health and well-being when he writes, "Science cannot tell us why, scientifically, we should value health. But once we admit that health is the proper concern of medicine, we can then study and promote it through science. . . . I think our concern for well-being is even less in need for justification than our concern for health is."[16]

But then from where does the assumption that humans prefer a life of well-being and flourishing over suffering and dying come? It is not an arbitrary element just tossed into the moral equation of determining right and wrong. It is discoverable from empirical science and astute observation that most people most of the time in most circumstances prefer to survive and flourish than to suffer and die, in the same way that they prefer education to ignorance, literacy to illiteracy, satiation to starvation, health to disease, freedom from pain to insufferable agony, freedom from cruel and unusual punishment to fairness and justice, and freedom from chains to chattel slavery.

How do we know that people have these preferences? By observing them, asking them, and noting how they behave historically—you know, empirical social science and history. In laboratories and historically, people almost always engage in behaviors that satiate their hunger, avoid disease, pursue pleasure, and escape bondage. That exceptions come to mind—the masochistic pursuit of pain as a form of pleasure, for example, or hunger strikes in protest of injustice—only reinforces the point that under *normal* conditions, such preferences are universal and part of human nature.

How do we know these things? Given a free and fair choice between democracy and autocracy, for example, people choose the former. A century of failed command economies has led nearly every nation—save those whose autocrats have yet to be overthrown—to switch to market economies because that is what people want. Why? Because they flourish under them. Compare East and West Germany between 1945 and 1990 and, even more dramatically, North and South Korea today; where would you rather live and work?

■ From *Is* to *Ought*

Morality involves how our actions affect the *survival and flourishing of sentient beings*. By *survival*, I mean the instinct to live. By *flourishing*, I mean having adequate sustenance, safety, shelter, and bonding and social relations for physical and mental health. Any organism subject to natural selection will by necessity have this drive to survive and flourish; if they didn't, they would not live long enough to reproduce and would therefore no longer be subject to natural selection. By *sentient*, I mean *emotive*, *perceptive*, *sensitive*, *responsive*, *conscious*, and therefore able to feel and to suffer. Our moral consideration should be based not primarily on what sentient beings are *thinking* but on what they are *feeling*. As the utilitarian philosopher Bentham articulated in one of the first rational arguments for animal rights: "The question is not, Can they *reason*? nor, Can they *talk*? but, Can they *suffer?*"[17] Since humans are animals, "survival and flourishing" includes the reduction of suffering as our moral starting point.

Given that moral principles must be founded on something *natural* instead of *supernatural* and that science is the best tool we have for understanding the natural world, and in applying evolutionary theory to the ultimate foundation of morality, it seems to me that *individual* sentient beings must be our starting point, because (1) the individual is the primary target of natural selection in evolution and (2) it is the individual who is most affected by moral and immoral acts. It is *individuals* who are entitled to rights, not races, genders, ethnicities, religions, or nations, because it is individuals who perceive, emote, respond, love, feel, and, most notably, suffer. Political rights involve the rights of *persons*, not collectives. Individuals vote, not genders or races or ethnicities. Individuals want to be treated equally under the law, not races. The Bill of Rights, in fact, was designed to protect *individuals* from being discriminated against as members of a group, such as by race, gender, and sexual orientation. Thus:

> *The survival and flourishing of individual sentient beings* is *the foundation for establishing values and morals, so determining the conditions by which sentient beings best survive and flourish* ought to be *the goal of a science of morality.*

To be sure, by nature we are a social species, so we enjoy and even need the company of others, such as families, extended families, friends, and communities. And we are a political species, so we revel in sorting ourselves into like-minded ideological tribes. But such consortiums should not be confused with or negate the value of the individual as the primary moral agent of our ethical concern, the axiomatic inheritor of legal rights, the principal participant in democracy, and the ultimate subject under the law. The unique individual is to politics what the atom is to physics and the organism is to biology—a fundamental unit of nature.[18]

I need to punctuate this point of individualism because in recent years, under the guise of "identity politics," liberals tend to treat individuals as members of an oppressed or oppressing group, as defined by race, ethnicity, gender, sexual orientation, religion, and political party. Similarly, under the pretense of "faith and flag," conservatives tend to sort people into such collectivities as nation, state, tribe, family, religion, and political party. The resulting Us vs. Them tribalism leads to such illiberal policies as speech censorship and destructive moralizing on the left and political populism and economic nationalism on the right. The identity politics of the alt-left is not dissimilar to the racial politics of the alt-right.

From this moral starting point, can we quantify human flourishing? We can. According to the World Bank, for example, the percentage of people living on less than $2.50 a day (poverty) and $1.25 a day (extreme poverty) has fallen by more than half since 1990 and is projected to disappear entirely by around 2035.[19] The end of poverty—imagine that![20] If the *survival and flourishing of individual sentient beings* are the foundation of values and morals, then we can say objectively and absolutely that ending poverty is real moral progress. On what basis can we make such a claim? *Ask the people who are no longer living in squalor*. They will tell you that surviving on more than $2.50 a day or $1.25 a day is better than suffering on less. Why is it better? Because it is in our nature to prefer flourishing to suffering. Or consider the fact that the number of polio cases has decreased from 350,000 in 1988, to 222 in 2012, to a few dozen in 2023.[21] Is that an absolute moral good? Ask the hundreds of thousands of people who were not paralyzed by polio. They'll tell you.

Or consider the almost unimaginable decline of violence of all types documented by Pinker in *The Better Angels of Our Nature*.[22] "Violent deaths of all kinds have declined, from around 500 per 100,000 people per year in pre-state societies to around 50 in the Middle Ages, to around 6 to 8 today worldwide, and fewer than 1 in most of Europe," Pinker explained to me in an interview in which I asked him to summarize the massive data sets he compiled. But what about the two World Wars, and the Holocaust, Stalin's gulags, and Mao's purges? "A very pessimistic estimate of the human damage from all wars, genocides, and war-induced and man-made famines in the twentieth century would be 60 per 100,000 per year—still an order of magnitude less than tribal warfare. And of course those numbers are dominated by 1914–1950 in Europe and 1920–1980 in East Asia, both of which have since calmed down."[23]

If that is not objectively quantifiable moral progress, then I don't know what is.

From My Perspective to Yours: The Principle of Interchangeable Perspectives

These examples demonstrate a logical transition from the way nature *is* (individuals struggling to survive and flourish in the dangerous environment of our evolutionary ancestry) to the way it *ought to be* (we should do more to enhance human survival and flourishing in the modern environment). Since this is-ought issue has been a contentious one among scholars ever since Hume first articulated it, I asked the philosopher Robert Pennock to assess my argument for a science of morality.

> The way the argument works is to say if you want to get a moral conclusion, you need at least one moral premise. It's not that there aren't factual premises—and this I took to be your main point, that science gives us some moral premises that make a difference—and that's exactly right. But the naturalistic fallacy doesn't say you can't have factual premises. It says you can't have *only* factual premises. You have to have something that has an *ought*, such that together with the *is*, you can get an *ought* in the conclusion. And I would say that the way you make your argument is actually bringing in *oughts* into your premises and so you're not actually denying the naturalistic fallacy. Really, you're accepting it but building in some *ought* premises from the beginning. And that's the right way to do it![24]

I concede the point that Pennock is making, namely that any case for right or wrong must begin with some built-in moral premise; in my theory's case, it is *the survival and flourishing of individual sentient beings*. If that's a moral premise, so be it, but it is one grounded in empirical science that anyone can observe for themselves. Pinker makes a similar point when he suggests that moral values might be something discoverable like abstract Platonic truths:

> On this analogy, we are born with a rudimentary concept of number, but as soon as we build on it with formal mathematical reasoning, the nature of mathematical reality forces us to discover some truths and not others. (No one who understands the concept of two, the concept of four and the concept of addition can come to any conclusion but that 2 + 2 = 4.) Perhaps we are born with a rudimentary moral sense, and as soon as we build on it with moral reasoning, the nature of moral reality forces us to some conclusions but not others.[25]

Along with having a natural desire to survive and flourish, we are social creatures living among other sentient beings who also want to survive and flourish. Reasoning moral agents in a game-theoretic matrix would eventually conclude that both should cooperate toward mutual benefit rather than compete to either a zero-sum outcome in which one gains and the other loses or both lose in a defection cascade. This line of reasoning was explored by Robert Wright in his book *Nonzero*, in which he documented an ever-increasing prevalence of nonzero-sum games through the history of life and civilization.[26] Over billions of years of natural history and thousands of years of human history, there has been an increasing tendency toward the playing of cooperative "nonzero" games between organisms. This tendency has allowed more nonzero gamers to survive. Although competition between individuals and groups was common in both biological evolution and human history, Wright argues that symbiosis among organisms and cooperation among people have gradually displaced competition as the dominant form of interaction. Why?

The answer is natural selection. Those who cooperated by playing nonzero games were more likely to survive and pass on their genes for cooperative behavior. From the Paleolithic period to the present, human groups have evolved from bands of hundreds, to tribes of thousands, to chiefdoms of tens of thousands, to states of hundreds of thousands, to nations of millions. This could not have happened through zero-sum exchanges alone. The hallmarks of humanity—language, tools, hunting, gathering, farming, writing, art, music, science, and technology—could not have come about through the actions of isolated zero-sum gamers. Thus, reasoning moral agents would conclude that cooperation was mutually beneficial. Pinker draws out the implications for moral realism:

> If I appeal to you to do anything that affects me—to get off my foot or tell me the time or not run me over with your car—then I can't do it in a way that privileges my interests over yours (say, retaining my right to run you over with my car) if I want you to take me seriously. Unless I am Galactic Overlord, I have to state my case in a way that would force me to treat you in kind. I can't act as if my interests are special just because I'm me and you're not, any more than I can persuade you that the spot I am standing on is a special place in the universe just because I happen to be standing on it.[27]

Combining self-interest and sociality with *impartiality*—what Pinker describes as "the interchangeability of perspectives"—we can derive a *principle of interchangeable perspectives* that is embodied in the Golden Rule discovered by many religions over thousands of years and rediscovered in different forms in Spinoza's viewpoint of eternity, the social contract of Thomas Hobbes, the work of Jean Jacques Rosseau and John Locke, Kant's categorical imperative, and Rawls's veil of ignorance.[28] The *principle of interchangeable perspectives* is also another way to formulate the *Golden Rule*: "As I would not want someone else to make *me* a slave, so I should not make someone else *be* a slave." In modern parlance, it is a description of the evolutionary stable strategy of *reciprocal altruism*: "I will scratch your back instead of being your master, if you will scratch my back and not make me a slave." It is the behavioral game theory strategy of *tit for tat*: "I won't make you a slave if you don't become my master."

The *principle of interchangeable perspectives* is also a restatement of Rawls's "original position" and "state of ignorance" arguments, which posit that in the original position of a society in which we are all ignorant of the state in which we will be born—male or female, Black or White, rich or poor, healthy or sick, Protestant or Catholic, slave or free—we should favor laws that do not privilege any one cohort because we don't know which category we will ultimately find ourselves in.[29] This can be restated in this context thusly: "As I would not want to live in a society in which I am a slave, so I will vote for laws that outlaw slavery." Abraham Lincoln put the principle of interchangeable perspectives into practice when he said during his October 15, 1858, debate with Stephen A. Douglas: "As I would not be a slave, so I would not be a master."[30] And in his Annual Message to Congress on December 1, 1862, he said: "In giving *freedom* to the slave, we *assure* freedom to the free."[31]

In an unpublished note penned in 1854, Lincoln outlined the argument in what to our modern ears sounds like a perfect articulation of a behavioral game theory analysis. In his refutation of the arguments made in his day that the races should be ranked by skin color, intellect, and "interest" (in reference to economic interest), Lincoln wrote the following:

> If A. can prove, however conclusively, that he may, of right, enslave B.—why may not B. snatch the same argument, and prove equally, that he may enslave A?
>
> You say A. is white, and B. is black. It is color, then; the lighter, having the right to enslave the darker? Take care. By this rule, you are to be slave to the first man you meet, with a fairer skin than your own.
>
> You do not mean color exactly?—You mean the whites are intellectually the superiors of the blacks, and, therefore have the right to enslave them? Take care again. By this rule, you are to be slave to the first man you meet, with an intellect superior to your own.

> But, say you, it is a question of interest; and, if you can make it your interest, you have the right to enslave another. Very well. And if he can make it his interest, he has the right to enslave you.[32]

This principle emerges time and again because it is, in a sense, a foundation of morality built into human moral nature and thus transcends culture and should be part of an empirical moral science. As Baruch Spinoza noted: "Those who are governed by reason desire nothing for themselves which they do not also desire for the rest of humankind."[33] Figure 7.1 well represents the principle of interchangeable perspectives.

Figure 7.1. The large, bold woodcut image of a supplicant male slave in chains appeared on the 1837 broadside publication of John Greenleaf Whittier's antislavery poem "Our Countrymen in Chains." The design was originally adopted as the seal of the Society for the Abolition of Slavery in England in the 1780s and appeared on several medallions for the society made by Josiah Wedgwood as early as 1787. This is just one of many examples of how moral truths—in this case the absolute immorality of the slave trade—are discovered in the fullness of time. Wikimedia Commons, source Library of Congress Rare Book and Special Collections Division

■ Testing Moral Truths

Now that we have established that there can be moral truths, let's examine the many ways they can be and have been tested. Many of the founding fathers of the United States, for example, such as Thomas Jefferson, Thomas Paine, Benjamin Franklin, James Madison, and John Adams, were either practicing scientists or were trained in the sciences. They deliberately adapted the scientific method of gathering data, running experiments, and testing hypotheses to their construction of the nation. Their understanding of the provisional nature of findings led them to develop a political system in which doubt and disputation were the centerpieces of a functional polity. They thought of political governance as a *problem-solving technology* rather than as a power-grabbing opportunity. They thought of democracy in the same way that they thought of science—as a method, not an ideology. They argued, in essence, that no one knows how to govern a nation (fallibilism), so a system is needed that allows for experimentation. Try this. Try that. Check the results. That is the heart of science. "The methods of science—with all its imperfections—can be used to improve social, political and economic systems," pronounced Carl Sagan in *The Demon-Haunted World*. "The great waste would be to ignore the results of social experiments because they seem to be ideologically unpalatable."[34]

Think about the 50 different states, each with its own constitution and set of laws. These are 50 different experiments. Every state has different gun control laws, for example, so we can treat these as experiments from which we can gather results and draw conclusions: States with more guns and fewer controls have higher homicide and suicide rates.[35] Every time an amendment to the Constitution is ratified and enacted into law, that is an experiment. The Nineteenth Amendment, which granted women the right to vote in 1920, worked, so we still abide by it. By contrast, the Eighteenth Amendment, which was passed in 1919 and prohibited alcohol to test the hypothesis that it would reduce drinking and crime, failed, so in 1933, the Twenty-First Amendment was enacted, overturning the

Eighteenth. Changing your mind when the evidence changes is a virtue in science.

These are not controlled laboratory tests, but they are nevertheless valuable experiments to social scientists, policymakers, and the public. For example, policy experiments showed that teaching abstinence in sex education classes does not stop teens from having sex,[36] and criminalizing abortions did not curb the practice.[37] In both cases, information and contraception work better.[38] We can't run laboratory-like experiments in real-world governance, but we can use the comparative method to compare the outcomes of different economic and political systems. Consider again the comparison of North and South Korea. In August of 1945, North and South Korea were divided at the thirty-eighth parallel. Both countries had equal annual average per-capita GNI (gross national income) and were in lockstep through the 1970s, at which point South Korea implemented economic measures to grow their economy, while North Korea continued its slide into a full-fledged dictatorship. Today, the per capita GNI of North Korea is 1.59 million won; in South Korea, it is 47.25 million won, a thirtyfold difference.[39] You can see the difference from space (figure 7.2): One is dark and impoverished, while the other is bright and flourishing.

That autocratic and theocratic regimes must build walls and concentration camps to maintain their dictatorial controls is empirical evidence for an unmistakable human preference. These, and many more in this vein (e.g., when women were given the chance to run companies and countries, they excelled), are examples from history and current events that serve as natural experiments that allow us to employ the comparative method of historical science to draw provisional conclusions about moral values.[40] In *The Science of Liberty*, Timothy Ferris notes of the architects of the United States: "The founders often spoke of the new nation as an 'experiment.' Procedurally, it involved deliberations about how to facilitate both liberty and order, matters about which the individual states experimented considerably during the eleven years between the Declaration of Independence and the Constitution."[41] We are all citizen scientists now.

Figure 7.2. In this satellite photograph taken from the International Space Station of the Korean Peninsula at night, January 24, 2024, South Korea's prosperity ends at the border and North Korea fades into darkness. In which Korea would you rather live? That everyone knows the answer reveals that there are discoverable objective moral truths. NASA's Earth Observatory, astronaut photograph ISS070 -E-80670. Public domain

All that said, I will admit that it is one thing to argue that a moral program grounded in human flourishing is a starting point based on empirical science; it is quite another to get into the weeds of moral issues to work out how science can determine—or at least inform—moral decisions. In the abortion issue, for example, whose survival and flourishing should we consider primary, the fetus's or the mother's? For historical and cultural reasons, I argue for the mother's,[42] but I'm not sure science—embryology, medicine, psychology, economics—can settle a dispute between pro-life and pro-choice advocates. In the end, we may be left with conflicting rights claims within one moral case (the rights of the fetus versus the rights of the mother) and/or conflicting moral systems (deontology vs. utilitarianism on lying) that are ultimately unresolvable by science.

The same may be true for other political hot-potato issues that are tossed back and forth each election cycle, such as immigration (how many people should be allowed into the country each year?), foreign aid (how much money and to which countries?), foreign wars (which nations should our military support or attack?), affirmative action (which type, which groups?), top-marginal federal income tax rate (94% in 1944, 70% in 1981, 50% in 1986, or 37% in 2025), and many others. These are political issues more than scientific matters, and as such, they depend more on election outcomes and the preferences of the people in power than on straight facts about the world.

Nevertheless, even such political issues as these are not completely decoupled from facts and data. Take social spending as a percentage of GDP (gross domestic product) of a country. As a moral issue as I've defined it here, we can think of social spending as an ethical imperative to help those in need and provide the homeless, mentally ill, physically handicapped, unemployed, and children with such necessities as shelter and housing, food, energy, education, job training, childcare, and medical care so they can survive and flourish. Liberals claim that we do not do enough to support citizens in need, while conservatives argue that too much social spending is enabling those who should be helping themselves (or that private charity should step up). There are elements of truth in both of these political positions, but the fact is that today, the strongest and fastest growing economies in the world allocate anywhere from 20% to 30% of their GDP to social expenditures, including (in order):[43]

> *France (31.5%), Finland (30.8%), Belgium (29%), Italy (28.9%), Denmark (28.7%), Austria (27.8%), Sweden (27.1%), Germany (25.3%), United Kingdom (21.5%), the United States (19.3%), Australia (19.1%), and Canada (17.1%).*

When social spending made through employers instead of government (on health care, retirement, and disability) is factored into the equation, the United States rises from twenty-fourth place to second in overall social expenditures. Nevertheless, the United States still boasts the largest economy in the world. Tellingly, a 2015 study on world human development between 1870 and 2007, conducted by the economist Leandro Prados de la Escosura, reported a positive correlation between the percentage of GDP that a nation belonging to the Organisation for Economic Co-operation and Development allocated to social spending and that nation's score on a composite measure of prosperity, health, and education.[44] Social spending has become an integral part of all advanced nations because, on the long arc of the moral universe, we have increasingly come to care about the survival and flourishing of our fellow human beings. That the exact number falls within that band of 20% to 30% of GDP, depending on which party is in power, does not obviate the overall trend and what it represents—an objective moral fact that it is good to care for those in need.

Most of the moral progress that has unfolded over the centuries—the abolition of slavery, torture, cruel and unusual punishment, capital punishment, corporeal punishment, witch crazes, inquisitions, pogroms, and violence in general, along with the recognition of and legal foundation for civil rights, women's rights, gay rights, children's rights, workers' rights, and even animal rights—was ultimately the result of the application of science and rationality to understanding causality and solving problems to increase the survival and flourishing of more people in more places.[45] This salubrious outcome was the result of a metaphysical assumption known as *scientific naturalism*, or in Pinker's description, *universal realism*—the principle that the world is governed by natural laws and forces that can be understood and that all phenomena are part of nature and can be explained by natural causes, including human cognitive, social, and moral phenomena.[46]

In the centuries following the Scientific Revolution and the Enlightenment, the gradual but systematic displacement of religious dogmatism, authority, and supernaturalism by scientific naturalism, particularly its application toward explaining the human world, led to the widespread adoption of *Enlightenment Humanism*, a cosmopolitan worldview that places supreme value on science and reason, eschews the supernatural, and relies exclusively on nature and nature's laws—including human nature and the laws and forces that govern us and our societies—for a complete understanding of the cosmos and everything in it, from particles to people.[47]

■ Moral Truths and Enlightenment Humanism

On April 4, 1864, President Lincoln wrote to the editor of the Frankfort, Kentucky, newspaper *Commonwealth*, Albert G. Hodges, who had journeyed to meet with Lincoln to discuss the recruitment of slaves as soldiers in Kentucky. At that time, Kentucky was a border state, and thus Lincoln's proclamation of the emancipation of the slaves the year before did not apply to them (although slaves who entered the military could gain their freedom). Lincoln made clear his position on the matter: "I am naturally anti-slavery. If slavery is not wrong, nothing is wrong. I can not remember when I did not so think, and feel."[48]

If slavery is not wrong, nothing is wrong. Call it Lincoln's axiom. In stating the obvious, the Great Emancipator was defending moral realism—again, the belief that ethical propositions refer to objective truths about the world, independent of subjective evaluations. Although a great many Americans disagreed with Lincoln, most notably those in the Southern states who at once benefited financially from the practice and believed Blacks were inferior to Whites, almost no one believes that today, and slavery is outlawed in every country on Earth. Why?

In 2017, I attempted to answer this question in the pages of the journal *Theology and Science*, in which my target article defending moral realism was critiqued by a physicist named George Ellis, to which I responded.[49] As a physicist steeped in the empirical practices of his profession, Ellis wondered how a social scientist might "discover" moral laws in human nature in a manner similar to a physical scientist discovering laws in nature. It's a good question, as is his query "Is it possible to say in some absolute sense that specific acts, such as the large scale massacres of the Holocaust, are evil in an absolute sense?" Here was my response:

> *If the Holocaust is not wrong, then nothing is wrong.*

Since Ellis is a physicist, I used an example from astronomy to make my point about discovering moral truths:

> It is my hypothesis that in the same way that Galileo and Newton discovered physical laws and principles about the natural world that really are out there, so too have social scientists discovered moral laws and principles about human nature and society that really do exist. Just as it was inevitable that the astronomer Johannes Kepler would discover that planets have elliptical orbits—given that he was making accurate astronomical measurements, and given that planets really do travel in elliptical orbits, he could hardly have discovered anything else—scientists studying political, economic, social, and moral subjects will discover certain things that are true in these fields of inquiry. For example, that democracies are better than autocracies, that market economies are superior to command economies, that torture and the death penalty do not curb crime, that burning women as witches is a falla-

> cious idea, that women are not too weak and emotional to run companies or countries, and, most poignantly here, that Blacks do not like being enslaved and that the Jews do not want to be exterminated.[50]

Why do Blacks not want to be enslaved? Why do Jews not want to be exterminated? The answer is in my moral starting point of *the survival and flourishing of individual sentient beings*. Any organism subject to natural selection will by necessity have this drive to survive and flourish. If it didn't, it would not live long enough to reproduce and would no longer be subject to natural selection. Why?

The answer is found in the deepest purpose of life: to push back against the entropy of nature, as described by the second law of thermodynamics. Entropy is a fundamental physical rule that closed systems (those not taking in energy) move from order to disorder, from organization to disorganization, from structured to unstructured, and from warm to cold. Although entropy can be temporarily reversed in an open system with an outside source of energy, such as heating cold food in a microwave, isolated systems decay as entropy increases.

The second law of thermodynamics is the first law of life. As the evolutionary psychologists Leda Cosmides, John Tooby, and Clark Barrett argue in their paper exploring the ultimate purpose of evolution: "The most basic lesson is that natural selection is the only known natural process that pushes populations of organisms thermodynamically uphill into higher degrees of functional order, or even offset the inevitable increase in disorder that would otherwise take place."[51] This "extropy" only happens in an open system with an energy source, such as the sun providing the energy to our planet that temporarily reverses entropy and replicating molecules like RNA and DNA that enable living organisms to send near-duplicates out into the world that provide fodder for natural selection.

Once this system is up and running, evolution can move away from the left wall of minimum order and simplicity and toward the right wall of maximum order and complexity. If you do nothing, entropy will take its course, and you will move toward a higher state of disorder (ultimately causing your demise). So, the most basic purpose in life is to combat entropy by doing something extropic—expending energy to survive, reproduce, and flourish.

Ellis disagrees with my moral premise, asserting that "science *per se* does not in any recognizable sense imply that survival and flourishing is either good or bad, because there is no scientific test for good or bad and no scientific proof that they are positive or negative in moral terms, i.e. that this is the way things *ought* to be."[52] Excuse me? We have, in fact, been running such experiments for centuries—the natural experiments of societies and their social, political, and economic systems. Every state or national constitution is an experiment in social and moral living. Different laws and systems produce different outcomes. We can study and learn from them, with our evaluative criteria grounded in human nature and our desire to survive and flourish.

Finally, intellectual humility requires me to acknowledge that it is possible that my theory of moral realism may be, in Ellis's words, "sociologically based—it is that of a WEIRD (Western, Educated, Industrialized, Rich, Democratic) culture—taken for granted by those living in such cultures, but not necessarily by others. People brought up in Eastern cultures are likely to make the opposite assumption."[53] I suppose it is possible that one day scientists may discover that humans do not have an instinct to survive and flourish, that most people do not want freedom, autonomy, and prosperity, that they don't mind starving and being disease-ridden and in pain, that they prefer ignorance to education and illiteracy to literacy, that women want to be lorded over by men, that some people like being enslaved, and that large populations of people don't object to being liquidated in gas chambers.

But I doubt it.

Through science and reason, we have followed a path of discovery that has led more people in more places to have better lives and enjoy more moral rights, respect, and consideration. That is moral progress grounded in moral truths.

8

Alien Truths UFOs and the Search for Sky Gods

■ The once-fringe topic of unidentified flying objects (UFOs), subject as it was to the giggle-factor typically accorded other such borderlands entities as Big Foot and the Loch Ness Monster, suddenly burst onto the social scene in the late 2010s as unidentified aerial phenomena (UAPs) and then in the 2020s as slightly modified unidentified anomalous phenomena (based entirely on a blurry video purportedly showing an object disappearing beneath the ocean surface, leading to claims that these alien spaceships are also capable of submarine activities), sparking scientific investigations, major media coverage, congressional hearings, and demands from politicians and pilots to get to the bottom of what is really going on in our skies.

For most commentators, it appeared that something new was afoot in the world—extraterrestrial beings, perhaps, or maybe Russian or Chinese spy planes, or US government secret military technologies, or maybe even interdimensional beings. But for those of us who have followed the UFO movement for decades, our *institutional memory* allows us to put these current claims and controversies into historical context.

Thus, it is when the *New York Times* published an article on "The Pentagon's Mysterious U.F.O. Program" in December of 2017,[1] and CBS's *60*

Minutes reported that "UFOs" were being "Regularly Spotted in Restricted U.S. Airspace" in May of 2021,[2] that I forthwith recalled similar UFO flaps in the past (since the early 1990s, I have been hearing that disclosure of alien visitation is coming any day now). But previous historical upsurges of sightings go back a century, to the 1890s groundswell of "mystery airships" spotted moving across the United States. These were later identified as dirigibles. Historian Mike Dash's description of the 1896–1897 series of these mysterious airships will sound familiar to those energized by the latest round of UAP videos:

> Not only were [the mystery airships] bigger, faster and more robust than anything then produced by the aviators of the world; they seemed to be able to fly enormous distances, and some were equipped with giant wings. . . . The files of almost 1,500 newspapers from across the United States have been combed for reports, an astonishing feat of research. The general conclusion of investigators was that a considerable number of the simpler sightings were misidentification of planets and stars, and a large number of the more complex the result of hoaxes and practical jokes. A small residuum remains perplexing.[3]

■ The Residue Problem

The final "small residuum" qualification hints at a reality in all skeptical and scientific investigations. No hypothesis or theory in any field accounts for 100% of the phenomena under investigation. This "residue problem" means that no matter how comprehensive a theory is, there will always be a residue of anomalies for which it cannot account. For example, in Leslie Kean's book *UFOs: Generals, Pilots and Government Officials Go on the Record*, the UFOlogist admitted that "roughly 90 to 95 percent of UFO sightings *can* be explained" as

> weather balloons, flares, sky lanterns, planes flying in formation, secret military aircraft, birds reflecting the sun, planes reflecting the

sun, blimps, helicopters, the planets Venus or Mars, meteors or meteorites, space junk, satellites, swamp gas, spinning eddies, sundogs, ball lightning, ice crystals, reflected light off clouds, lights on the ground or lights reflected on a cockpit window, temperature inversions, hole-punch clouds, and the list goes on![4]

So the entire extraterrestrial hypothesis for explaining UFOs and UAPs is based on a residue of data left over after this list has been exhausted. What's left? Not much.

Kean begins by asking readers to consider "with an open and truly skeptical mind" that such sightings represent "a solid, physical phenomenon that appears to be under intelligent control and is capable of speeds, maneuverability, and luminosity beyond current known technology" and that the "hypothesis that UFOs are of extraterrestrial or interdimensional origin is a rational one and must be taken into account, given the data we have."[5] She opens her exploration "on very solid ground, with a Major General's firsthand chronicle of one of the most vivid and well-documented UFO cases ever"—the UFO wave over Belgium in 1989–1990. That major general is Wilfried de Brouwer, and here is his account of the first night of sighting: "Hundreds of people saw a majestic triangular craft with a span of approximately a hundred and twenty feet and powerful beaming spotlights, moving very slowly without making any significant noise but, in several cases, accelerating to very high speeds."[6]

First, how does he know it had a span of 120 feet? What measurement instrument was used? Regardless, even seemingly unexplainable sightings such as de Brouwer's can have quotidian explanations. Perhaps it was an early experimental model of a delta-wing bomber (US, Soviet, or otherwise) that secret-keeping military agencies were understandably loath to reveal. Or maybe it was three sources of aerial lights (flares? small planes?) that, from the perspective of a ground observer, appeared triangular, with the mind filling in the space in between the lights—as what happens in the Kanizsa illusion (figure 8.1).

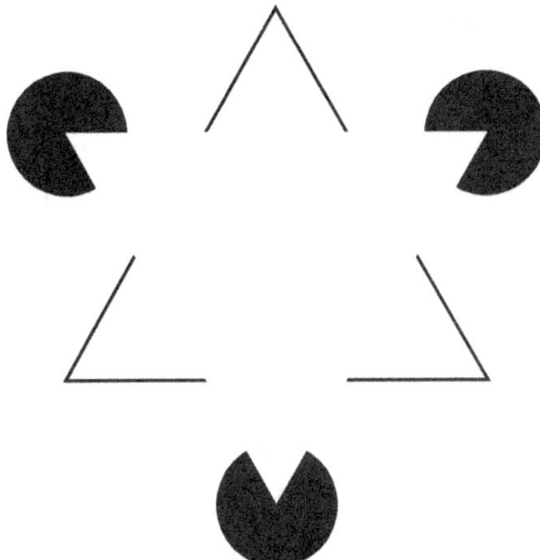

Figure 8.1. The Kanizsa illusion, popularized by the Italian artist Gaetano Kanizsa in a 1976 *Scientific American* article, demonstrates how the mind fills in the gaps of information to "see" a triangle where none exists. This effect explains some triangular-shaped UFO/UAP sightings. *Skeptic* magazine

The one and only photograph associated with the Belgian event seems to show a triangular craft that appears to be more than a Kanizsa illusion, but the UFO investigator Robert Sheaffer discovered that it was, in fact, a faked photograph of a small Styrofoam model with three spots affixed to it.[7] Since the fake photograph was inspired by "real" sightings, we still need to deal with those in order to get to the truth, so let's compare de Brouwer's narrative to Kean's summary of the same incident: "Common sense tells us that if a government had developed huge craft that can hover motionless only a few hundred feet up, and then speed off in the blink of an eye—all without making a sound—such technology would have revolutionized both air travel and modern warfare, and probably physics as well."[8]

Note how de Brouwer's 120-foot craft became "huge" in Kean's retelling, how "moving very slowly" was changed to "can hover motionless," how "without making any significant noise" shifted to "without making a sound," and how "accelerating to very high speeds" was transformed into "speed off in the blink of an eye." This language transmutation is common in UFO narratives, making it harder for scientists to provide terrestrial explanations.

■ Pilots, Astronauts, and Eyewitness Accuracy

One reason for Kean's confidence in her assertion that at least some UFOs and UAPs represent alien spacecraft is that she thinks pilots and astronauts "represent the world's best-trained observers of everything that flies. What better source for data on UFOs is there? . . . [They] are among the least likely of any group of witnesses to fabricate or exaggerate reports of strange sightings." Based on such eyewitness reports, Kean concludes that UFOs and UAPs show movements that could only be made if they were flown by intelligent pilots. "These incidents clearly demonstrate that in no way are these examples of natural events, but rather that UFOs are phenomena with a deliberate behavior. The physical nature of UFOs has been proved."[9] Has it?

According to the NASA space journalist and historian James Oberg, in his review of Kean's book, far from it. Oberg starts by referencing the renowned UFO investigator J. Allen Hynek's study on eyewitnesses, which

> found that the best class of witnesses had a 50 percent misperception rate, but that pilots had a much higher error rate: 88 percent for military pilots and 89 percent for commercial pilots, the worst of all categories listed. Pilots could be counted on for an accurate identification of *familiar* objects—such as aircraft and ground structures—but Hynek said "it should come as no surprise that the majority of pilot misidentifications were of astronomical objects."[10]

In *The Hynek UFO Report*, the astronomer concluded: "Surprisingly, commercial and military pilots appear to make relatively poor witnesses." Oberg also cited the authors of a Russian UFO study that came to the same conclusion.

> Yulii Platov of the Soviet Academy of Science and Col. Boris Sokolov of the Ministry of Defense looked into a series of sightings in 1982 that caused air defense units to scramble jet fighters to intercept the UFOs. Platov and Sokolov said the sightings were sparked by military

balloons that rose to higher-than-expected altitudes. "The described episodes show that even experienced pilots are not immune against errors in the evaluation of the size of observed objects, the distances to them, and their identification with particular phenomena," Platov wrote.[11]

More recently and poignantly (because of his fame and status), the astronaut and pilot Scott Kelly, at a NASA press conference dealing with the latest UAP flap, threw cold water on the myth of extraordinary perceptual powers of pilots and astronauts:

> In my experience of flying over 15,000 hours in 30 something years in airplanes and in space, the environment that we fly in is very conducive to optical illusions, so I get why these pilots would look at that Go Fast video and think it was going really really fast. I remember one time I was flying off Virginia Beach Military operating area and my RIO [Radar Intercept Officer], who sits in the back of the Tomcat, was convinced we flew by a UFO. I didn't see it, so we turned around to go look at it. It turns out it was a Bart Simpson balloon.
>
> My brother Mark Kelly, a former NASA astronaut and also now a U.S. Senator, shared a story with me about an experience he had years ago that when he was the commander of STS 124; they were getting ready to close the payload bay doors of the Space Shuttle and they see something in the payload bay and they thought it was a tool, maybe a bolt—they couldn't quite figure it out—and they were potentially going to have to go and do a spacewalk to retrieve it. But before they did that my brother grabbed the camera and they took a picture of it, and when they blew up the picture they realized that this is not a bolt or a tool in the payload bay; it was actually the International Space Station that was 80 miles away.
>
> There are cases where pilots have rendezvoused on a buoy because they thought that was their wingman. It's just a very very challenging environment to work, especially at night.[12]

Perception problems are one thing. Deception issues are quite another. Consider the most famous alien abduction case on record—that of Travis Walton on November 5, 1975, in Arizona (made into a major motion picture called *Fire in the Sky*[13])—which I wrote about in the context of appearing with Travis on a 2008 television show called *The Moment of Truth.*[14] Lie detector tests were administered to claimants who agreed to appear on the show. Apparently, Walton was so confident in his belief that he was abducted by aliens, he must have thought that his body would not betray him. Unfortunately for him, while recounting his abduction experience, he failed the polygraph test. Subsequently, I received an email from one Kelley Waldrip, who grew up with Walton and confirmed that he simply made up his abduction story:

> I happened across your assessment of Travis Walton's alleged abduction aboard a UFO in 1975. Your suspicion that it was a hoax is completely correct. Travis and I were in Jr. High together back in the early 60's and he was constantly dreaming up schemes to deceive folks that a UFO was visiting our little town in northern Arizona. Not having seen him for decades, I actually reminded him of that in 2006 via email and he simply changed the subject, not wanting to crack his golden egg I suppose. I did find his on-line bio rather telling as well: we were in the same grade in school and presumably the same age. I noticed that his bio lists him as having been born five years after me. That would have put him in first grade while I was in sixth. My guess is this little chronological slippage is telling.[15]

What Does "Real" Mean?

When UFO enthusiasts breathlessly state that this latest wave of UAP sightings was confirmed as "real" by no less an authority than the *New York Times*, the assumption is that the "paper of record" launched an investigation of its own, independent of UFOlogists. That is not what happened. If you check the byline for that and related articles in that paper, one of the coauthors is none other than Kean, who, as we have seen, is anything but a neutral and objective narrator of the UFO phenomena and the government's response to it. Although coauthor Helene Cooper does work for the paper as a correspondent for Pentagon matters, the other coauthor, Ralph Blumenthal, left the paper in 2009 and wrote a book titled *The Believer: Alien Encounters, Hard Science, and the Passion of John Mack*, the late Harvard psychiatrist who uncritically accepted alien abduction stories as accounts of real close encounters of the fourth kind.[16] And while the *New York Times* article was an accurate work of reportage, it didn't go very far, quoting only one skeptic—Oberg. This was at least better than *60 Minutes* in their coverage of the UAP flap that astonishingly—given their reputation as one of the most respected sources in all media—failed to interview a single scientist familiar with the sightings under investigation.

When *60 Minutes* correspondent Bill Whitaker asked Luis Elizondo, who directed the Pentagon's Advanced Aerospace Threat Identification Program, "So what you are telling me is that UFOs, Unidentified Flying Objects, are real?," Elizondo replied: "The government has already stated for the record that they're real. I'm not telling you that. The United States government is telling you that."[17] The word *real* is doing a lot of work here. No one—not the media, not the military, and certainly not the US government—is saying that these sightings represent real alien visitors. What they are confirming as "real" is the videos. But when UFO believers and the public hear the word *real*, their brains tend to autocorrect to *alien* or *Russian* or *Chinese assets*, instead of an ordinary effect of cameras and visual illusions or, simply, unexplained anomalies.

In my own classification system to explain UFO and UAP sightings, I distill them into three hypotheses:

- *Ordinary terrestrial* (balloons, camera/lens effects, visual illusions, etc.)

- *Extraordinary terrestrial* (Russian or Chinese spy planes or drones capable of feats of physics and aerodynamics unheard of in the United States)
- *Extraordinary extraterrestrial* (alien intelligence)

Let's consider each of these hypotheses and see which one has the highest credence.

Ordinary Terrestrial

The first video in this latest flap was that of Lieutenant Commander Alex Dietrich, who reported seeing an unidentified aircraft about 70 miles west of San Diego in 2004. Her explanation of what she thinks she saw is emblematic of the entire phenomena and reinforces my point about the residue problem: "Just because I'm saying that we saw this unusual thing in 2004, I am in no way implying that it was extraterrestrial or alien technology or anything like that. . . . I think that the [US government] report's going to be a huge letdown. I don't think that it's going to reveal any fantastic new insight."[18] Indeed, the report was predictably unrevealing of anything alien.

The three most widely viewed and discussed videos were filmed by infrared cameras mounted on Navy F/A-18 jets over the Atlantic seaboard and off the coast of San Diego. They were taken by the Navy Advanced Targeting Forward Looking Infrared (ATFLIR) camera pods attached to the fuselage of the jets, and the videos are now known as "Flir1" (San Diego, 2004), "Gimbal," and "Go Fast" (Florida coast, 2015).

"Flir1" (figure 8.2) is the 2004 *Nimitz* video taken by Lieutenant Chad Underwood. According to *Popular Mechanics*, it first came to light in 2007 on a UFO website.[19] It was elevated into public consciousness when it was reposted in Kean's *New York Times* article and again in 2019 by the former Blink-182 front man guitarist Tom DeLonge's UFO organization, To the Stars Academy of Arts and Science.[20] In response, the Navy acknowledged

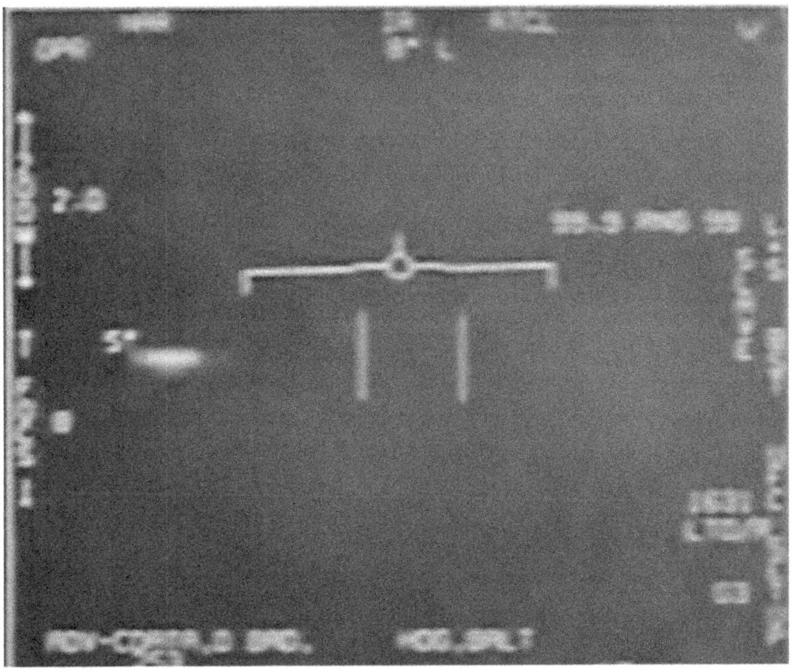

Figure 8.2. "Flir1" video screenshot, November 2004.
United States Department of Defense

that the videos were "real," meaning that they are real videos and not hoaxes.[21] Finally, in 2020, the Pentagon posted the three videos "in order to clear up any misconceptions by the public on whether or not the footage that has been circulating was real, or whether or not there is more to the videos."[22] So, these "new" videos people reference are anything but new.

The heavy lifting on analyzing these videos was done by Mick West, a former video game designer, host of the Metabunk.org website, and a former columnist for *Skeptic*.[23] West's analysis is a remarkable body of work, and one can only hope the Pentagon has at the very least considered it as part of their investigations. In the "Flir1" video, for example, the object appears to zoom almost instantly off the screen, interpreted by some to indicate extraordinary speed and turning ability far beyond anything our jets are capable of. Note that in the upper left of the screen, the camera "zoom" indicator doubles from one to two at the moment the object "zooms" to the left. When West slowed down the video replay from zoom two to one, the extraordinary maneuver becomes quite ordinary.

"Flirl" and "Gimbal," says West, are what one would see if a jet were flying away from the camera, thus accounting for the eyewitness accounts that the object showed no directional control surfaces or exhaust. And their appearance being described as saucerlike and the shape of a "Tic Tac" candy, West continues, is due to glare on the lens of the camera. As he told the *San Diego Union-Tribune*, "What we're seeing in the distance is essentially just the glare of a hot object," most likely that "of an engine—maybe a pair of engines with an F/A-18—something like that." (To be sure, not everyone accepts West's conclusions. See, for example, the UFOlogist Robert Powell's analysis in his book *UFOs*;[24] Powell told me, "You are correct in your quoting of Mick. Whether his assertions are correct is very debatable."[25]) As well, West notes, sudden acceleration of the aircraft could cause the Flir camera to lose lock on the object, thereby making it look like the objects themselves are making extraordinary maneuvers: "The supposed impossible accelerations in the 'Tic-Tac' video were revealed to coincide with (and hence caused by) sudden movements of the camera, leading to the conclusion that the object in the video was not actually doing anything special."[26]

The "Go Fast" (figure 8.3) video purportedly shows an object with no heat source (and therefore one that is propelled by some unconventional engine) that appears to move impossibly fast just above the surface of the ocean.

West used what he describes as "10th-grade trigonometry" to show that, in fact, the object was actually well above the ocean surface at around 13,000 feet and was probably just a weather balloon traveling at about 30 to 40 knots. "Because of the extreme zoom and because the camera is locked onto this object . . . the motion of the ocean in this video is actually

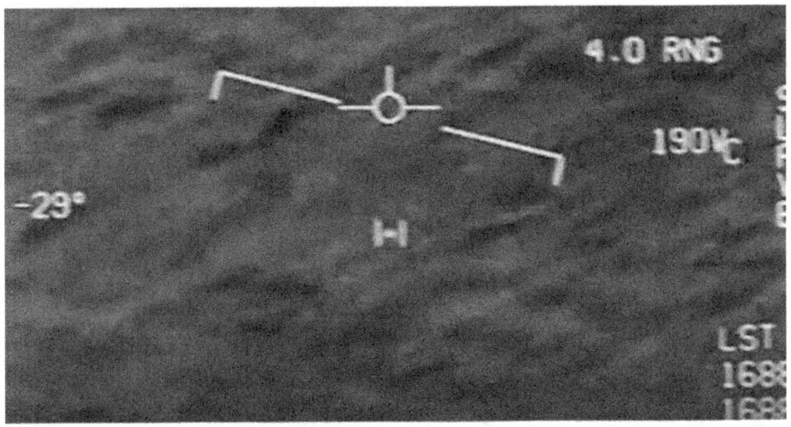

Figure 8.3. "Go Fast" video screenshot, January 2015.
United States Department of Defense

exactly the same as the motion of the jet plane itself. You're seeing something that's actually hardly moving at all, and all of the apparent motion is the parallax effect from the jet flying by."[27]

In the "Gimbal" (figure 8.4) video, an object appears to skim effortlessly over background clouds then come to an abrupt stop and rotate in midair with no apparent propulsion systems to pull off such a maneuver.

Again, astoundingly, West appears to be the only person to notice that when the "Gimbal" object rotates, background patches of light in the scene also rotate in perfect union with the object. "I think what's clear about Gimbal is it's very hot—it's consistent with two jet engines next to each other and the glare of these engines gets a lot bigger than the actual aircraft itself so it gets obscured by it," West explains, adding that "at the start of the video, it looks like the object is moving rapidly to the left because of the parallax effect, and the rotation was a camera artifact, and that the 'flying saucer' was simply the infrared glare from the engines of a distant aircraft that was flying away."[28] When he looked up the patents for that

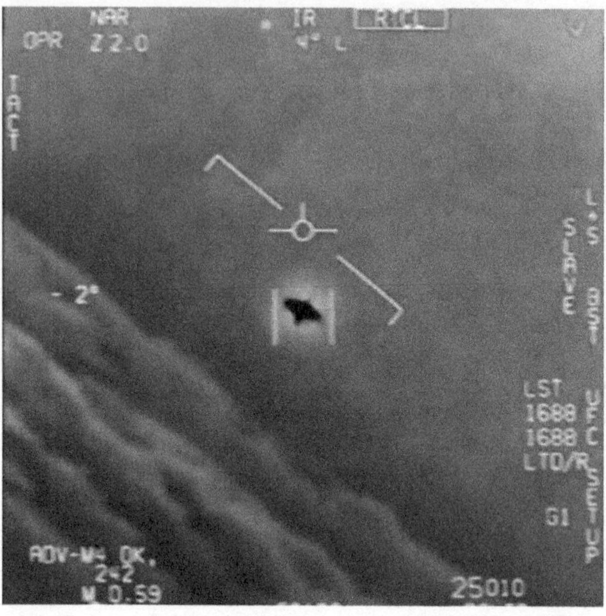

Figure 8.4. "Gimbal" video screenshot, January 2015. United States Department of Defense

camera, West found that the gimbal mechanism was responsible for the apparent rotation.[29]

Since then, two more videos by the UAP Task Force were released, one showing a flying triangle (figure 8.5) and the second an apparently zigzagging submersible sphere (figure 8.6). As the media and public gawked at yet another triangle-shaped UFO, West noted that it was filmed at night beneath the flight path into Los Angeles International Airport and that the object blinked in perfect unison with commercial airliners flying into Los Angeles from Hawaii. The triangular shape, he surmised, was most likely the result of a triangle-shaped lens aperture and the "bokeh" effect, or the soft out-of-focus background generated by shooting an object with a fast lens and wide aperture.[30] In fact, there were other triangle-shaped objects

Figure 8.5. "Flying Triangle" video screenshot, 2019. United States Department of Defense

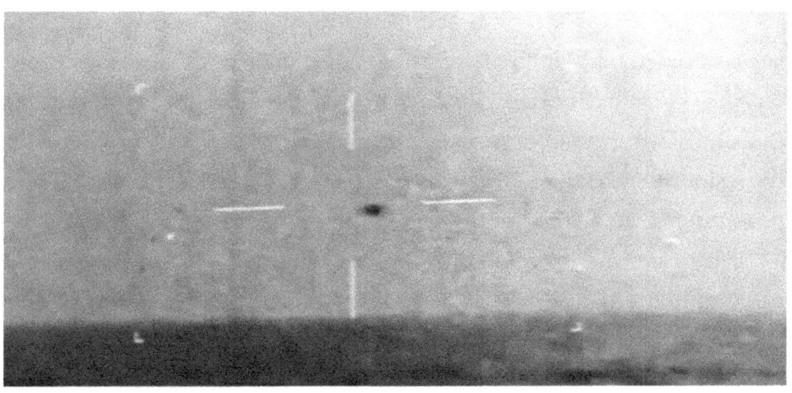

Figure 8.6. "Submersible Sphere" video screenshot, 2019. United States Department of Defense

in the image that correspond perfectly to celestial objects that West identified as the planet Jupiter and some known stars.

As for the "zigzagging" object, also filmed off the coast of California from the combat ship *Omaha*, you can see in West's video analysis that it is the camera that is zigzagging, not the object, and it doesn't "submerse" into the water, it simply disappears beyond the horizon (furthermore, the video is so grainy that whatever is being filmed isn't clear at all).[31]

Proponents of UAPs point out that the sightings were not just filmed but also witnessed by pilots and, in the case of the 2004 encounter near San Diego, by a couple of sailors aboard the guided missile cruiser *Princeton*, who reported to *Popular Mechanics* that they saw on their new radar systems aircraft that appeared to descend from 60,000 feet to 50 feet in a matter of seconds (leading the aforementioned Dietrich to divert her jet to intercept the "bogies"). (According to Powell, "The decision to intercept the bogies came from the *Princeton*-based . . . radar systems. The pilots found the bogie at the location they were sent to, so that's quite a coincidence that the radar and the pilot's visual detection systems matched up."[32])

But who knows what was going on with the new radar system? Perhaps it needed calibration or adjustment (although, according to the sailors, the system had been recalibrated), or maybe the military will one day explain it, or it may forever remain in the realm of unsolved mysteries in the residue of anomalies. In any case, just being witnessed is not enough to be accepted as truth. This entire UFO subject revolves around the fact that our senses can and do fail us all the time. We don't gain knowledge only based on our (highly unreliable) senses, as René Descartes reminded us centuries ago: "Whatever I have accepted until now as most true has come to me through my senses. But occasionally I have found that they have deceived me, and it is unwise to trust completely those who have deceived us even once."[33] Figure 8.7, the reflection of a ceiling light in a window that appears to be a UFO in the sky, well illustrates the point.

That both *60 Minutes* and Fox News would run photographs of what are obviously mylar balloons as evidence of either threatening foreign assets or extraterrestrial visitation to Earth does not help the cause of the UFOlogists who want to be taken seriously (figure 8.8 and figure 8.9).

Figure 8.7. The reflection of a ceiling light in a window appears to be a UFO in the sky. Photograph by William Bull. Reproduced with permission

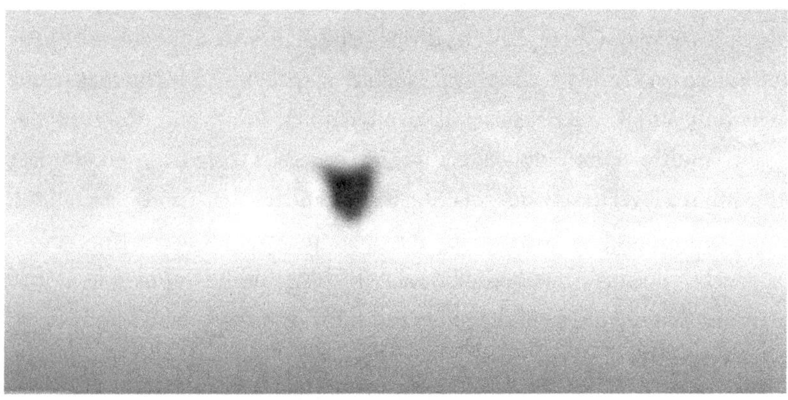

Figure 8.8. *60 Minutes* featured this photograph of a mylar balloon as one of many UAP images purported to be mysterious, foreign assets, or extraterrestrials.

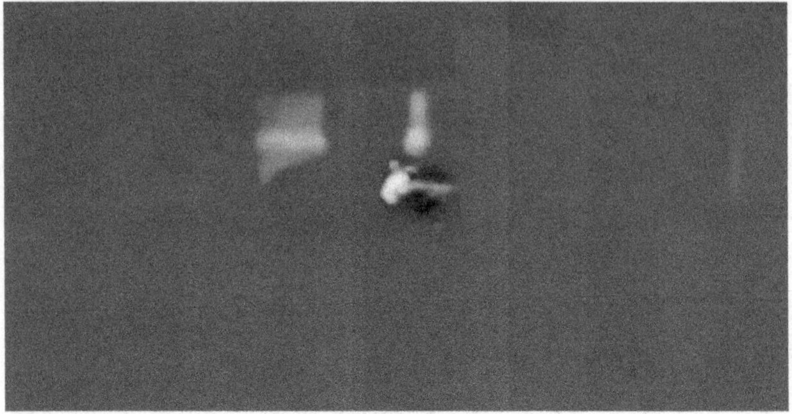

Figure 8.9. Fox News featured this photograph of a mylar balloon as one of many UAP images purported to be mysterious, foreign assets, or extraterrestrials.

■ Extraordinary Terrestrial

An alternative to ordinary explanations for UAP sightings is that they represent Russian or Chinese assets, drones, spy planes, or some related but as yet unknown (to us) technology capable of speeds and turns that seemingly defy all known physics and aerodynamics. Pilots and observers describe "multiple anomalous aerial vehicles" accelerating from 80,000 feet down to sea level in seconds, making instantaneous turns and even sudden stops, or shooting off horizontally at hypersonic speed, breaking the sound barrier but not making a sonic boom, which should be impossible, not to mention that it would kill the pilots instantly. And these vehicles appear to be able to do so with no apparent jet engine or visible exhaust plume, suggesting that they're using some antigravity technology unavailable to even the most advanced experimental programs worked on at DARPA (Defense Advanced Research Projects Agency). When *60 Minutes* correspondent Whitaker asked former Navy pilot Lieutenant Ryan Graves, who had seen with his own eyes UAPs buzzing around Virginia Beach in 2014, "Could it be Russian or Chinese technology?," Graves responded, "I don't see why not." He added, "If these were tactical jets from another country that were hangin' out up there, it would be a massive issue."[34] David Fravor, Top Gun Navy pilot and commander of the F/A-18F squadron on the USS *Nimitz*, told *60 Minutes*, "I don't know who's building it, who's got the technology, who's got the brains. But there's something out there that was better than our airplane."[35]

The hypothesis that the objects are terrestrial and developed by some other nation or corporation or some genius working in isolation is highly unlikely, given what we know about the evolution of technological innovation, which is cumulative from the past. In his seminal work, *The Evolution of Technology*, the historian George Basalla busts the myth of the inventor working in isolation, dreaming up new and innovative technologies out of sheer creative genius (the ping of the light bulb flashing brilliantly in the mind). All technologies, Basalla demonstrates, are developed out of either preexisting artifacts (artificial objects) or already existing naturfacts (organic objects): "Any new thing that appears in the made world is based on some object already in existence," he explains.[36] But some artifact had to be first—an invention that comes from no other invention, *ex nihilo* as it were. If this is the case, then that artifact, Basalla shows, likely came from a naturfact. (Barbed wire is a famous example. Its inventor, Michael Kelly, in 1868 explained: "My invention [imparts] to fences of wire a character approximating to that of a thorn-hedge. I prefer to designate the fence so produced as a thorny fence."[37])

In *How Innovation Works*, Matt Ridley demonstrates through numerous examples that innovation is an incremental, bottom-up, fortuitous process that is a result of the human habit of exchange rather than an orderly, top-down process developing according to a plan. Innovation is different from invention, Ridley argues, because "it is the turning of inventions into things of practical and affordable use to people that makes innovation possible."[38] Innovation, he continues, "is always a collective, collaborative phenomenon, not a matter of lonely genius. It is gradual, serendipitous, recombinant, inexorable, contagious, experimental and unpredictable. It happens mainly in just a few parts of the world at any one time."[39] Examples include steam engines, jet engines, search engines, airships, vaping devices, vaccines, cuisine, antibiotics, mosquito nets, turbines, propellers, fertilizer, computers, dogs, farming equipment, fire, genetic engineering, gene editing, container shipping, railways, cars, safety rules, wheeled suitcases, mobile phones, powered flight, chlorinated water, toilets, vacuum cleaners, the telegraph, radio, social media, block chain, the sharing economy, artificial intelligence, and hyperloop tubes.

It is simply not possible that some nation, corporation, or lone individual—no matter how smart and creative—could have invented and innovated new physics and aerodynamics to create an aircraft of any sort that could be, essentially, centuries ahead of all known present technologies. That is not how innovation works. It would be as if the United States were using rotary phones while the Russians or Chinese had smart phones, or if we were flying biplanes while they were flying stealth fighter jets, or if we were sending letters and memos via fax machine while they were emailing files via the internet, or if we were still experimenting with captured German V-2 rockets while they were testing SpaceX-level rocketry. These are impossible scenarios. We would know about all the steps leading to such technological wizardry.

Consider the Manhattan Project, arguably the most secretive program in US history to date, which led to the successful development of atomic bombs in 1945. The Russians had an atomic bomb by 1949. How? They stole our plans through a German theoretical physicist and spy named Klaus Fuchs. Modern tech companies like Apple, Google, Intel, and Microsoft are notoriously secretive about their inventions, forcing employees to sign nondisclosure agreements, enforcing extensive security protocols for their offices, and protecting intellectual property rights through countless lawsuits. And yet, all of our computers, smart phones, computer chips, and software programs are essentially the same, or at least in close parallel development. Countries and companies steal, copy, back engineer, and innovate each other's ideas and technologies, leaving no one company or country very far ahead or behind any other.

■ Extraordinary Extraterrestrial

Could these UAPs and UFOs represent visitations by extraterrestrial intelligences, or ETIs? Let's first separate two questions that most people confuse: (1) Are aliens out there somewhere in the cosmos? (2) Have aliens come here? When I state my skepticism about the latter, people assume I'm also skeptical about the former. "Do you seriously think we're alone in this vast cosmos?" is a common rejoinder I hear when I say something like "UFOs are not ETIs." So, let me state for the record that although we have no definitive evidence to answer either question in the affirmative, *I think it highly likely that aliens are out there somewhere in the cosmos, but they have not come here*. There's a lot to unpack that goes a long way toward explaining why these UAPs very probably are not ETIs.

To the first question, the law of large numbers suggests that aliens are very likely out there. A 2016 analysis of the Hubble Ultra Deep Field by NASA and the European Space Agency estimated that there are ten times the number of galaxies previously known (about one hundred billion), meaning that there are at least one trillion galaxies in the universe,[40] each of which has at least one hundred billion stars, for a total of a hundred million trillion stars—100,000,000,000,000,000,000,000—an almost inconceivably large number. The discoveries made by the Kepler Space Telescope revealing that nearly all stars have planets add many more zeroes to that already Brobdingnagian figure for the number of possible places where life could evolve into an intelligent communicating species. We also now know that it takes only a few million years for stars and planets to coalesce out of clouds of dust and gas to form solar systems. In our galaxy alone, this happens about once a month. In the universe with the aforementioned number of stars, this would mean a thousand new solar systems are *born every second*. In her book *Cosmos: Possible Worlds*, Ann Druyan captured the concept thus: "Snap your fingers. That's a *thousand new solar systems* right there. Snap. A thousand new solar systems . . . Snap. A *thousand new solar systems* . . . Snap. A *thousand new solar systems* . . . Snap. Snap. Snap."[41]

How many of these stars have Earth-like planets orbiting their sun-like star in a habitable zone conducive to the evolution of intelligent life with which we might communicate? This number is usually calculated using the eponymous Drake equation, proposed in 1961 by the radio astronomer Frank Drake for estimating the number of technological civilizations that reside in our galaxy:

$$N = R \times f_p \times n_e \times f_l \times f_i \times f_c \times L$$

In this equation, N = the number of communicative civilizations, R = the rate of formation of suitable stars, f_p = the fraction of those stars with planets, n_e = the number of Earth-like planets per solar system, f_l = the fraction of planets with life, f_i = the fraction of planets with intelligent life, f_c = the fraction of planets with communicating technology, and L = the lifetime of communicating civilizations.[42]

In the literature of the search for extraterrestrial intelligence (SETI), a conservative 10% figure is often used for the different factors in the equation, where, in a galaxy of 100 billion stars, there will be 10 billion sun-like stars, 1 billion Earth-like planets, 100 million planets with life, 10 million planets with intelligent life, and 1 million planets with intelligent life capable of radio technology.

Although most SETI astronomers are realistic about the limitations of such estimates, I was puzzled to encounter numerous caveats about L—the lifetime of technological civilizations—such as this one from SETI Institute astronomer Seth Shostak: "The lack of precision in determining these parameters pales in comparison to our ignorance of L."[43] Similarly, Mars Society President and space exploration visionary Robert Zubrin says that "the biggest uncertainty revolves around the value of L; we have very little data to estimate this number and the value we pick for it strongly influences the results of the calculation."[44] Estimates of L by astronomers reflect this uncertainty, ranging from 10 years to 10 million years, with a mean of about 50,000 years.

Using a conservative Drake equation calculation where $L = 50{,}000$ years (and $R = 10, f_p = 0.5, n_e = 0.2, f_l = 0.2, f_i = 0.2, f_c = 0.2$), $N = 400$ civilizations, or 1 per 4,300 light years. Applying Zubrin's optimistic (and modified) Drake equation, $N = 5{,}000{,}000$ galactic civilizations, or 1 per 185 light years. Zubrin's calculation assumes the Milky Way galaxy has 400 billion stars, of which 10% are suitable G and K type stars not part of multiple star systems, with almost all having planets, and with 10% of these containing an active biosphere, and 50% of those as old as Earth. Estimates of N range wildly in between these figures of 400 and 5 million, from Planetary Society SETI scientist Thomas R. McDonough's 4,000[45] to Carl Sagan's 1 million galactic civilizations.[46]

In fact, I have argued that we have copious empirical data on the lengths of civilization from history. To compute my own value of L, I compiled the lengths of 60 civilizations (the number of years from inception to demise), including Sumer, Mesopotamia, Babylonia, the eight dynasties of Egypt, the six civilizations of Greece, the Roman Republic and Empire, and others in the ancient world, plus various civilizations since the fall of Rome, including the nine dynasties (and two Republics) of China, four in Africa, three in India, two in Japan, six in Central and South America, and six modern states of Europe and America. For all 60 civilizations in my database, there was a total of 25,234 years, or $L = 420.5$ years. For more modern and technological societies, L became shorter, with the 28 civilizations since the fall of Rome averaging 304.5 years (table 8.1).

I should point out that since I first published these calculations in *Scientific American*,[47] a number of SETI scientists—most notably Jill Tarter and Shostak—countered that when a civilization falls and a new one arises, they don't have to start over with science and technology because knowledge of such gets passed along. Here is how Powell articulated the argument after reviewing my analysis:

> The development of technology does not begin or end with the downfall of each civilization. I don't think you can then use the number 304.5 to calculate the average length of a technological civilization in the Drake equation. You could argue that there is a "length" to the time at which civilizations can communicate with each other. If you assume a civilization lasts 50,000 years, that doesn't mean that the civilization at year 1 is even capable of engaging a civilization at year 50,000. Imagine the technological changes in our own civilization across that time period.[48]

Table 8.1. Civilizations and Their Durations Through Human History

Civilization	Years	Civilization	Years
Sumeria, 2800–1900 BC	900	Greece, 2900–146 BC	2,754
Mesopotamia, 2800–1200 BC	1,600	Minoan, 2900–1150 BC	1,750
Babylonia, 1900–1100 BC	800	Mycenean, 1600–1150 BC	450
Hittite, 1600–717 BC	883	Dark Ages, 1100–750 BC	350
Israel, 1000 BC–AD 70, David–Herod	1,070	Archaic, 750–500 BC	250
Persia, 550–323 BC	227	Hellenic, 479–323 BC	156
Parthia, 250 BC–AD 225	475	Hellenistic, 323–146 BC	177
Maurya 321–185 BC	136	Rome, 509 BC–AD 312	821
"Axial Age," 600–400 BC	200	Republic, 509–31 BC	478
Egypt, 3100–30 BC	3,070	Empire, 31 BC–AD 312	343
Early Dynastic, 3100–2686 BC	414	Byzantine empire, 312–1453	1,141
Old Kingdom, 2686–2181 BC	505	Sassanid Persia, 226–642	416
1st Intermediate, 2181–2040 BC	141	Ottoman, 1350–1918	568
Middle Kingdom, 2133–1786 BC	347	Africa	–
2nd Intermediate, 1786–1567 BC	219	Axum, 300–700	400
New Kingdom, 1567–1085 BC	482	Ghana, 900–1100	200
Late Dynastic, 1085–341 BC	744	Mali, 1200–1450	250
Ptolemaic, 332–30 BC	302	Songhai, 1460–1591	131

It's a good point, but scientific and technological space exploration and alien search programs have to be organized, funded, and run by specific political entities, which do have limited lifespans. So, plugging these figures into the Drake equation goes a long way toward explaining why ET has yet to visit or call. Where $L = 420.5$ years, $N = 3.35$ civilizations in our galaxy; where $L = 304.5$ years, $N = 2.44$ civilizations in our galaxy.[49] Given the enormous size of our galaxy (100,000 light years in length and 50,000 light years in width) and the vast distances between the stars, if there were only a few intelligent and communicating civilizations, the probability of making contact with one is astronomically low.

Table 8.1. (*continued*)

Civilization	Years	Civilization	Years
India	–	Japan	–
Harappan, 3000–1900 BC	1,100	Shogunate, 1338–1867	529
Mauryan empire, 332–185 BC	147	Meiji Restoration, 1868–1937	69
Mughal empire, 1483–1757	274	Central/South America	–
China	–	Olmec civilization, 800–300 BC	500
Xia dynasty, 2205–1818 BC	387	Toltec empire, 300–600	300
Shang dynasty, 1523–1027 BC	496	Mayan civilization, 300–1300	1,000
Zhou dynasty, 1027–771 BC	256	Aztec empire, 1400–1519	119
Han dynasty, 206 BC–AD 220	426	Inca empire, 1438–1538	100
Sui dynasty, 581–618	37	Spanish empire, 1519–1810	291
Tang dynasty, 618–907	289	Modern nation-states	–
Yuan dynasty, 1280–1367	87	United States, 1776–2002	226
Ming dynasty, 1368–1644	276	Germany, 1871–2002	131
Qing dynasty, 1644–1911	267	England, 1066–2002	936
Republic of China, 1911–1949	38	France, 1789–2002	213
People's Republic, 1949–2002	53	Italy, 1870–2002	132
		Israel, 1948–2002	54

BC + AD total: 25,234 years ÷ 60 civilizations = 420.56 years, average length of a civilization
AD only total: 8,527 years ÷ 28 civilizations = 304.53 years, average length of a civilization

Bayesian Reasoning About UFOs

Some UFOlogists claim that there is extraordinary evidence for alien visitation in the form of tens of thousands of UFO sightings. But Shostak points out that this actually argues *against* UFOs being ETIs, because to date, not *one* of these tens of thousands of sightings has materialized into concrete evidence that UFO sightings equal ETI contact.[50] Lacking physical evidence or nonblurry/nongrainy photographs and videos, more sightings equals *less confidence*, because with so many unidentified objects purportedly zipping around our airspace, we surely should have captured one by now, and we haven't. And where are all the high-definition photographs and videos captured by passengers on commercial airliners? The aforementioned Graves told *60 Minutes* correspondent Whitaker that they had seen UAPs "every day for at least a couple of years." If true, given that nearly every passenger has a smart phone with a high-definition camera, there should be thousands of clear and unmistakable photographs and videos of these UAPs. To date, there is not one. Here, *the absence of evidence is evidence of absence.*

In a 500-page history of the UFO/UAP phenomena—Garrett Graff's *UFO: The Inside Story of the US Government's Search for Alien Life Here and Out There*[51]—it becomes clear and is especially noteworthy that after 75 years of serious searching, we still have no definitive and unmistakable evidence for ETIs, so it is reasonable to maintain a low credence in the UFOs = ETIs hypothesis. Graff admitted to me, "I sort of came into this subject as a general skeptic." Though he is not leaving it "as a believer," he is nevertheless "open to the possibility of there being sort of interesting and weird answers in here." After a career writing about government security programs, the FBI, 9/11, Watergate, and Raven Rock (the government's Cold War doomsday plans), he concludes that if the government is covering up anything, it is that they don't know what's going on in our skies. As he explained the problem to me:

> The challenge for me with government conspiracies is they presuppose a level of competence that is not on display in the rest of the

> work that the government does. I just don't believe that the government is capable of keeping a secret at scale like this for any meaningful period of time. For example, my next book is a history of D-Day, Operation Overlord—the biggest, most important secret that the US government had. They had six, eight, ten complete breaches of secrecy in the six or eight months before. One guy literally accidentally mailed a copy of the invasion plans to his mom in Chicago. One officer got drunk and accidentally started talking about the invasion at a cocktail party. Another officer left a briefcase behind on a bus that he ended up chasing after down the street trying to recover the invasion documents. That's one operation in one six-month period. So to me, I just don't see the capability of the US government to keep any meaningful secrets about this UFO program over a long period of time. And yet you have a conspiracy around UFOs that would employ thousands of people over decades and not one has leaked anything, or left a briefcase full of UFO secrets in an Uber or a taxi cab, or accidentally mailed documents to the wrong person, or written a tell-all memoir, or gone on *60 Minutes* with firsthand knowledge.[52]

After studying this phenomenon for over 30 years, I suspect there is something much deeper that touches on mythology, religion, and the desire to believe we are not alone. And this desire to believe is often stronger than the desire for truth.

■ Sky Gods for Skeptics

In *The Plurality of Worlds*, the science historian Steven Dick suggested that when Newton's mechanical universe replaced the medieval spiritual world, it left a lifeless void that was filled with the modern search for ETI.[53] In *Are We Alone?*, the physicist Paul Davies noted: "What I am more concerned with is the extent to which the modern search for aliens is, at rock-bottom, part of an ancient religious quest."[54] Basalla made a similar observation in

Civilized Life in the Universe: "The idea of the superiority of celestial beings is neither new nor scientific. It is a widespread and old belief in religious thought."[55] In *Contact with Alien Civilizations*, Michael A. G. Michaud proposes that "one of the drivers behind our search for other intelligent beings is our desire to find or attribute purpose to our existence. We have an innate yearning to be identified as part of some ill-defined grander scheme of things."[56] Here is how Carl Sagan expressed the sentiment in an interview with CBS anchor Walter Cronkite:

> It used to be possible to believe in a personal, benevolent, powerful, all-knowing God who cared about individuals who you could pray to. But now, there's very few people who really believe that, I think. Science, for good or for ill, has destroyed a lot of the traditional theologies. And yet people have the same needs to believe that they always did, perhaps more so because of the times we live in. Well, the flying saucer myths are a really clever compromise. It's a way of having beings that come from the sky that are worried about us, that are powerful, that are going to step in and prevent us from destroying ourselves.[57]

In *The Myth and Mystery of UFOs*, the historian and UFO author Thomas Bullard, while admitting that the evidence for aliens is "sloppy ambiguous, and unsatisfactory . . . and ufology is a fine mess, crowded with charlatans, true believers, gullibility, and unsubstantiated claims," nevertheless contends:

> UFO stories echo unmistakable leitmotifs of the great mythological themes: culture-bearers and saviors from the sky, supernatural enemies and the end of the world, visits to and from the otherworld, rituals of initiation and transformation, interbreeding with otherworld entities, magical events and trickster figures like Men in Black. The initiatory journey of the shaman echoes through the examinations, conferences, and otherworld visits of abductees, apocalyptic configurations through UFO conspiracy theories. Whether these similarities are borrowed or

> coincidental may serve as a subject of contention, but at least a psychosocial position that they depend on cultural influence—for their form if not their substance—has defensible grounds.[58]

What might those psychosocial factors be? To find out, the psychologist Clay Routledge and his colleagues conducted a four-part study in which they found an inverse relationship between religiosity and ETI beliefs—those who report low levels of religious belief but high desire for meaning show greater belief in ETIs. In Study 1, subjects who read an essay "arguing that human life is ultimately meaningless and cosmically insignificant" were statistically significantly more likely to believe in ETIs than those who read an essay on the "limitations of computers." In Study 2, subjects who self-identified as either atheist or agnostic were statistically significantly more likely to report believing in ETIs than those who reported being religious (primarily Christian). In Studies 3 and 4, subjects completed a religiosity scale, a meaning in life scale, a well-being scale, an ETI belief scale, and a religious supernatural belief scale. "Lower presence of meaning and higher search for meaning were associated with greater belief in ETI," the researchers reported, but ETI beliefs showed no correlation with supernatural beliefs or well-being beliefs. From these studies, the authors conclude:

> ETI beliefs serve an existential function: the promotion of perceived meaning in life. In this way, we view belief in ETI as serving a function similar to religion without relying on the traditional religious doctrines that some people have deliberately rejected. That is, accepting ETI beliefs does not require one to believe in supernatural forces or agents that are incompatible with a scientific understanding of the world.[59]

In other words, if you don't believe in God but seek deeper meaning outside of our world, the thought that we are not alone in the universe "could make humans feel like they are part of a larger and more meaningful cosmic drama."[60]

Given that there is no more evidence for aliens than there is for God, believers in either one must take a leap of faith or suspend judgment until evidence emerges to the contrary to change one's credence (and as of a 2024 Pentagon report, there is still no evidence whatsoever of alien visitation[61]). Until then, I'll give the last word to Dietrich, who witnessed the 2004 UAP incident from a USS *Nimitz* fighter jet, as I think it well sums up 75 years of UFOlogists' search for aliens: "I think they enjoy the anticipation more than actually finding answers."[62]

PART III

KNOWN UNKNOWABLES

■ We can be as honest as we are ignorant. If we are, when asked what is beyond the horizon of the known, we must say that we do not know. We can tell the truth, and we can enjoy the blessed freedom that the brave have won. We can destroy the monsters of superstition, the hissing snakes of ignorance and fear. We can drive from our minds the frightful things that tear and wound with beak and fang. We can civilize our fellow-men.

—**Robert Ingersoll**, *The Works of Robert G. Ingersoll*, vol. 1, *Lectures*

9

The Truth About Consciousness

What Is It Like to Be You?

■ Living in Santa Barbara on the California coast, I regularly see dolphins playfully swimming and surfing the warm waters inside the Channel Islands, breaching the surface, doing flips in the air, and riding the bow wave of whale-watching boats. On a trip to a Mexican resort, I once had the opportunity to swim alongside and even touch dolphins under the watchful eyes of their trainers and caretakers of their aqueous artificial home. Such experiences have led me to wonder what it's like to be a dolphin.

Consciousness is often defined as "what it's like to be something," inspired by the philosopher Thomas Nagel's 1974 classic paper, "What Is It Like to Be a Bat?" As he explained the problem: "An organism has conscious mental states if and only if there is something that it is like to *be* that organism—something that it is like *for* the organism."[1] Let's make dolphins our subject of inquiry. If I added echolocation to my sensory systems, perhaps I would be able to "see" the shapes of things with sound waves, and that would nudge me a bit closer to dolphin-ness. Strapping to my feet one of those giant monofins to serve as a tail would allow me to feel what it's like to power through a viscous aquatic medium, which would be made all the smoother if I donned one of those rubbery Olympic full-body swimsuits to mimic the dolphin's sleek, smooth, rubbery skin texture. Adding a snorkel that serves as a blowhole for breathing, an appetite for squid (sushi?), and the ability to make clicks and whistle sounds might nudge me further along the dolphin-ness scale.

But the only way to have the full-on qualitative experience of dolphinness is to actually *be a dolphin* with all that entails anatomically, physiologically, neurologically, and cognitively. In that case, then, I would no longer be a human wondering what it's like to be a dolphin. I'd just be a dolphin and very likely not asking what it's like to be a human. This is what is called the *hard problem of consciousness*. As first proposed by the philosopher David Chalmers, the problem is trying to explain how we are able to experience the world from inside a wet neurochemical brain machine.[2] The easy problem of consciousness would be to explain how, for example, the color red is processed in the retina of the eye and then transduced into neurochemical processes back to the visual cortex of the brain. The hard problem is explaining how it is we can experience "redness."

That qualitative experience is called *qualia*, and in the history of philosophy, this is also known as the mind-body problem—how nonmaterial mind emerges from material body. As Nagel reflected, "Without consciousness the mind-body problem would be much less interesting. With consciousness it seems hopeless."[3] The neuroscientist Christof Koch put it this way: "How can activity in the brain trigger feelings? It's just squishy stuff. How can mere meat, as cyberpunk novels dismissively refer to the body, engender sentience? Putting it more generally, how can anything physical give rise to something nonphysical, to subjective states?"[4]

The hard problem is not only hard for all these anatomical, physiological, neurological, and cognitive reasons; I put it into the category of a *known unknowable* because it is logically impossible to solve for the simple reason that it would violate Aristotle's law of identity—*A is A*. Thus: *A cannot also be non-A*. You cannot at one and the same time be one thing (a human) and another thing (a dolphin). If I were able to shape-shift from human to dolphin, I would not retain my humanness while inside the body and brain of a dolphin. I would just be a dolphin, full stop. Put another way, asking what it's like to be one thing precludes one from knowing what it's like to be a different thing. It's conceptually contradictory. Understanding how the brain machinery works is different from experiencing the brain machinery itself.

The hard problem's thought experiment of wondering what it's like to be something is also conceptually flawed in that it implies a form of *dualism* in which my soul or homunculus or mini-me transports into the body of a dolphin to experience its physical and mental state of being. This is not possible because there is no ghost in the machine, no soul in the body, and no mind in the brain, as if these are different entities that can separate and travel elsewhere. This *essentialism* about the self, as it is called, leads us to intuitively feel like we have a soul or mind, separate from the body and brain. So we get the humor of films like *All of Me*, in which the gendered soul of Steve Martin's character switches places with that of Lily Tomlin so that each knows what it's like to be the other sex (with all the gender-bending comedy that follows), or the film *Freaky Friday*, in which the teenage essence of Lindsay Lohan swaps places with the middle-aged mom essence of Jamie Lee Curtis, and hilarity ensues as the middle-aged mom is suddenly filled with teenage angst mingling with her youthful peers, and the immature teenager suddenly finds herself in adult situations for which she is ill equipped.[5]

Novelists have explored similar themes. In Franz Kafka's *Metamorphosis*, a man falls asleep and wakes up as a giant insect, while his human personality remains intact inside the bug (as imagined by artists for the book's many covers—figure 9.1). But that is not what would happen. After the metamorphosis from human to arthropod, the essence of humanness would simply dissolve away while the essence of cockroach took its place. Yet, such *Gedankenexperiments* fill us with imaginative worlds we can never experience in real life. Here is how the psychologist Paul Bloom explains the process:

> In fact most people around the world believe that an even more radical transformation actually takes place. Most people believe that when the body is destroyed, the soul lives on. It might ascend to heaven, or descend to hell, go off into some sort of parallel world, or occupy some other body, human or animal. Even those of us who do not hold such views have no problems understanding them. But they are only coherent if we see people as separate from their bodies.[6]

Here, the distinction in worldviews is that between *dualism* and *monism*. *Dualists* believe that we consist of two substances—body and soul, brain and mind (called "substance dualism"). *Monists* contend that there is just one substance—a body and a brain—from which consciousness is an

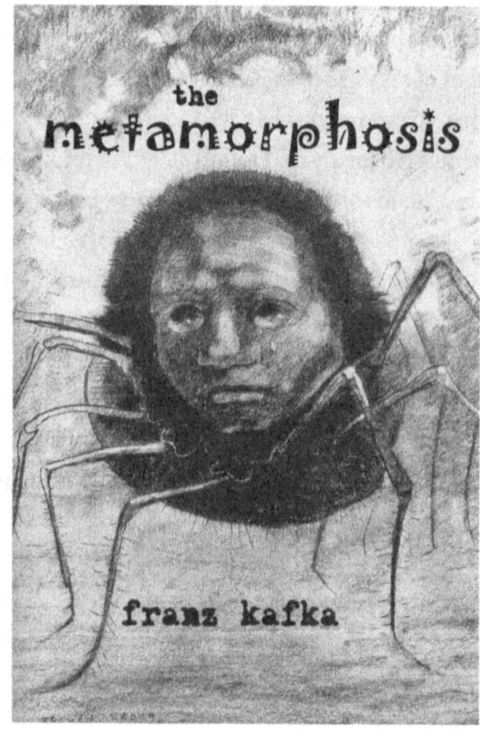

Figure 9.1. One of the many book covers for Franz Kafka's *Metamorphosis* depicting the dualistic error that our self is separate from our body. You are your body. Art by Odilon Redon, *The Crying Spider*, charcoal drawing. Cover design by Jack Lyon, reproduced with permission of Waking Lion Press

emergent property; *mind* is just the term we use to describe what the brain is doing, and the *soul* is just the pattern of information that represents our thoughts, memories, and personalities. As such, *monists* hold that the death of the body—the disintegration of the material body and the degradation of memory patterns in the brain—means the death of the soul. By contrast, *dualists* assert that the soul, like the mind, is a separate entity from the body, so even after the death of the body, the soul will continue.

Most people are *dualists* because dualism is intuitive—it just feels like there is something else inside of us, in the same way that the thoughts floating around up there in our skulls feel like our mind is separate from our brain. Thus, Bloom calls us "natural-born dualists," as reflected in our language when we use phrases such as "my body aches" (rather than "I ache") or "my mind is muddled" (rather than "I am muddled"), as if "my body" and "my mind" are separate things.[7]

Not everyone agrees that the hard problem of consciousness is an insoluble one. In psychology labs, neuroscientists have continued working on the problem, even after, in 2023, Koch lost his bet with Chalmers that the hard problem would be solved in a quarter century.[8] This, despite his decades-long search for the neural correlates of consciousness—that is, the neurons and neural networks associated with conscious experiences,[9] which are not limited to our species.[10] There are, in fact, at least 22 theories of consciousness as documented by Anil Seth and Tim Bayne in their review article of the subject, including these:

> *higher-order theory, self-organizing meta-representational theory, global workspace theories, integrated information theory, information closure theory, dynamic core theory, neural Darwinism, predictive processing, neuro-representationalism, active inference, attention schema theory, electromagnetic field theory, and orchestrated objective reduction theory.*[11]

When I mentioned this fact to Koch in my podcast conversation with him about the hard problem of consciousness—noting that this variety of explanations suggests we are nowhere near a solution—he countered by noting that Wikipedia has an entire entry titled "Interpretations of Quantum Mechanics" with a long list of its own: Copenhagen, many worlds, quantum information theories, relational quantum mechanics, QBism, consistent histories, ensemble interpretation, De Broglie-Bohm theory, transactional interpretation, von Neumann–Wigner interpretation, quantum logic, modal interpretations of quantum theory, time-symmetric theories, and more. Inasmuch as quantum mechanics is one of the soundest and most tested theories in the history of science, it's a fair point.[12]

The psychiatrist Ralph Lewis has pruned the 22 theories of consciousness down to 4 he thinks have the best chance of succeeding:

Higher-order theories (HOTs): thoughts become conscious when basic perceptions ("lower-order" representations) become re-represented as higher-order representations at higher levels of the brain, specifically in the prefrontal cortex.

Global workspace theories (GWTs): perceptions, thoughts, emotions, etc., become conscious when they gain access to a "workspace," or to apply another analogy, when they make it into the "spotlight"—as if the mind were a theater where conscious thought is the activity in the spotlight on the stage at a given moment.

Integrated information theory (IIT): how parts of a brain interact to create a unified experience. Consciousness is theorized to be related to how much information is integrated among the different parts of the brain. IIT tries to mathematically measure this. The more information that is connected and integrated, the more conscious the system is thought to be. IIT attempts to explain the quality of conscious experience, suggesting that the unique pattern of relationships between the elements of the system is what defines a particular conscious experience.

Re-entry and predictive processing theories: conscious mental states are associated with top-down signaling [that] refers to the process

> by which higher-level brain regions send information, expectations, or context to lower-level brain regions. This communication helps shape how the brain perceives and interprets bottom-up information received via its sense organs from the world around it.[13]

Which of the 22 (or 4) theories are likeliest to be true? Lewis cautions that "it would be unrealistic for us to expect it to have been completely solved at this early stage in the still-young science of consciousness," and he may be right. Then again, Lewis identifies a conceptual problem in the entire enterprise—that is, a problem with the concept of consciousness itself—when he notes that "as soon as the first cell evolved there was an inside and an outside, and therefore the beginnings of a subjective-objective divide between the body and the outside world."[14] That is, how can something or someone *outside* of something or someone know what it's like *inside* that system?

I return to this conceptual problem at the end of this chapter—when I conclude that it is ultimately an insoluble one—but this is what Eastern Wisdom traditions have been telling us for some time when they invert the problem to argue that consciousness is primary and the fundamental property of the universe from which everything else is derived and is on the outside of. Here is how Deepak Chopra described it in his book *You Are the Universe*: "Consciousness is fundamental and without cause. It is the ground state of existence. As conscious beings, humans cannot experience, measure, or conceive of a reality devoid of consciousness."[15]

In support of this consciousness-first position, Chopra identifies a number of world-class physicists who seem to agree:

- Roger Penrose: Consciousness is the phenomenon whereby the universe's very existence is known.[16]
- Werner Heisenberg: The atoms or elementary particles themselves are not real; they form a world of potentialities or possibilities rather than one of things or facts.[17]

- Freeman Dyson: Atoms in the laboratory are weird stuff, behaving like active agents rather than inert substances. They make unpredictable choices between alternative possibilities according to the laws of quantum mechanics. It appears that mind, as manifested by the capacity to make choices, is to some extent inherent in every atom.[18]

In *Then I Am Myself the World*, Koch would seem to agree, especially after he altered his consciousness with a psychedelic called 5-MeO-DMT, also known as the "toad" (because it is excreted from the glands of a species of desert toad), the effects of which were near instantaneous:

> Within seconds, my entire field of view became engulfed by dark, swirling smoke. The space around me fractured into a thousand hexagons and shattered. As I was sucked into a black hole, my last thought was that with the dying of the light, I too would die. And I did. I ceased to exist in any recognizable way, shape, or form. No more Christof, no more ego, no more self; no memories, dreams, desires, hopes, fears—everything personal was stripped away. Nothing was left but a nonself.[19]

After this experience, the renowned neuroscientist, steeped in the world of hard-nosed materialistic science, reassessed his worldview, noting that "science tries to retrofit the 'subjective' world of experiences onto this 'objective' world. That is, without adding anything else to its worldview, it wants to explicate consciousness as arising out of the mindless actions of a gazillion molecules. It is here, however, that science runs into metaphysical difficulties. Indeed, this approach has it backward. Primacy goes to consciousness, not to the objective world."[20]

Strictly speaking, all of these observations are true, in the sense that if there is no one in the forest observing a falling tree, then the impact on the ground will make no sound, if we define sound as the vibration of air stimulating the hearing apparatus of sentient beings. But if we take all conscious beings out of the equation, trees, atoms, and universes do not cease to exist. We just have a different definition of sound, trees, atoms, and universes. In like manner, it is one thing to define the existence of atoms or spiders as percepts forming concepts in brains, but that doesn't mean atoms and spiders would not exist without those perceiving brains. We are talking at two different levels of analysis, both equally valid but neither one gainsaying the other. They are complementary, not contradictory.

Mystical Experiences and External Reality

The subject of internal mystical experiences versus external objective reality came up at the 2023 HowTheLightGetsIn festival in London, during a panel discussion on the role of spiritual experience in our lives. I shared the stage with the psychologist John Vervaeke and the philosopher Sophie Grace Chappell. Vervaeke asserted that spiritual practices and the cultivation of wisdom are crucial in our lives, while Chappell, a self-proclaimed Christian, said "reality is not divided into the natural and the supernatural. Reality is inexhaustible!" Both quoted the noted philosopher Ludwig Wittgenstein at length, while I quoted Douglas Adams: "Isn't it enough to see that a *garden* is beautiful without having to believe that there are *fairies* at the bottom of it too?"[21]

To emphasize the necessity of external validation of internal truths in a less than formal manner, I added the modifier *woo-woo* to my description of many spiritual practices, which was perhaps a tad impolite to my copanelists, but a summary of the event by the philosopher Ricky Williamson nevertheless makes my point:

> This final argument from Shermer is a typical anti-spiritual retort. "Show us the evidence." Well Michael, here it is: The mystical experience. The mystical experience, much like any other type of experience, offers clear evidence of spiritual reality. But what is the mystical experience? Philosophical arguments for spirituality, or even for God, are

> of far less value in my estimation when compared to the empirical evidence of the mystical experience. Spiritual reality can be well-hidden when in a "normal" frame of mind, not much about regular reality hints at the presence of this possible, radical other, but when you see it, when you have a mystical experience, the experience is undeniable.[22]

Note the circular reasoning: Evidence for a "spiritual reality" can be found in the "mystical experience," and "the mystical experience is evidence of spiritual reality." How can we get out of this tautology? We can't. So Williamson turns to quotes from people who have had mystical experiences:

> [Mystical experiences are] those peculiar states of consciousness in which the individual discovers himself to be one continuous process with God, with the Universe, with the Ground of Being, or whatever name he may use by cultural conditioning or personal preference for the ultimate and eternal reality. (Alan Watts)

> [The mystical experience] has been variously denoted by the names ecstasy, rapture, illumination, union with God. (Arthur Schopenhauer)

Note the language: "Ground of Being," "ecstasy," "rapture," "union with God." What do these words mean to the authors? It beats me. I would have to have similar experiences myself, and even then . . .

I acknowledge, of course, that such *experiences* are undeniably real to the experiencers, but do those experiences represent something entirely inside the skull of the experiencers, or are they also out in the world? I have written elsewhere about my 1983 alien abduction experience after going 83 straight hours without sleep and racing a bicycle over 1,200 miles nonstop in the Race Across America—the 3,000-mile nonstop transcontinental bicycle race. At the time it happened, it was very real to me, but after a refreshing sleep break, my mind returned to normal, and I realized that my support crew members were not, in fact, body-snatching aliens.[23]

But Williamson, defending Vervaeke's "Transcendent Naturalism," is dissatisfied with my call for external validation of internal states of mind: " 'Other people can't see your hallucinations though, so they can't be real,' you might claim. But nobody can see my personal experience of the colour red either, and yet the colour red is surely no hallucination. I, and others, have argued that what we call hallucinations, might reveal something true about reality elsewhere."

It's true, the color red is no hallucination, but there is no way for me to know if your experience of red is the same as mine, as there is no ghost in the machine that can enter your skull to see if your red looks the same as mine. Is this type of external validation ultimately unattainable and does it doom us to nothing but internal experiences? Williamson thinks it does:

> As is well documented, during the mystical experience, the subject-object distinction breaks down. The idea that "I am in here" and "the world is out here" disappears. For my consciousness of the world takes up the very same space as that which I call my mind. There is, in perception, no "inside" the mind and "outside" to the world. Look around you. All you can see is the outside! All you see is the room, and the window, and the sky. You do not see the interior of your mind—unless the world itself makes up that interior.[24]

Nonsense! First, this book is one long argument for escaping the internal truth trap. External validation is not only attainable, it is what the principles of rationality and the scientific method were designed to achieve. Second, simply apply the Copernican principle—"we're not special"—to yourself: "I'm not special." If you express thoughts and feelings that I can observe, understand, and respond to, there's nothing special about the wiring in my brain that precludes you from having similar internal experiences. It's a good bet that your red looks like mine and that your emotions feel similar to mine. If I see you crying in apparent despair over something painful, I know from experience what those expressions feel like, so chances are good that this is also your internal state of mind, and with empathy, I can feel your pain.

But what if the spiritual or mystical experience is more like an alien abduction than the color red? "What we cannot do, if we are to live in accordance with what is true, is deny that the mystical experience exists altogether," Williamson insists, "as the anti-spiritual do when they say such things as, 'show us the evidence.' The evidence is there. You are only ignoring it, ignorant of it, or disbelieving of those who claim to have had this experience."[25] Not so! My commitment to *universal realism* begins with the foundational assumption that there is an external reality that exists separately from our internal perceptions of it and that we can know something about that reality, however imperfectly. The color red is a common part of our daily existence; alien abductions are not.

The Weak Consciousness Principle Versus the Strong Consciousness Principle

Since you have to be conscious to experience anything, when Chopra proposes that consciousness and the universe are equivalent, in the sense that it is an "undeniable fact that any universe is only knowable through the human mind's ability to perceive reality," he is stating the obvious. Call this the *weak consciousness principle*: *You have to be conscious to experience consciousness*. But Chopra goes further than this when he says that "if all human knowledge is rooted in consciousness, perhaps we are viewing not the real universe based on limitations of the brain"; he adds "that the apparent evolution of the cosmos since the big bang has been totally dependent upon human consciousness." Chopra contends that making the brain the cause of the mind is a fundamental mistake. He holds that this logic collapses once you look more closely. Here is how he explained it to me in an email (in response to his review of this chapter):

> Let's imagine a world where the only musical instrument in existence is the piano. Under such circumstances, you couldn't play Bach or Mozart without a piano, yet obviously, it would be absurd to say that

> the piano actually composes music. It is the instrument, not the cause. Likewise, we only have one instrument of thought, the brain, but there is no proof that it is anything but an instrument. Just as every note of Mozart emerges from a piano, every mental function emerges as a correlate in the brain, but that is all.[26]

Call this the *strong consciousness principle*. It seems to me that this is reversing the causal arrow, from perception to determination, from being consciously aware of the universe and trying to understand it to our own consciousness bringing about the universe.

In my understanding of the *neural correlates of consciousness*, the hypothesis that the brain gives rise to consciousness has vastly more evidence for it than the hypothesis that consciousness creates the brain. Damage to the fusiform gyrus of the temporal lobe, for example, causes prosopagnosia, or face blindness, and stimulation of this same area causes people to see faces spontaneously. Stroke-caused damage to the visual cortex region called V1 leads to loss of conscious visual perception. Changes in conscious experience can be directly measured by fMRI (functional magnetic resonance imaging), EEG (electroencephalogram), and single-neuron recordings. Neuroscientists can predict human choices from brain scan activity before the subject is even consciously aware of the decisions made. Using brain scans alone, neuroscientists have even been able to reconstruct on a computer screen what someone is seeing.[27] In other words, *brain activity gives rise to conscious experience.*

Thousands of lab experiments, in conjunction with naturally occurring experiments in the form of brain tumors, strokes, accidents, and injuries, confirm the hypothesis that neurochemical processes produce subjective experiences. In other words, *neural activity gives rise to qualia.*

A scientific challenge to this position was presented by the cognitive scientist Donald Hoffman in a 2008 paper titled "Conscious Realism and the Mind-Body Problem." Conscious realism, Hoffman explains, "asserts that the objective world, i.e., the world whose existence does not depend on the perceptions of a particular observer, consists entirely of conscious agents." Consciousness is fundamental to the cosmos and gives rise to particles and fields. "It is not a latecomer in the evolutionary history of the universe, arising from complex interactions of unconscious matter and fields," Hoffman continues. "Consciousness is first; matter and fields depend on it for their very existence."[28]

Where is the evidence for consciousness being fundamental to the cosmos? Here, Hoffman turns to how human observers "construct the visual shapes, colors, textures and motions of objects." Our senses do not construct an approximation of physical reality in our brains, he argues, but instead operate more like a graphical user interface system (GUI) that bears little to no resemblance to what actually goes on inside the computer. In this model, our senses operate to construct reality, not reconstruct it. Further, this view "does not require the hypothesis of independently existing physical objects."[29]

Hoffman has developed his ideas into a full-blown theory he calls the interface theory of perception (ITP), which he presents more forcefully in his 2019 book, *The Case Against Reality*.[30] Like most scientists, Hoffman rejects solipsism—the belief that only one's mind is known to exist—but unlike most scientists, he does not accept the model of *veridical perception*, which holds that natural selection shaped our senses to give us a reasonably accurate model of the world.[31] Instead, ITP contends that percepts are a species-specific user interface that directs behavior toward survival and reproduction, not truth.[32] Hoffman's computer analogy is that the physical environment is like the desktop and the objects in nature are like desktop icons. Our senses, he says, form a biological user interface—a gooey GUI—between our brains and the outside world, transducing physical stimuli such as photons of light into neural impulses processed by the visual cortex as things in the environment. GUIs are useful because you don't need to know what's inside computers and brains; you just need to know how to interact with the interface well enough to accomplish your task. Adaptive function, not veridical perception, is what is important.[33] In other words, evolution designed us to want to have more babies, not to determine Truth.

Hoffman's holotype is the Australian jewel beetle *J. bakewelli.* Females are large, shiny, brown, and dimpled. So, too, are discarded beer bottles called "stubbies," and males will mount them until they die by heat, starvation, or ants. The species was on the brink of extinction because its senses and brain were designed by natural selection not to perceive reality (it's a beer bottle, you idiot!) but to mate with anything big, brown, shiny, and dimply. Like beetles, Hoffman says, humans are easily fooled by illusions because our brains did not evolve to give us an exact replica of reality.[34]

ITP is a provocative idea, but I am skeptical. First, how could a more accurate perception of reality *not* be adaptive? Hoffman's answer is that evolution gave us an interface to hide the underlying reality because, for example, you don't need to know how neurons create images of snakes; you just need to jump out of the way of the snake icon. But how did the snake icon come to look like a snake in the first place? The answer is natural selection. And why did some nonpoisonous snakes evolve to mimic poisonous species? Because predators avoid *real* poisonous snakes. Mimicry only works if there's an objective reality to mimic.

This is, in fact, another example of the *correspondence theory of truth* or "the view that truth is correspondence to, or with, a fact" and "more broadly to any view explicitly embracing the idea that truth consists in a relation to reality."[35] This is also called *ontological realism*, or the belief that there is a world external to human minds and that this world is knowable. For what it's worth, this is the position held by the majority of professional philosophers. In a 2023 survey of 3,226 philosophy professors and graduate students,[36] half (50.8%) agreed with the correspondence theory of truth. Further, three-quarters (75.1%) reported that they accept or lean toward *scientific realism*, or "a commitment to the idea that our best theories have a certain epistemic status: they yield knowledge of aspects of the world, including unobservable aspects."[37]

Still, in the history of philosophy and science, it would not be the first time that a majority of thinkers were wrong (think geocentrism before Copernicus or creationism before Darwin). Hoffman, along with Chopra and many others who share this worldview, believes that the tide is turning against ontological realism, scientific realism, and the correspondence theory of truth. "A rock is an interface icon, not a constituent of objective reality," Hoffman asserts. But a real rock chipped into an arrow point and thrown at a four-legged meal really works, even if you don't know physics and calculus. Is that not veridical perception with adaptive significance? Also, there's a reason those desktop icons look as they do—documents have little bent corners like real paper, and folders have raised tabs because that's how they used to be sorted into drawers. If you were inside your computer looking out, wouldn't it be more accurate to "see" documents as bent pieces of paper than as something else entirely? Evolution can and does select for reproductive success *and* more accurate models of reality, even if they're not perfect representations.

As for jewel beetles, stubbies are what ethologists call *supernormal stimuli*, which exaggerate real-world objects that elicit a response. Examples include silicone breast implants in women and testosterone-enhanced bodybuilding in men. Supernormal stimuli operate only because evolution designed us to respond to *normal stimuli*, which must be accurately portrayed by our senses to our brains in order to work. Hoffman says perception is species specific and that we should take predators "seriously, but not literally." A dolphin's icon for "shark" no doubt looks different from a human's—presumably it would be a sonar pattern of waves instead of a visual pattern of light—but there really are sharks, and they really do have powerful tails on one end and a mouthful of teeth on the other end, and this is true no matter how your sensory system works.

Hoffman often describes reality as an "illusion."[38] How, then, are we fooled by illusions created by artists, magicians, and perceptual psychologists, and why are we startled when thus fooled? It is only by having some grasp of what reality is *really* like that the illusion works. M. C. Escher is the iconic artist of this genre; consider, for example, his depiction of an aqueduct system in which the water flows uphill (figure 9.2).

When magician David Copperfield appears to walk through a brick wall, we're startled because we understand that real brick walls don't allow it. If IPT were correct, these illusions would not surprise and delight us as they do.

Finally, why present this problem as an either-or choice between fitness and truth? Adaptations depend in large part on a relatively accurate model of reality. The fact that science progresses toward, say, eradicating diseases and landing spacecraft on Mars must mean that our perceptions of reality are growing ever closer to the truth, even if it is with a small *t*. Thus, the interface theory of perception is in alignment with the *weak consciousness principle* but not the *strong consciousness principle*. In the end, I agree with Steven Pinker's assessment of the hard problem of consciousness: "Our best science tells us that consciousness consists of a global workspace

Figure 9.2. Visual illusions such as this 1961 lithograph by M. C. Escher, in which water appears to flow uphill in an aqueduct system, show that reality is not an illusion and that humans have some grasp of what reality is like; otherwise, such illusions would not be jarring to our sensibilities. M.C. Escher's "Waterfall"

representing our current goals, memories, and surroundings, implemented in synchronized neural firing in fronto-parietal circuitry. But the last dollop in the theory—that it subjectively *feels like* something to be such circuitry—may have to be stipulated as a fact about reality where explanation stops."[39]

With all these facts in mind—themselves part of the answer to the easy problem of consciousness, for which neuroscientists have made great progress—the hard problem is asking us a question that is impossible to answer: *What's it like to be the neural wiring?* That is, *What's it like to be you?* How should I know? I'm not you and never can be. I can *imagine* what it's like to be you, and I can apply the Copernican principle to myself—I'm not special—and reasonably infer that your internal states are similar to mine if I see in your actions and emotions patterns similar to those that I express. But the final step of knowing *what it's actually like to be you*—or a dolphin or bat or anything—is one thought too many. Only you can experience you.

In my assessment of the hard problem, then, consciousness is a known unknown that is very likely unknowable, at least as the concept is conceived of at present, and thus the truth about consciousness may never be known. And that brings us to the next known unknowable—namely, free will and determinism and to what extent we are self-determining volitional beings.

10

The Truth About Free Will

Determinism, Self-Determinism, and Your Future Self

■ In 1985, the physiologist Benjamin Libet conducted a series of experiments that involved taking EEG readings of subjects' brains engaged in a task that required them to press a button at random intervals whenever they felt like it during the session. The results were revealing: Several seconds before the "decision" was consciously made by the subject, the brain's motor cortex was activated.[1] Libet's research has held up well during the replication crisis in psychology. The neuroscientist John-Dylan Haynes, for example, employed fMRI brain scans in a 2011 study in which subjects situated inside the scanner observed a series of random letters and were instructed to press one of two buttons whenever they wanted. Participants were then told to verbally report which letter was on the screen when they "decided" to press the button. The results were equally striking: The time between brain activation and conscious awareness of a "choice" was several seconds and even a full seven seconds in some cases.[2]

In these studies and others, scientists measuring subjects' brains knew which decision they would make *before the subjects themselves knew it!* For example, in a 2011 study, Itzhak Fried and his UCLA colleagues recorded activity in a tiny network of neurons in the brains of subjects who were instructed to command their fingers to move. Astonishingly, the neuroscientists could detect neural activity related to the finger movement a full 15 seconds before subjects reported making the decision to move their finger! Narrowing down their search, they found activity in a tiny clump of 256 neurons in the medial frontal cortex that enabled them to predict with 80% accuracy which choice a subject would make a full seven seconds before the subjects themselves knew.[3]

If these results don't sound spooky, then you're not thinking hard enough about them. What they imply is that we are not free to choose in the way we think we are. We *feel* free, but that's just what our higher conscious self believes, because it doesn't know about the inputs feeding into it from our lower self below, which has apparently already made the choice.

Here is how the neuroscientist Sam Harris articulated it in his widely read book, *Free Will*: "Our wills are simply not of our own making. Thoughts and intentions emerge from background causes of which we are unaware and over which we exert no conscious control. We do not have the freedom we think we have."[4]

In his book *Determined: A Science of Life Without Free Will*, the Stanford University biologist Robert Sapolsky articulated the deterministic position even more succinctly: "We are nothing more or less than the cumulative biological and environmental luck, over which we had no control, that has brought us to any moment."[5]

Remember these exact definitions, as I return to them shortly.

■ Determinism

The principle of determinism holds that every event in the universe has a prior cause. If all effects have causes, including human thoughts and actions, then where in the causal chain does the act of choice enter? Libertarian free will (as it's called, having nothing to do with the political party) holds that there is some part of you that makes choices that is somehow disconnected from the machinery of the brain running the mind and thus can break into the causal chain. But very few philosophers or scientists endorse libertarian free will because it is another form of dualism—a ghost in the machine, a mind in the brain, a homunculus in the human. The problem is that even if there were a Mini-Me inside of me calling the shots, his little brain would have to be just as determined as my big brain, so by this line of reasoning, for Mini-Me to have free will, he would have to have a mini-Mini-Me inside of him pulling his strings, and mini-Mini-Me would himself need an itty-bitty mini-Mini-Me inside of his brain . . . ad infinitum.

And if you believe in souls, this fails in the same way as Mini-Me does. A soul inside of you pulling your strings does not grant you freedom; it just means the soul is in charge. In any case, such a soul would mean that there's a mini-soul inside the soul directing its actions, and a tiny mini-soul inside the mini-soul, and so forth. It would seem that if determinism is true, then we do not have free will. Here is how Sapolsky characterizes the problem, deeply informed as it is by a half century of studies of animal and human behavior in the lab and in the wild, with countless unbreakable links in variegated causal chains:

> Once you work with the notion that every aspect of behavior has deterministic, prior causes, you observe a behavior and can answer why it occurred: as just noted, because of the action of neurons in this or that part of your brain in the preceding second. And in the seconds to minutes before, those neurons were activated by a thought, a memory, an emotion, or sensory stimuli. And in the hours to days before that behavior occurred, the hormones in your circulation shaped those thoughts, memories, and emotions and altered how sensitive your brain was to particular environmental stimuli. And in the preceding months to years, experience and environment changed how those neurons function, causing some to sprout new connections and become more excitable, and causing the opposite in others.[6]

Sapolsky wants to go even further down the causal chain to adolescence, when "a key brain region was still being constructed, shaped by socialization and acculturation." And deeper still: "Further back, there's childhood experience shaping the construction of your brain, with the same then applying to your fetal environment. Moving further back, we have to factor in the genes you inherited and their effects on behavior." But he's not done yet!

> That's because everything in your childhood, starting with how you were mothered within minutes of birth, was influenced by culture, which means as well by the centuries of ecological factors that influenced what kind of culture your ancestors invented, and by the evolutionary pressures that molded the species you belong to. Why did that behavior occur? Because of biological and environmental interactions, all the way down.[7]

By *all the way down*, Sapolsky means the hundreds of thousands of years of our species' existence, the millions of years of primate evolution, millions more years of mammalian evolution, billions of years of cellular evolution, all the way back to the origin of life itself nearly four billion years ago. In fact, Sapolsky's broader argument for determinism is "it's turtles all the way down."

Science would seem to support this deterministic position, inasmuch as its goal is to discover natural laws that govern the universe, of there being chains of connected causes and effects that form a "causal net"—a *network* of cause-and-effect linkages throughout the past and into the future. This causal net involves all phenomena, past, present, and future, throughout the cosmos, from atoms to molecules, cells, organisms, persons, planets, stars, and galaxies, all the way out to the edge of the observable universe. Without assuming that the universe is determined, in fact, scientists could not explain the past nor predict the future, and this includes psychologists and neuroscientists attempting to explain and predict human behavior.

Why does this matter? As Sapolsky told me in our podcast conversation, "a huge amount of the world's misery is due to the fact that people who had bad luck are treated as if they had something to do with it. And that we all then congratulate ourselves on the notion that the world is just in that regard because we can be the agents of our own actions when we're not."[8]

And yet, we feel free. We feel like we make choices. Even a hard determinist like Sapolsky struggles with the intuition of volition we all have, as he confessed to me:

> I'm a total determinist and just a little bit of the time I'm able to actually function as if that's the case. It's hard. It's hard because we're people of our place and time. I've got no trouble at all with the notion that there's no such thing as witches. But no matter how much I believe in this [determinism] stuff, it's still kind of nice when someone says to me, "good job," about something that I've done, and to truly step out from some notion of agency going on there.[9]

How can we square this circle? We can't. It's a known unknown that is probably unknowable, at least as I've outlined it here, because of the limitations of our language and concepts, namely "determined" and "free." It seems like it must be one or the other. The attempt to make them compatible is called, appropriately enough, *compatibilism*, which Sapolsky rejects, indicting those who embrace it: "I suspect that most of them know this as well. When you read between the lines, or sometimes even the lines themselves in their writing, a lot of these compatibilists are actually saying that there has to be free will because it would be a total downer otherwise, doing contortions to make an emotional stance seem like an intellectual one."[10]

Compatibilism

Are the determinists right? Or are our intuitions about feeling free right? Is there a legitimate middle ground? What do professional philosophers think? To find out, in 2009, the philosophers David Bourget and David Chalmers asked 3,226 philosophy professors and graduate students to weigh in on 30 different subjects of concern in their field, including a priori knowledge, aesthetic value, the external world, God, laws of nature, knowledge, the mind, moral realism, and even philosophical zombies.[11] On the topic of "free will: compatibilism, libertarianism, or no free will," the survey found the following results:

Accept or lean toward compatibilism,	59.1%
Accept or lean toward libertarianism,	13.7%
Accept or lean toward no free will,	12.2%
Other,	14.9%

In a 2013 follow-up meta-analysis of philosophers' beliefs about such timeless issues,[12] Bourget and Chalmers conclude: "There is famously no consensus on the answers to most major philosophical questions." While many timeless philosophical issues do not reach the 70% level the researchers set as a low bar for consensus, compatibilism did. Now, from a scientific perspective, it shouldn't matter how many people support one or another position; only the quality of the evidence and arguments should matter. As Einstein said in response to a 1931 book skeptical of relativity theory, titled *A Hundred Authors Against Einstein*, "Why one hundred? If I were wrong, one would have been enough."[13]

But there is something revealing about these figures: If the most qualified people to assess a problem are not in agreement on an answer—and the free-will/determinism problem has been around for thousands of years—it may be that it is an insoluble one, a known unknowable.

In any case, the freedom to choose to do otherwise is what most people (not just philosophers) mean by free will, and in this sense, despite what they say and write, most determinists do believe in free will when it comes to actually living their lives. And except for those extreme cases of mental illness, chemical addiction, or brain damage, we all have this type of volition. Our choices may be part of the determined causal net of the universe, but they are still *our* choices that *we* make, and so they are *self-determined*, and we should be held accountable for them. The justification for this compatibilist position comes from the observation that the universe is *determined but not predetermined*, the future is unlike the past, and your present self can alter the causal net of the universe for your future self. Call it *self-determinism*.

Self-Determinism as a Self-Organized Emergent Property

Since philosophers love to employ thought experiments to test ideas, here's one for you to consider (feel free to plug yourself and your spouse or significant other into the situation): John Doe is an exceptionally moral person who is happily married to Jane. The chances of John ever cheating on Jane is close to zero. But the odds are not zero because John is human, so let's say—for the sake of argument—that John has a one-night stand while on the road and Jane finds out. How does John account for his actions? Does he, per the standard deterministic explanation for human behavior (as in Harris's and Sapolsky's definitions), say something like this to Jane?

> *Honey, my will is simply not of my own making. My thoughts and intentions emerge from background causes of which I am unaware and over which I exert no conscious control. I do not have the freedom you think I have. I could not have done otherwise because I am nothing more or less than the cumulative biological and environmental luck, over which I had no control, that brought me to the moment of infidelity.*

Could John even finish the thought before the stinging slap of Jane's hand across his face terminated the rationalization? If free will is *the power to do otherwise*, as it is typically defined by philosophers,[14] both John and Jane know that, of course, he could have done otherwise, and she reminds him that should such similar circumstances arise again, he damn well better make the right choice—or else.

Consider the "could you have done otherwise?" question in a rewind of the tape of your life. If it is a read-only memory (ROM) tape, then no, you could not have done otherwise, because that's just a replay of a recording of what already happened. If the entire universe is a ROM tape, and everything would repeat exactly as it originally happened in a replay, then determinism is true, free will is an illusion, and there is no compatibilist work-around. In this universe, it was determined from the moment of the Big Bang that I would type these words and you would read them.

But this is not the universe we live in. In our universe (unlike the one in which thought experiments are run), the second law of thermodynamics and entropy means that time flows forward, and no future scenario can ever perfectly match one from the past. As Heraclitus's idiom informs us, "you can't step into the same river twice," because you are different and the river is different. What you did in the past influences what you choose to do next in future circumstances (the technical name for this is "learning"), which are always different from the past. So, while the world is determined, we are active agents in determining our decisions going forward in a *self-determined* way, in the context of what already happened and what might happen. Our universe is not predetermined but rather *post-determined*, and we are part of the causal net of the myriad determining factors to create that post-determined world. Self-determinism, far from being a downer, is the ultimate upper, as it means we can do something about the future—namely, we can change it!

In his book *Why Free Will Is Real*, Christian List outlines the three requirements of free will, or what I am calling *self-determination*: (1) *intentional agency*—the capacity to form an intention to pursue different possibilities; (2) *alternative possibilities*—the capacity to consider several possibilities for action (this is the "could have done otherwise" element); and (3) *causal control*—the capacity to take action to move toward one of those possibilities. "If we wish to establish whether someone can be held responsible for something he or she did, we need to know not only whether the person has the capacity of free will in general but also whether what he or she did resulted from its exercise," List explains.

> Specifically, we need to know whether what the person did was freely performed, as characterized by the three bullet points. . . . Was it an intentional action? Could the person have done otherwise? Was the person in control? Or, if what the person did was not freely performed, we need to know whether the person's free will was at least implicated in the run-up to it: Was there a free decision to get drunk in the first place, for instance? Of course, moral responsibility might well require more than that . . . but I do take the presence of free will somewhere along the relevant chain of events to be a necessary condition for a salient form of moral responsibility.[15]

The rest of this chapter makes the case that free will as such is real, even in a determined universe, through the concept of self-determination, an idea well-developed by the psychologist Kennon Sheldon in his 2022 book, *Freely Determined*, in which he summarized 35 years of research on "the self-stated personal goals that people report—that is, the broad objectives they are pursuing in life, from what career they'll try to enter and what values they'll uphold to what exercise targets they'll try to hit." Here is how Sheldon characterizes such self-determination:

> At any moment, we can decide to adopt a new purpose, course, or aim, and these decisions can potentially change everything, leading to major improvements in our lives. Of course, not all of our goals are portentous and life changing. Nor are we always successful at achieving them. No matter: the point is that, moment to moment, we're constantly selecting just one of the many possibilities in front of us, taking actions that divert the universe into a particular course that never would have happened otherwise. Making choices between imagined alternatives might even be the most profound capacity of human brains.[16]

In my podcast conversation with Daniel Dennett, the renowned defender of compatibilism, he explained that "determinism doesn't tie your hands, nor does it prevent you from making and then reconsidering decisions, turning over a new leaf, learning from your mistakes. Determinism is not a puppeteer controlling you. If you're a normal adult, you have enough self-control to maintain your autonomy, and hence responsibility, in a world full of seductions and distractions."[17]

What about people with brain damage, or those suffering from extreme drug addiction or alcoholism, or those with a brain tumor that led to their bad behavior, like Charles Whitman in the school tower shooting his fellow students? Harris says, "it's tumors all the way down," echoing Sapolsky's descriptor that "it's turtles all the way down." Dennett identifies the error in this line of reasoning:

> Well, I like the way you put it very much, Michael, because I think you put your finger on the mistake that Sapolsky is making there. And Harris makes it too. No, it's not tumors all the way down. It's machinery all the way down. But there's good machinery and there's bad machinery. And if we have bad machinery, then yes, we're disabled to some degree. But what about people who have good machinery? They're not disabled. Why can't we hold them responsible? Now, some people are, alas, through no fault of their own, not responsible for what they do. And that might well include people with terrible, terrible youths, who didn't get a good upbringing, or who had a horrific upbringing. And so we have to, as society, we have to decide, okay, given that this is a dangerous person, what's the humane, good thing to do? I don't think there's an algorithm or a bright line for distinguishing somebody whose brain is good enough from somebody whose brain is a little too disabled. We just have to make the decision.
>
> We do it all the time. You've got to be 16 to get a driver's license. Some 15-year-olds would be perfectly safe as drivers. Some 21-year-olds would not. But the law has to have a bright line and so it chooses

> one. We might argue whether we want to raise it or lower it, the way the drinking age has been raised or lowered, or the way the driving age has been raised or lowered. We have to have a policy and we have to stick to it and we can change it as we learn more and more. But what we don't do is just say, oh, it's disability all the way down. No, you're not disabled, I'm not disabled. I want to be held responsible. I think you want to be held responsible too.[18]

In his book *Free Agents*, the geneticist and neuroscientist Kevin Mitchell shows that the determinist's reductionistic approach to understanding human thought and behavior, from neurons to molecules to atoms, or neuroscience, chemistry, and physics—"is not just wrong—it's wrong-headed." Why? "A purely reductionist, mechanistic approach to life completely misses the point." How?

> Basic laws of physics that deal only with energy and matter and fundamental forces cannot explain what life is or its defining property: living organisms do things, for reasons, as causal agents in their own right. They are driven not by energy but by information. And the meaning of that information is embodied in the structure of the system itself, based on its history. In short, there are fundamentally distinct types of causation at play in living organisms by virtue of their organization. That extension through time generates a new kind of causation that is not seen in most physical processes, one based on a record of history in which information about past events continues to play a causal role in the present.[19]

Do determinists really fall into the trap of pure reductionism? They do. Here is the determinist Sapolsky defending his belief that free will does not exist because single neurons don't have it: "Individual neurons don't become causeless causes that defy gravity and help generate free will just because they're interacting with lots of other neurons." In fact, billions of interacting neurons is exactly where self-determinism arises. But Sapolsky is having none of that: "A lot of people have linked emergence and free will; I will not consider most of them because, to be frank, I can't understand what they're suggesting, and to be franker, I don't think the lack of comprehension is entirely my fault."[20]

Determinists like Harris and Sapolsky have physics envy. The history of science is littered with the failed pipe dreams of ever-alluring reductionist schemes to explain the inner workings of the mind—schemes increasingly set forth in the ambitious wake of Descartes's own famous attempt, some four centuries ago, to reduce all mental functioning to the actions of swirling vortices of atoms supposedly dancing their way to consciousness. Such Cartesian dreams provide a sense of certainty, but they quickly fade in the face of the complexities of biology. We should be exploring consciousness and choice at the neural level and higher, where the arrow of causal analysis points up toward such principles as emergence, self-organization, and autocatalytic feedback loops. For example:

Water is a self-organized emergent property of a particular arrangement of hydrogen and oxygen molecules.

Life is a self-organized emergent property of prebiotic chemicals.

Complex life is a self-organized emergent property of simple life, where simple prokaryote cells self-organized to become more complex eukaryote cells (the little organelles inside cells were once self-contained independent cells).

Multicellular life is a self-organized emergent property of single-celled life and so on up the chain of complexity to colonies, social units, societies, consciousness, language, law, economies, and political systems.

Consciousness is a self-organized emergent property of billions of neurons firing in patterns in the brain.

Language is a self-organized emergent property of thousands of words spoken in communication between language users.

Economy is a self-organized emergent property of millions of people pursuing their own self-interests without any awareness of the larger system in which they work.

Free will, volition, and choice are not to be found in atoms, molecules, or individual neurons but in the collective action of billions of neurons bundled into neural networks of information out of which real choices are made.

As I like to ask determinists: Where is *inflation* in the laws and principles of physics, biology, or neuroscience? It's not there, because inflation is an emergent property arising from millions of individuals in economic exchange, a subject properly described by economists, not physicists, biologists, or neuroscientists.

■ Free Will, Free Won't, and Degrees of Freedom

If we define free will as the power to do otherwise, think of *free won't* as the power to *veto* one impulse in favor of another. *Free won't* is the capacity to reject a particular action arising from the unconscious neural network, such that any decision to act one way instead of another way is an authentic choice. We have limitations, it's true—we cannot just do anything we choose—but for the most part, we have veto power. We have the capacity to say "no"; we can act this way instead of that way, and that is a real choice.

Support for *free won't* may be found in a 2007 study conducted by the neuroscientists Marcel Brass and Patrick Haggard, who used fMRI brain scans while subjects made choices. But at the last moment, the subjects could change their minds and override their initial decision to press a button. When the subjects chose to veto their initial decision, the scientists discovered that a specific area of the brain lit up—the left dorsal frontomedian cortex, an area that is normally active during decision-making behavior, especially during the intentional inhibition of a choice. Tellingly, there were no differences between the brain regions active in preparation for a voluntary action and those involved in inhibiting such actions. "Our results suggest that the human brain network for intentional action includes a control structure for self-initiated inhibition or withholding of intended actions."[21] That is free won't.

Even Libet himself—the instigator of this line of research that has led so many neuroscientists to abandon belief in free will—in the end came down in favor of human nature containing a volitional element: "The role of conscious free will would be, then, not to initiate a voluntary act, but rather to control whether the act takes place. We may view the unconscious initiatives for voluntary actions as 'bubbling up' in the brain. The conscious-will then selects which of these initiatives may go forward to an action or which ones to veto and abort."[22]

What this research suggests is that the neural architecture of choice can be modified by experience—in other words, training and practice—which means that in the long run, with better neuroscience and technology, we could not only teach people how to impede their maladaptive impulses to, say, eat unhealthy foods, drink alcohol excessively, take dangerous drugs, or engage in risky sexual behavior, investments, and sports, but also, in principle, we could train criminals to learn to veto their early and dangerous choices in order to make more socially acceptable decisions. And the choice is real in this way: Regardless of which part of our brain makes our choices, they are still *our* choices, and even the apparently subconscious ones can be overridden by conscious effort.

Instead of framing the issue as free will versus determinism, think of it in terms of *degrees of freedom*—a range of options that an organism has as a result of its complexity and the number of intervening variables acting upon it. Insects, for example, have very few degrees of freedom and are guided mostly by fixed instincts. Reptiles and birds have more degrees of freedom enabled by modifiable instincts that are subject to environmental triggers in critical periods (imprinting), with subsequent life experience allowing for learned responses to changing environments. Mammals, especially the great apes, have many more degrees of freedom through considerable neural plasticity and learning, but humans have vastly more degrees of freedom because of our massive cortex and our highly developed culture.

This version of free will is one that has been explored extensively by Dennett in his book *Freedom Evolves*.[23] Dennett argues that free will arises from a number of our characteristics of cognition, including a sense of being *self-aware* and aware that others are self-aware, *symbolic language* that allows us to communicate the fact that we are aware and self-aware, *complex neural circuitry* that allows for many behavioral options arising out of numerous neural impulses, a *theory of mind* about others that enables us to think about what they're thinking about, and *evolved moral emotions* about right and wrong choices, and these factors led to the evolution of a neural architecture for behavioral choice.[24] Out of this collection of cognitive characteristics comes the kind of free will worth wanting because we can, and do, weigh the consequences of the many courses of action available to us at any given moment. We are aware that we (and others) consciously make these choices, and we hold ourselves (and others) accountable.

Exceptions prove the principle. Some people—psychopaths, the brain damaged, the severely depressed, or the chemically addicted—have fewer degrees of freedom than other people. The law recognizes such degrees of freedom, for example, by distinguishing between various grades of murder, which are classified according to circumstance and intent. *First-degree murder* is the unlawful killing of one human being by another, with malice aforethought—intentional and premeditated. *Second-degree murder* is the unlawful killing of one human being by another, but *without* malice aforethought. *Voluntary manslaughter* is the unlawful killing of one human being by another *without* prior intent to kill and committed under circumstances that would "cause a reasonable person to become emotionally or mentally disturbed," as in a crime of passion. *Involuntary manslaughter* is neither deliberate nor premeditated and is reserved for fatal accidents due to negligence—for example, deaths caused by drunk driving. Finally, there are *lawful killings*, such as those that occur in war or as a result of self-defense or capital punishment by a state. All of these ways in which a human life is cut short take into account circumstances, intent, and moral degrees of freedom.[25]

Your Future Self: Self-Determination Through Willpower and Won't Power

In an episode of the hit animated television series *The Simpsons*, Marge Simpson warns her husband that he might regret the drinking binge he's about to go on, to which Homer replies: "That's a problem for future Homer. Man, I don't envy that guy." All of us have future selves. Or, more accurately, there is no fixed self but rather an ever-changing self, and the fact that we can project ourselves into the future means we can not only anticipate how our future selves might act, we can take measures today to alter how our future selves behave.

Since the future can never perfectly match the past in a universe like ours, governed by the second law of thermodynamics while the world (and you by extension) are determined, your future self is not *predetermined*. Thus, you can alter the causal net of the future by choosing to restructure the present as you move through it. How? Well, you can start by making your bed. Seriously. That was the advice of Admiral William H. McRaven in his 2014 commencement address at the University of Texas at Austin that went viral with millions of views. The Navy SEAL veteran explained the principle:

> If you make your bed every morning you will have accomplished the first task of the day. It will give you a small sense of pride and it will encourage you to do another task and another and another. By the end of the day, that one task completed will have turned into many tasks completed. Making your bed will also reinforce the fact that little things in life matter. If you can't do the little things right, you will never do the big things right. And, if by chance you have a miserable

> day, you will come home to a bed that is made—that you made—and a made bed gives you encouragement that tomorrow will be better.[26]

In self-help parlance, these are called "small wins," which cumulatively build into larger wins and ultimately lead to the fulfillment of one's goals. Each step in the causal chain requires some level of self-control over your present self in order to bring about the outcomes desired by your future self. It may seem odd to think of yourself as a past self, present self, and future self, but as suggested in this language, your "self" is not fixed from birth, destined to a future over which you have no control. We live not only in space but in time, and as such, no matter the preconditioning factors nudging you along a given pathway—your genes, upbringing, culture, luck, and contingent history—there is always wiggle room to alter future conditions. The river of time flows ever onward, and you are part of its future.

If your present self knows that the temptation for dessert is going to be hard to resist for your future self in the early evening, your earlier self can make sure there are no sweets in the house. If you have difficulty getting up and around in the morning but desire to do an early workout, your present self can lay out your workout clothes the night before so that your weak and groggy future self at zero dark thirty has fewer excuses for procrastination. If your present inner Odysseus knows that the Siren songs of temptation will be too much to resist for your future Greek king, you can plug your ears with wax, or if you want to hear the Siren songs but don't trust your future self, you can have yourself lashed to the ship's mast. This is called *Odyssean self-control* (figure 10.1).[27]

The pioneering researcher of self-control (and by extension self-determination) is the legendary psychologist Walter Mischel, whose book *The Marshmallow Test* is part memoir (Mischel recounts how he quit his three-pack-a-day smoking habit), part science (the extensive research on self-control is artfully summarized), and part self-help (he offers handy tips for increasing your willpower).[28] The now famous "marshmallow test"

Figure 10.1. Odysseus and the Sirens, photograph of Ulixes mosaic at the Bardo National Museum in Tunis, Tunisia, second century AD. "Odyssean self-control" is an example of free will, or self-determinism, in which, like Odysseus, we can choose to either plug our ears with wax or have ourselves strapped to the ship's mast, in order to avoid future temptations. Wikimedia Commons, file name GiorcesBardo54.jpg

was devised by Mischel as a straightforward way to measure self-control at the Bing Nursery School at Stanford University (where Mischel was a professor) in the late 1960s. In its simplest form, children ages four to six were given a choice between one marshmallow now or two marshmallows 15 minutes later. Some kids ate the marshmallow right away, but most engaged in unintentionally hilarious examples of how to overcome temptation (type the text string "marshmallow test" in a YouTube search box to view numerous videos). They averted their gaze, covered their eyes, squirmed in their seats, or sang to themselves. They made grimacing faces, tugged at their ponytails, picked up the marshmallow and pretended to take a bite. They sniffed it, pushed it away from them, covered it up. If paired with a partner, they engaged in dialogue about how they could work together to reach the goal of doubling their sugary pleasure. About a third of the original subjects, the researchers reported, deferred gratification long enough to get the second treat.

When this research was first published, it was characterized as a study of "delay of gratification," and there was not much controversy surrounding the experiments.[29] That changed in 2006, when Mischel and his colleagues published a follow-up paper reporting 40 years later that the children who were able to delay gratification had higher SAT scores and GPAs, made more money after college, had more successful careers, enjoyed happier marriages, and—tellingly, given the temptation target of the original experiment—even had a lower body-mass index.[30]

Suddenly, people started paying attention. *New York Times* columnist David Brooks considered the implications in a piece called "Marshmallows and Public Policy."[31] *Sesame Street* featured Cookie Monster controlling his impulses to indulge so that he could become a member of the Cookie Connoisseurs Club. Investment companies used the marshmallow metaphor to encourage potential clients to delay gratification and save for retirement. Some parents started buying their toddlers T-shirts that said "Don't Eat the Marshmallows" and "I Passed the Marshmallow Test."

It was too much. No single variable—such as self-control—can explain success or failure. Critics pointed out that Mischel's original subjects—children of Stanford University professors and graduate students—were not exactly a representative sample from the general population. Other scientists noted that variations in home environment could account for self-control differences: Stable homes and one-child families encourage delay of gratification because the second marshmallow will be more predictably delivered, whereas in unstable homes and those with multiple siblings, if you don't nab a marshmallow now, there might not be any left in 15 minutes.

Mischel addressed his critics, noting that studies in nonelite schools found similar results, and he acknowledged the power of the environment to shape our ability to delay gratification and that "self-control can be nurtured in children and adults, so that the prefrontal cortex can be used deliberately to activate the cool system and regulate the hot system."[32] This metaphor of "hot" and "cool" systems in the brain is meant to convey how the brain evolved to handle different environments—"one hot to deal with immediate rewards and threats" and "the other cool to deal with delayed consequences." Mischel describes the way they work together: "As one becomes more active, the other becomes less active. The challenge is to know when it's best to let the hot system guide your course, and when (and how) to get the cool system to wake up."[33]

How do you cool your hot system? You physically distance yourself from temptation in both space and time. For example, clear your fridge of tempting treats you know you shouldn't eat. Get a full night's sleep and eat a healthy diet to maintain the energy level you need—exercising willpower, researchers have found, burns a lot of actual calories. Pat yourself on the back for even the smallest triumphs of self-control (like making your bed). And don't be afraid to enlist help from friends or family members who understand or share your weaknesses and will encourage you to resist temptation and reinforce your self-control mechanisms.

These and many other techniques of self-determination are documented by the psychologist Roy Baumeister in his book *Willpower*, coauthored with the science writer John Tierney.[34] They solved a riddle I have long pondered, namely why it is that religious people live longer, happier, and healthier lives—is it really possible that the almighty rewards His followers in such a manner? No. First, religions offer the ultimate delay-of-gratification strategy (eternal life). Baumeister and Tierney cite research showing that "students who spent more time in Sunday school scored higher on laboratory tests of self-discipline" and that "religiously devout children were rated relatively low in impulsiveness by both parents and teachers."[35] Of course, many religions require a certain level of self-discipline to even become a member, so those being measured later by social scientists may be a self-selected group who are already high in self-control and willpower.

The underlying mechanisms of setting goals and monitoring one's progress, however, can be tapped by anyone, religious or not. Meditation, in which you count your breaths up to ten and then do it over and over, Baumeister and Tierney note, "builds mental discipline. So does saying the rosary, chanting Hebrew psalms, repeating Hindu mantras." Brain scans of people conducting such rituals show strong activity in areas associated with self-regulation and control of attention. In his lab, Baumeister has demonstrated that self-control can be increased with the practice of resisting temptation, but you have to pace yourself, because, like a muscle, self-control can become depleted after excessive effort, leaving you more likely to succumb to a subsequent temptation. Finally, Baumeister and Tierney add that religion acts as a monitor of behavior and a feedback system, and it gives people a sense that someone is watching over them—God or other members of their religion.[36] For nonbelievers, family, friends, and colleagues serve as the watchers—those who will look upon misbehaviors with disapproval.

There is another self-determination strategy captured by the novelist F. Scott Fitzgerald when he asserted that "action is character," by which he meant that what you do is who you are, and stronger character shapes future action through discipline, which in turn builds stronger character in a positive feedback loop. Cognitive psychologists call this "embodied cognition"; action *becomes* character. Here is how the science writer Amy Alkon explains the principle in her humorous way: "Embodied cognition research shows that who you are is not just a product of your brain. It's also in your breathing, your gut, the way you stand, the way you speak, and, while you're speaking, whether you make eye contact or dart your eyes like you're about to bolt under a car like a cat."[37]

Your mind is a product of both your brain and your body. How you move, breathe, and carry yourself can transform not only how you see yourself but how other people see you; as Amy says, "becoming the new you mostly takes behaving as the person you want to be." By applying these principles to changing her own life, Amy is living proof "that behaving differently is what it takes to stop going through life as a linguine-spined suck up." By acting and behaving in a new way, you push out of your mind the old ways of being that you want to change. Your present self can alter your future self through current thoughts and actions.

This theory of emotion—called the James-Lange theory, after William James and Carl Lange—says that actions come first, followed by feelings. Let's say you're out on a walk down a single-track mountain trail and you come across a snake. Do you feel afraid and turn and run? No, says this theory. You instinctively turn and run, and *then* you feel afraid. The conscious processing of all the bodily changes and actions takes time, so it has to follow from the bodily response to, in this case, a threat.[38] In experiments where people are shown an image of a threatening stimuli (like a snake) that flashes by so quickly that they are not consciously aware of what they saw, the subjects still experience the bodily changes that accompany threat. The lower neural pathways in your brain operate very rapidly to trigger bodily movements that are then interpreted by the higher neural pathways in your brain in which conscious awareness comes into being.[39] The body and the mind together create our emotions, and the conscious awareness of what is going on comes after the actions you take in response to your environment.

Whatever your state of being is in the *present* can be willfully altered to create a different *future*. How far into the future should you look? Behavioral economists have identified a problem called *future discounting*, or *myopic (nearsighted) discounting*, and research shows that most of us discount the future too steeply—for example, by electing to spend too much now instead of saving more for later. People are notoriously bad at long-term investing and selecting smart retirement plans. The reason is that in the world in which we evolved, life was, in the words of the fifteenth-century political theorist Thomas Hobbes, "nasty, brutish, and short." Why save for a fabulous seventy-fifth birthday party when the chances were good that you'd be dead by 50? For most of our ancestors, a bird in the hand was worth two in the bush. In that world, it was better to eat one marshmallow now. A bumper sticker captures the psychology of temptation: "Life is short. Eat dessert first."

In today's world, however, there is a good chance you will live a long life, so there is some justification to figuring out how to delay gratification, save for the future, plan for retirement, and expect your future self to be around for a while. That is, we need to be paid to delay gratification. How much? In one study by the behavioral economist Richard Thaler, subjects were given a choice between taking $15 today and some higher amount in the future and then asked what that higher figure would have to be if the future were one month, one year, or ten years. The median responses were $20 in one month, $50 in one year, and $100 in ten years.[40] In the jargon of economics, the *utility* of the original offer diminishes over time—*diminishing utility*—so the future value of it must be increased today.

I recall one such choice I was offered in the 1980s, when I was bike racing and had a chance to participate in a television commercial as a background extra along with other cyclists. One of the producers came around with a wad of $100 bills and offered us one right then and there, or else we could fill out a bunch of paperwork, mail it in to the company, and wait four to six weeks to receive a check for $150. We all opted for the cash on the spot. Why? First, the transaction costs of the larger offer were high—reading and signing contracts, filling out financial forms, and the like. Second, the future uncertainties were also high—I didn't know the producer or the production company, and since we were just extras anyway, what recourse did we have if they reneged on the deal? In this intertemporal choice, $100 now was worth more to my present self than $150 was to my future self.

■ Sacred Self-Control and Your Two Selves

Why should this intertemporal choice effect exist at all? The answer is that there are uncertainties about the future that increase the further you project yourself out, and in the environment of our evolutionary ancestry, the future beyond a few days or weeks was unpredictable and largely unknown. Since most exchanges in our Paleolithic past were in basic commodities such as food, clothing, tools, jewelry, and social favors, the informal means of conflict resolution and trust enforcement were not always reliable, and there were no social institutions in place to create long-term trust and enforce future payoffs and expected reciprocity. So, the future discounting effect is ultimately due to the uncertainty of Paleolithic futures. The result is that too many of us fail to save for retirement, consume the calorie-rich dessert, sleep in instead of work out, drink too much, eat too much, play too much, and engage in risky behaviors that have short-term payoffs but long-term consequences.

The world is full of temptations, and as Oscar Wilde quipped, "I can resist everything except temptation." The nineteenth-century African explorer Henry Morton Stanley dealt with his temptations by having what he called a "sacred task" (his was the abolition of slavery), believing "self-control is more indispensable than gunpowder." Select your sacred task, monitor and pace your progress toward that goal, eat and sleep regularly to increase your willpower, be organized and well groomed (Stanley shaved every day in the jungle), and surround yourself with a supportive social network that reinforces your efforts.

Such sacred salubriousness is the province of anyone who wills themselves to loftier purposes. As the economist Thomas Schelling observed: "People behave sometimes as if they had two selves, one who wants clean lungs and long life and another who adores tobacco, or one who wants a lean body and another who wants dessert. The two are in continual contest for control."[41] Martin Luther King Jr. put it this way: "Each of us is two selves. The great burden of life is to always try to keep that higher self in command. . . . And every time that old lower self acts up and tells us to do wrong, let us allow that higher self to tell us that we were made for the stars, created for the everlasting, born for eternity."[42] That higher self is who McRaven invoked in the final life lesson of his commencement address:

> In SEAL training there is a bell. A brass bell that hangs in the center of the compound for all the students to see. All you have to do to quit—is ring the bell. Ring the bell and you no longer have to wake up at 5 o'clock. Ring the bell and you no longer have to do the freezing cold swims. Ring the bell and you no longer have to do the runs, the obstacle course, the PT—and you no longer have to endure the hardships of training. Just ring the bell. If you want to change the world don't ever, ever ring the bell.[43]

Interestingly, one of Mischel's lesser-known marshmallow experiments had a similar setup, with a bell that the children could ring to call back the experimenter to deliver them from temptation. "At the end of that causal chain," Mischel concluded, "it is the individual who is the agent of the action and decides when to ring the bell."[44]

That agent of action is you. Act accordingly.

11

The Truth About God

Arguments For and Against the Divine

■ Studies by religious scholars tell us that the vast majority of people in the Western world who believe in God associate themselves with some form of monotheism,[1] in which God is understood to be all powerful (omnipotent), all knowing (omniscient), and all good (omnibenevolent); to have created out of nothing the universe and everything in it; and to be uncreated and eternal, a perfect noncorporeal spirit who created matter and life, who loves, and who can grant eternal life to humans.[2]

Do you believe this God exists (*theism*)? Do you believe that this God does not exist (*strong atheism*)? Do you not believe that this God exists (*weak atheism*)? Do you believe it is not possible to know if this God exists (*agnosticism*)?[3]

There are other positions to take on the God question—for example, *deism* (the belief in the existence of a supreme being but not necessarily a personal God) or *pantheism* (the belief that the universe itself is a divine unity)—but these cover the vast majority of what people believe in the Western world. The difference between *strong atheism* and *weak atheism* is a matter of a positive assertion that God does not exist (which is difficult to prove) versus a negative assertion of a simple lack of belief in God. The latter is what many people think an *agnostic* is, but I use the term as it was originally defined in 1869 by the biologist and anthropologist Thomas Henry Huxley—"one who holds that the existence of anything beyond and behind material phenomena is unknown and so far as can be judged unknowable, and especially that a First Cause and an unseen world are subjects of which we know nothing." Huxley explained how he derived his position:

> When I reached intellectual maturity and began to ask myself whether I was an atheist, a theist, or a pantheist. . . . I found that the more I learned and reflected, the less ready was the answer. They [believers] were quite sure they had attained a certain "gnosis,"—had, more or less successfully, solved the problem of existence; while I was quite sure I had not, and had a pretty strong conviction that the problem was insoluble.[4]

Practically speaking, I am an atheist in the weak sense. I simply do not believe in God, even while acknowledging that I cannot prove God does not exist in the strong sense. Epistemologically, I am closer to being an agnostic than a strong atheist, inasmuch as I think that the God question may ultimately be an insoluble one in the scientific truth sense.

Debating God

Given the aforementioned definition of God, there are two things that I know for certain: (1) I am not God, and (2) you are not God. Given *Cromwell's rule* of Bayesian reasoning (from chapter 3) to "never assign a 0 or 1 probability to anything, just in case we're wrong," I also know for certain that (1) you do not know with 100% certainty that God exists, and (2) I do not know with 100% certainty that God does not exist. Nevertheless, some historical and geographic facts may lead us to conclude that it is more likely humans created God than vice versa:

- Had we lived 10,000 years ago, no one would be a Jew, a Christian, or a Muslim, since no such beliefs existed anywhere in the world at that time.
- Had we been born today in, say, India, China, or Japan instead of the United States or some other Western country, chances are high that few of us would be Christian.
- Even in the modern West, there are over 10,000 distinct religions of 10 general varieties, with Christians found among an astonishing 33,820 different denominations.[5]

Given this almost unfathomable level of religious diversity, it seems obvious that any claim to sole possession of objective truth is fleeting. Clearly, these many different religions cannot all be right. Or, more to the point, none of them are justified true beliefs in any objective empirical sense, whereas all of them may be subjectively true for the individual believers in them. *In that sense, I believe in the God that exists in the minds of believers, since for them, that God is all knowing, all powerful, and all good and affects their lives in measurable ways, both good and evil.*

This highlights the difference between believing something and knowing something. Anyone can believe anything they like, but knowing the truth about something is another matter entirely. Religious "knowledge," in this sense, is based on belief, not evidence and truth. Nevertheless, when asked why they believe in God, most people attribute their belief to what they perceive to be cogent arguments and evidence, so I address these here in the context of seeking the truth about the divine.

Philosophical Arguments for God

What follows are the nine most common philosophical arguments for the existence of God and counterarguments for each. They are necessarily abbreviated, inasmuch as entire chapters—and even books—have been published dealing with each one. The first five arguments are historically the most referenced, as they were initially presented by the great Catholic theologian and philosopher St. Thomas Aquinas in his classic *Summa Theologica*.[6] The work is massive, dealing with hundreds of topics—morality, the resurrection, good and evil, the passions, love, habits, virtues, law, and more—but it is most cited for its five proofs of God.

1. Prime Mover Argument

Everything in the universe is in motion. "Now whatever is in motion is put in motion by another, for nothing can be in motion unless it is in potency to that towards which it is in motion." Thus:

> whatever is moved must be moved by another. If that by which it is moved be itself moved, then this also must be moved by another, and that by another again. But this cannot go on to infinity, because then there would be no first mover. . . . Therefore, it is necessary to arrive at a first mover which is moved by no other. And this everyone understands to be God.[7]

COUNTERARGUMENT

The universe is everything that is, ever was, or ever shall be. Thus, God must be within the universe or *is* the universe. In either case, God would himself need to be moved, and thus the regress to a prime mover just begs the question of what moved God. If God does not need to be moved, then clearly not everything in the universe needs to be moved. Maybe the initial creation of the universe was its own prime mover. In inflationary cosmology, all motion began with the Big Bang, so why not postulate *that* as the prime mover and leave the supernatural out of it? (And, as discussed in the next chapter, there are additional purely natural explanations for the origin of the universe that do not require the intervention of a deity.) If God is neither the universe itself nor within the universe—but rather is outside of space and time and therefore unknowable in any rational or empirical manner—then these arguments do not support or refute God, since by definition it is not possible for a natural being to understand a supernatural entity.

2. First Cause Argument

Aquinas's "second way" begins with the presumption that "in the world of sense we find there is an order of efficient causes. There is no case known (nor indeed, is it possible) in which a thing is found to be the efficient cause of itself, because in that case it would be prior to itself, which is impossible." This cause-and-effect sequence cannot be regressed forever, so there had to be a first cause, a causal agent who needed no other cause. "Therefore it is necessary to admit a first efficient cause, to which everyone gives the name of God."[8]

COUNTERARGUMENT

As with the prime mover counterargument, if God is within the universe or *is* the universe, God would also need to be caused, and thus the regress to a first cause just begs the question of what caused God. If God does not need a cause, then clearly not everything in the universe needs a cause. Maybe the universe itself does not need a cause in the normal sense of that word (again, see the next chapter for scientific theories of the cause of the universe). Many cosmologists think it possible that the universe sprang into existence uncaused out of a quantum vacuum, not unlike many quantum effects, such as the release of photons of light from atoms. And, again, if God is a supernatural being outside of space and time and therefore unknowable in any empirical truth manner, then these arguments are pointless.

3. Possibility and Necessity Argument

Aquinas's "third way" argues that in nature, it is possible for things to be or not to be. But not everything could be in the realm of the possible, for then there could be nothing.

> Therefore, if everything is possible not to be, then at one time there could have been nothing in existence. Now if this were true, even now there would be nothing in existence, because that which does not exist only begins to exist by something already existing. There-

> fore, if at one time nothing was in existence, it would have been impossible for anything to have begun to exist.[9]

Since we can all look around and see that things exist, "there must exist something the existence of which is necessary. But every necessary thing either has its necessity caused by another, or not. Now it is impossible to go on to infinity in necessary things which have their necessity caused by another." Therefore, Aquinas concludes in this tongue-twisting ratiocination, "This all men speak of as God."

COUNTERARGUMENT

Why is it not equally plausible that God, like the universe, is possible but not necessary and as such could just as well not exist? Aquinas's arguments presume a monotheistic deity that must be supernatural or somehow both part of our universe and outside of it, but why delimit the definition of the deity as such? As Carl Sagan noted in *The Varieties of Scientific Experience*:

> Now, think again of all the possibilities. Worlds without gods, gods without worlds, gods that are made by preexisting gods, gods that were always here, gods that never die, gods that do die, gods that die more than once, different degrees of divine intervention in human affairs, zero, one, or many prophets, zero, one, or many saviours, zero, one, or many resurrections, zero, one, or many gods.[10]

Why not regress the argument from necessity another step and conclude that Yahweh was not necessary, but instead, some other creator deity above the God of the Abrahamic religions has of itself its own necessity? About the limitations of such argumentation, Sagan notes:

> Now, by the way, on this issue of who's older, God or the universe, there's actually a three-by-three matrix: God can have always existed but will not exist for all future time. God might have no beginning but might have an end. God might have a beginning but no end. God might have no beginning and no end. Likewise for the universe. The universe might be infinitely old but it will end. The universe might

> have begun a finite time ago but will go on forever, or it might have always existed and will never end.[11]

4. Perfection/Ontological Argument

In his "fourth way," Aquinas argued that there are gradations from less to more good, true, and noble. "There is then, something which is truest, something best, something noblest. Therefore there must also be something which is to all beings the cause of their being, goodness, and every other perfection. And this we call God." This is known as the *ontological argument* and was first presented by St. Anselm, the eleventh-century archbishop of Canterbury, who, in his *Proslogion*, defined God as "something than which nothing greater can be conceived."[12] Reversing the argument, Anselm says it is equally impossible to think of God as nonexistent: "For something can be thought of as existing, which cannot be thought of as not existing, and this is greater than that which can be thought of as not existing."[13]

COUNTERARGUMENT

First, David Hume refuted this argument over two centuries ago: "Nothing, that is distinctly conceivable, implies a contradiction. Whatever we conceive as existent, we can also conceive as non-existent. There is no being, therefore, whose non-existence implies a contradiction. Consequently there is no being, whose existence is demonstrable."[14]

Second, regarding Aquinas's rendering of the argument—"there is then, something which is truest, something best, something noblest. Therefore there must also be something which is to all beings the cause of their being, goodness, and every other perfection," which we call God—why couldn't the opposite be true? In my rendering:

> *There is, then, something which is falsest, something worst, something ignoblest. Therefore there must also be something that is to all beings the cause of falsity, badness, and ignobility. And this we call God.*

Third, what does it mean to be perfect? Obviously no nonperfect human can know, yet we are the creators of the concept itself. We can envision some maximal level of perfection and then argue that God must be above this, but what does that mean? No natural finite being like us can possibly know. In any case, here is my rendering of the ontological argument for God's existence, followed by another syllogistic sequence that reveals its shortcoming:

- It is a conceptual truth that God is a being than which none greater can be imagined.
- God exists as an idea in the mind.
- A being that exists as an idea in the mind *and in reality* is greater than a being that exists only as an idea in the mind.
- Therefore, God exists in reality.

Let's make the same argument for Satan's existence:

- It is a conceptual truth that Satan is a being besides which none worse can be imagined.
- Satan exists as an idea in the mind.
- A thing that exists as an idea in the mind *and in reality* is greater than a being that exists only as an idea in the mind.
- Therefore, Satan exists in reality.[15]

Once you go down this path of concocting syllogisms unmoored from reality, it's easy to concoct similar such "proofs" of God's existence—and nonexistence. Here are a couple I came up with:

Paradox of Perfection

- If God exists, then he is perfect.
- Perfect beings must create perfect things.
- God created the universe.
- The universe is not perfect.
- Therefore, God is not perfect or does not exist.

Paradox of Omnipotence

- If God can create a stone so big that he cannot lift it, then he is not omnipotent.
- If God cannot create a stone so big that he cannot lift it, then he is not omnipotent.
- Therefore, God is not omnipotent.
- Or God is just another flawed being.
- Or God does not exist.

To my ears, this is all just word play, armchair ratiocination of what we can or cannot conceive of without once looking out the window to see what is actually in nature that may confirm or disconfirm our imaginary ideas.[16]

5. Design/Teleological Argument

Aquinas's "fifth way" deals with "the governance of things." "We see that things which lack knowledge, such as natural bodies, act for an end, and this is evident from their acting always, or nearly always, in the same way, so as to obtain the best result. Hence it is plain that they achieve their end not by chance, but by design." Thus, Aquinas concludes in this precursor to the intelligent design (ID) movement, "Therefore some intelligent being exists by whom all natural things are ordered to their end; and this being we call God."

COUNTERARGUMENT

Modern design arguments are more sophisticated and involve the intricacies of apparent design in nature, so I deal with those in more detail in the section on scientific arguments for God. But, generally speaking, such design arguments from nature are untenable because they are based on designed human artifacts whose design can be traced back to the natural designer, such as a watchmaker. But we have no evidence whatsoever of a supernatural designer, beyond the circular argument that natural objects appear designed and thus require a designer to explain them. In fact, as we shall see, science has more than adequately explained through the theory of evolution how apparently designed features like eyes and wings came to be. As Dan Barker points out, the argument "We have never observed design without a designer" is a tautology, another way of saying "We have never observed things that were designed by intelligence that were not designed by intelligence." And that, Barker notes, "smuggles intelligence into the premise that is aimed at concluding intelligence."[17]

Let us move on to other theological arguments that came after Aquinas.

6. Pascal's Wager Argument

At the age of 31, the French philosopher Blaise Pascal had what he termed a "mystical experience" that changed his life. Not content to rest his belief entirely in the mystical (and knowing this would never convince fellow skeptics such as René Descartes), he formulated what has become known as Pascal's wager: If we wager that God does not exist and he does, then we have everything to lose and nothing to win. If we wager that God does exist and he does, then we have everything to gain and nothing to lose. Pascal was not naive enough to believe that people would then just place the bet or that God would just accept the gamblers into His heavenly casino. He realized that belief comes through action, so he argued that you also needed to go through the religious rituals, and in time, you would come to really believe.[18]

COUNTERARGUMENT

First, this is not strictly a proof of God, since Pascal himself admitted that one still needs faith. Second, believing in God and going through the motions of religious rituals is not a case of "nothing to lose," starting with the time and effort it takes to do all this when one could be doing something else (opportunity costs). Finally, what if there were some other divine being or some other religion whose sacraments and sacrifices were different from those of the Christian faith? You might be eternally punished for placing your wager on the wrong religion.

7. Mystical Experience Argument

This is another rendition of a subjective truth: "I know God exists because I have experienced him." Such mystical experiences and conversions are historically common. Saul's conversion to Paul on the road to Damascus birthed Christianity. Constantine's "vision" at the Milvian Bridge preceding his victory over Maxentius in AD 312 cemented the Christian religion into the Roman world. Augustine heard voices telling him to "Pick it up, read it; pick it up, read it!," upon which "I got to my feet . . . to open the Bible and read the first passage I should light upon." The passage told him to sell his belongings and give the money to the poor. This he did, and as he notes in his *Confessions*, "as the sentence ended, there was infused in my heart something like the light of full certainty and all the gloom of doubt vanished away." John Calvin reported in his *Commentary on the Psalms* that he had "a sudden conversion." Martin Luther was reportedly struck to the ground by a lightning bolt and cried in terror, "St. Anne, help me! I will become a monk."

COUNTERARGUMENT

I dealt with mystical experiences in chapter 9. As we saw, there is no way to go from those internal subjective truths to external objective truths, so there is no justification for belief in them beyond what one gets out of such experiences personally. It would be the equivalent of arguing, per my thought experiment in chapter 2 about the invisible dragon in my garage, "I feel the presence of the dragon" or "I feel the dragon's love," which is not objective evidence but subjective emotion. In any case, neuroscientists have long noted that these experiences are most likely the result of temporal lobe seizures or some other aberration in neural physiology and thus cannot be considered proof of anything divine.[19]

8. Fideism, or the *Credo Quia Consolans* Argument

Of all the philosophical arguments for God, perhaps this stands as the most honest in its admission of the personal nature of belief: *Credo Quia*

Consolans—"I believe because it is consoling." As noted in chapter 5 in the discussion of fideism as a religious truth, at its core it says that (1) in issues of extreme importance to human existence, (2) when the evidence is inconclusive one way or the other, and (3) you must make a choice, it is acceptable to take a leap of faith for personal, subjective, and emotional reasons.

COUNTERARGUMENT

This is an argument for one's personal belief, which, by definition, cannot be extrapolated to others' beliefs. Like the mystical experience argument, it is an internal subjective truth that is proof of nothing externally divine. Another flaw is that fideism reduces belief to personality type—some need it, some don't, depending on temperament and context. If beliefs are to be based on emotion rather than argument or evidence, this would seem to eliminate the need for reason and science altogether. In that case, why not just say that God is an unknowable concept and an unsolvable mystery and go about your life believing (or not) without the need for evidence or proofs?

9. Moral Argument

Humans are moral beings and animals are not. Where did we get this moral sense of right and wrong? Through the ultimate moral being—God. Without God, without the highest of higher moral authorities, anything goes, and there would be no basis for morality and no reason to be moral.

COUNTERARGUMENT

I dealt with this argument in chapter 7, in which I made the case for a universal secular morality grounded in human nature and culture that has no need of divine intervention or providence. More briefly, when confronted with this argument, I sometimes retort: "What would you do if there were no God? Would you lie, cheat, steal, rob, rape, and murder, or would you continue being a good and moral person?" If the answer is that you would turn to such abhorrent behavior, then this is an indictment of your moral character, and we would be well advised to steer a wide course around you.

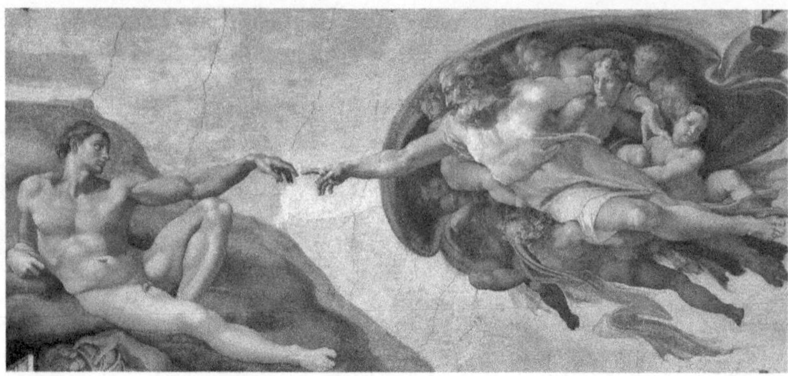

Figure 11.1. *The Creation of Adam*, a panel on the ceiling of the Sistine Chapel in Vatican City, Rome, painted circa 1511 by the Italian Renaissance artist Michelangelo. The idea of the universe having a beginning naturally leads many people to conclude that a creation requires a creator. Wikimedia Commons, file name Michelangelo - Creation of Adam.jpg

If the answer is that you would continue being good and moral, then apparently you can be good without God.

One of the best single source refutations of all these arguments by a professional philosopher may be found in Rebecca Newberger Goldstein's 2010 book, *36 Arguments for the Existence of God: A Work of Fiction*.[20] She shows that the cosmological argument "is a prime example of the Fallacy of Passing the Buck: invoking God to solve some problem, but then leaving unanswered that very same problem about God himself." As for a first cause of everything, Goldstein notes that "to apply this concept to the universe itself is to misuse the concept of cause, extending it into a realm in which we have no idea how to use it. As the logician Charles Peirce put it, 'Universes are not as numerous as blackberries.' " This is why, as visualized in figure 11.1, it is almost impossible to picture God as anything other than a superpowerful human, even with the sublime artistic genius of a Michelangelo.

As for the ontological argument, Goldstein, channeling Immanuel Kant, points out that it treats "existence" as a property, like "being skinny" or "having ten toes." Thus, she notes, "the ontological argument relies on a bit of word-play, assuming that 'existence' is just another property, but logically it is completely different. If you really could treat 'existence' as just part of the definition of the concept of God, then you could just as easily build it into the definition of any other concept." She uses the example of a "trunicorn," or "a horse that (a) has a single horn on its head, and (b) exists." So, thinking of a "trunicorn" means it must exist, but it doesn't, so this entire line of reasoning is barking mad.

■ Scientific Arguments for God

Science and religion are, at present, largely separate spheres of knowledge divided by, more than anything else, a difference in epistemological methodologies. Science is a process of inquiry aimed at building a testable body of knowledge open to rejection or confirmation; its "truths" are provisional. Religion is the affirmation of a set of beliefs aimed at providing a community of people with shared morals and meaning; its truths are final, confirmed by faith. "Faith is the substance of things hoped for, the evidence of things not seen" (Hebrews 11:1). "We walk by faith, not by sight" (II Corinthians 5:7). "Blessed are they that have not seen, and yet have believed" (John 20:29). Attempts at reconciling science and religion fail for the fundamental reason that religion ultimately depends on faith, or believing regardless of the evidence, which is the antithesis of science.

Nevertheless, because we now live in the Age of Science and no longer in the Age of Faith, temptations abound to use science to bolster faith. The intelligent design theorist Stephen Meyer, for example, in his book *The Return of the God Hypothesis*, argues that God belongs in the realm of empirical scientific truths based on "three scientific discoveries that reveal the mind behind the universe." They are:

> (1) Evidence from cosmology suggesting that the material universe had a beginning; (2) evidence from physics showing that from the beginning the universe has been "finely tuned" to allow for the possibility of life; and (3) evidence from biology establishing that since the beginning large amounts of new functional genetic information have arisen in our biosphere to make new forms of life possible—implying . . . the activity of a designing intelligence.[21]

Let's consider these and related science-based arguments for God's existence and counterarguments for each.

1. Design Inference

There is a distinct difference between objects that are naturally designed and those that are intelligently designed.

Mount Rushmore is made entirely of natural material (rock), but no one would infer that the natural forces of erosion account for the design of four US presidents' faces. This is an example of what intelligent design theorists call a *design inference*. Of course, there are lots of examples of natural forces that do account for designed-looking objects: the eroded mountain on Mars that under coarse-grained resolution looks like a face; the "Nun Bun" found by a Tennessee baker that resembles Mother Teresa; the image of the Virgin Mary on the side of a bank building in Clearwater, Florida, or on a cheese sandwich in a Las Vegas casino. Although such artifacts were created entirely by natural forces, almost no one infers that there is an intelligent designer behind them. How can we tell the difference between natural and artificial design? According to Meyer:

> Inferences to design thus employ the standard uniformitarian method of reasoning used in all historical sciences, many of which routinely detect intelligent causes. Intelligent agents have unique causal powers that nature does not. When we observe effects that we know only agents can produce, we rightly infer the presence of a prior intelli-

gence even if we did not observe the action of the particular agent responsible.[22]

COUNTERARGUMENT

One, the inference to design is subjective. Sometimes it is obvious, and other times it is not. The difference between a rock and a watch is obvious; the difference between a randomly chipped rock and an intentionally chipped stone tool made by an *Australopithecine* three million years ago is not so obvious. The inference to design is specific to each claim. In the chipped-stone problem, for example, a rock that has been chipped on both sides in a symmetrical fashion is more likely to have been intelligently designed than naturally flaked. Nevertheless, archaeologists occasionally infer false positives, and there is no surefire design inference algorithm that applies to all archaeological problems, let alone one that applies to all scientific fields. The set of criteria used by archaeologists to determine whether a stone was chipped by chance or design is completely different from the set of criteria used by astronomers to determine whether a signal from space is natural or artificial.

Two, we perceive nature to be intelligently designed because of our vast experience with human artifacts that we know are intelligently designed, since we can observe them being made. By contrast, we have no experience with an intelligent designer outside of the human realm or with a supernatural agent outside of inferring his existence through gaps in our knowledge of (thus far) unexplained mysteries. For a watch, I can go to the factory and see it being designed and built. There is no such factory for life or the universe.

2. Irreducible Complexity

Evolution cannot account for the stepwise gradual increase in complex systems.

In *On the Origin of Species*, Darwin wrote, "If it could be demonstrated that any complex organ existed which could not possibly have been formed by numerous, successive, slight modifications, my theory would absolutely break down."[23] Creationists have been in search of Darwin's exception ever since. Lehigh University biochemist Michael Behe, for example, thinks he has found several examples of living properties that he says are irreducibly complex, by which he means "a single system composed of several well-matched, interacting parts that contribute to the basic function, wherein the removal of any one of the parts causes the system to effectively cease functioning." Behe asserts:

> An irreducibly complex system cannot be produced directly (that is, by continuously improving the initial function, which continues to work by the same mechanism) by slight, successive modifications of a precursor system, because any precursor to an irreducibly complex system that is missing a part is by definition nonfunctional. Since natural selection can only choose systems that are already working, then if a biological system cannot be produced gradually it would have to arise as an integrated unit, in one fell swoop, for natural selection to have anything to act on.[24]

The human eye is a favorite example among creationists because of its purported irreducible complexity—take out any one part, they claim, and it will not work. How could natural selection have created the human eye, when none of the individual parts themselves have any adaptive significance? Or consider the bacteria flagellum—Behe's type specimen of irreducible complexity and intelligent design; the little tail that propels cells is complex and composed of many parts, so the removal of any one of them would cause the system to cease working. The bacteria flagellum is not like a machine, it *is* a machine, and it has no antecedents in nature from which it could have evolved in a stepwise Darwinian manner.

Irreducible complexity leads to an inference of intelligent design—an inference that Behe claims "is so unambiguous and so significant that it must be ranked as one of the greatest achievements in the history of science," which he immodestly equates with the discoveries of "Newton and Einstein, Lavoisier and Schrodinger, Pasteur, and Darwin."[25]

COUNTERARGUMENT

First, when Behe says that "any precursor to an irreducibly complex system that is missing a part is by definition nonfunctional," he is committing the fallacy of bait-and-switch logic, says the philosopher of science Robert Pennock. He is shifting the basis of his reasoning from something that is true "by definition" to something that is proved through empirical evidence. Every time someone finds an example in nature that is simpler than Behe said it could be, he redefines irreducible complexity to *that* simpler level of complexity.[26] In other words, irreducible complexity is whatever Behe says it is, depending on the example at hand.

Second, the evolutionary biologist Jerry Coyne identified a number of biochemical pathways that have been claimed by Behe to be impossible to explain without an intelligent designer but in fact "have been rigged up with pieces co-opted from other pathways, duplicated genes, and early multi-functional enzymes." Behe, for example, claims that the blood-clotting process could not have come about through gradual evolution. Coyne shows that, in fact, thrombin "is one of the key proteins in blood clotting, but also acts in cell division, and is related to the digestive enzyme trypsin."[27] In other words, thrombin evolved for one purpose and was later co-opted for other purposes.

Third, Behe's irreducible complexity is a more sophisticated version of an argument made against Darwin in the nineteenth century known as *the problem of incipient stages*. Fully formed wings are obviously an excellent adaptation for flight that provide all sorts of advantages for animals who have them; but of what use is half a wing? For Darwinian gradualism to work, each successive stage of wing development would need to be functional, but stumpy little partial wings are not aerodynamically capable of flight. Darwin answered his critics thus:

> Although an organ may not have been originally formed for some special purpose, if it now serves for this end we are justified in saying that it is specially contrived for it. On the same principle, if a man were to make a machine for some special purpose, but were to use old wheels, springs, and pulleys, only slightly altered, the whole machine, with all its parts, might be said to be specially contrived for that purpose. Thus throughout nature almost every part of each living being has probably served, in a slightly modified condition, for diverse purposes, and has acted in the living machinery of many ancient and distinct specific forms.[28]

This solution, in which a feature that originally evolved for one purpose is co-opted for a different purpose, is called *exaptation*.[29] The incipient stages in wing evolution had uses other than for aerodynamic flight; half wings were not poorly developed wings, they were a well-developed something else—a thermoregulating device being one likely adaptive use. The first feathers in the fossil record, for example, are hairlike and resemble the insulating down of modern bird chicks.[30] Since modern birds probably descended from bipedal therapod dinosaurs, wings with feathers could have been employed for regulating heat—holding them close to the body enables heat retention, and stretching them out releases heat.[31] The most famous transitional fossil in evolutionary history, *Archaeopteryx*, has wings whose surface area is large enough to support its body, asymmetrical feathers capable of attaining lift, and a shoulder that allows enough flexibility for an adequate upstroke of the wing necessary for flight. Nevertheless, *Archaeopteryx* retains many dinosaur features, including a functional grasping hand, for which the "wing" was probably originally adapted before being exapted for flight.[32]

Similar reasoning explains the incipient stages in the evolution of eyes, blood clotting, the flagellum motor, and the other structures claimed by proponents of intelligent design to be inexplicable through evolutionary theory. For the human eye, for example, it is not true that it is irreducibly complex and that the removal of any part results in blindness. Any form of light detection is better than none—lots of people are visually impaired by a variety of different diseases and injuries, yet they are able to utilize their restricted visual capacity to some degree and would certainly prefer this to blindness.

3. Microevolution and Macroevolution

Life shows signs of intermittent design intervention that account for large-scale changes.

Natural selection can account for minor changes within a species but cannot produce new species, new body forms, or new lineages. Creationists have been making this argument ever since Darwin, and some intelligent design theorists today present a more sophisticated version of the argument that several billion years ago, an intelligent designer created the first cell prepackaged with the necessary genetic information to produce all of the irreducibly complex systems we see today. Then, the laws of nature and evolution took over to create diversity within species. But when totally new and more complex species, body forms, and lineages appear in the fossil record, they are evidence of when the intelligent designer (God) stepped in to intervene with a new design element.

COUNTERARGUMENT

First, within evolution biology, there has been considerable debate about whether the microevolutionary process of natural selection operating on individuals within populations can by itself account for the diverse macroevolutionary forms of life. Today, the new science of evolutionary developmental biology—evo-devo—reveals that the wide diversity of forms evolved through an interaction of the embryological development of forms and the subsequent pruning of these forms by natural selection. For example, it turns out that the bodily architecture of vertebrates is the product of blueprint *Hox* genes that direct the construction of repeating parts, such as ribs and vertebrae. In embryological development, various structures form—or do not form—depending on whether the *Hox* genes are expressed or not. Natural selection operates on expressed forms only, since these result in organisms that survive long enough to pass on their genes for the future expression of those forms.

Similarly, the wide variety of eyes found throughout the animal kingdom—from the compound eyes of flies to the camera eyes of vertebrates—evolved under the control of the commonly shared *Pax-6* gene, which directs the production of photoreceptor cells and light-sensing proteins. Each type of complex eye we find today evolved from simpler photoreceptive structures in a distant common ancestor of arthropods, cephalopods, and vertebrates. The evo-devo biologist Sean B. Carroll explains:

> The ancestor possessed two kinds of light-sensitive organs, each one endowed with a distinct type of photoreceptor, as well as with light-sensitive proteins called R-opsin and C-opsin, respectively. One organ was a simple two-celled prototype eye; the other, called the brain photoclock, was a part of the animal's brain and played a role in running the animal's daily clock. The arthropod and squid retinas incorporated the photoreceptor from the simple prototype eye, whereas the vertebrate eye incorporated both kinds of photoreceptor into its retina.[33]

Likewise, and more generally, instead of an extensive genetic tool kit with genes for constructing each and every bodily structure, evo-devo shows that a small set of gene complexes, such as the *Hox* genes and the *Pax-6* genes, are expressed in novel ways that can generate large-scale changes in a non-incremental fashion. This explains why the human genome is not especially different from the mouse genome. It is not the *number* of genes that counts so much as it is *how* genes are turned on or off. Evolution involves old genes developing new tricks.

Second, to turn the tables on intelligent design theorists, how does ID theory explain micro and macro forms? Did ID/God personally tinker with the DNA of every single organism in a population, or did it tweak the DNA of just one organism and then isolate that organism to start a new population? When and where did ID/God intervene in the history of life? Did ID/God create each genus and then evolution created each species? Or did ID/God create each species and evolution create each subspecies? Most ID theorists accept natural selection as a viable explanation for microevolution—the beak of the finch, the neck of the giraffe, and the varieties of subspecies found on Earth. If ID/God created species, then why not subspecies? By contrast, if natural selection can create subspecies, then why not species, genera, families, and on up the classification scale to kingdoms?

4. Undone by Entropy

The second law of thermodynamics makes evolution impossible.

According to the laws of physics, entropy increases—systems change from hot to cold, from ordered to disordered, and from complex to simple. Yet, evolutionists state that the universe and life moves from chaos to order and from simple to complex, the exact opposite of the entropy predicted by the second law of thermodynamics. The creationist Henry Morris stated the argument thus: "Evolutionists have fostered the strange belief that everything is involved in a process of progress, from chaotic particles billions of years ago all the way up to complex people today. The fact is, the most certain laws of science state that the real processes of nature do not make things go uphill, but downhill. Evolution is impossible."[34]

COUNTERARGUMENT

First, on any scale other than the grandest of all—the 3.5-billion year history of life on Earth—species do not evolve from simple to complex, and nature does not simply move from chaos to order. The history of life is checkered with false starts, failed experiments, and extinctions, local and mass. It is anything but the textbook foldout of linear progress from single cells to humans.

Second, the second law of thermodynamics applies to closed, isolated systems. Since the Earth receives a constant input of energy from the sun—it is an open-dissipative system—entropy may decrease and order increase. Thus, as an open system, life on Earth evolved without violating natural law.[35]

Third, Earth's open-dissipative system slips in and out of thermodynamic equilibrium, and the sciences of nonlinear dynamics and complexity theory show that systems can spontaneously self-organize into more complex systems when they are in states of thermodynamic nonequilibrium. By being out of balance, energy flowing in and out of the system triggers parts to interact with one another locally, and these coupled interactions reverberate throughout the system to sustain it. Autocatalysis, or feedback loops, can cause a system to grow in complexity. From these self-organized autocatalytic interactions emerge complexity and order.[36] All of this happens without any top-down input. Evolution no more breaks the second law of thermodynamics than one breaks the law of gravity by leaping into the air.

5. Belied by Chance

Evolution is random, and randomness cannot produce complex specified design.

Even the simplest life forms are too complex to have come together by random chance. Take a simple organism consisting of merely 100 parts. Mathematically, there are 10^{158} possible ways for the parts to link up. There are not enough molecules in the universe, or time since the Big Bang, to account for these possible ways to come together in even this simple life form, let alone to produce human beings. It is the equivalent of the monkey typing *Hamlet*, or even "to be or not to be," by random chance.

COUNTERARGUMENT

Natural selection is not "random"; it preserves the gains and eradicates the mistakes. The eye evolved from a single, light-sensitive cell into the complex eye of today through thousands of intermediate steps, many of which still exist in nature. In order for a monkey to type the first 13 letters of Hamlet's soliloquy by chance, it would take 26^{13} number of trials for success. This is 16 times as great as the total number of seconds that have elapsed in the lifetime of the solar system. But if each correct letter is preserved and each incorrect letter eradicated, the process operates much faster. My mentor Richard Hardison constructed a computer program in which letters were "selected" for or against, and it took an average of only 335.2 trials to produce the sequence of letters TOBEORNOTTOBE, or less than 90 seconds. *Hamlet* in its entirety can be typed in about 4.5 days![37] Independently of Hardison, and around the same time, Richard Dawkins conducted the same computer experiment for his book *The Blind Watchmaker*, except he used a different phrase—"Methinks it is like a weasel."

6. Bayesian God

An equation estimates a probability for God's existence.

There is an argument for God using Bayes's theorem that is discussed in a book called *The Probability of God* by the physicist Stephen D. Unwin.[38] Unwin rejects most scientific attempts to prove the divine, concluding that this "is not the sort of evidence that points in either direction, for or against." Instead, Unwin employs "Bayesian probabilities," starting with a 50% probability that God exists (because 50/50 represents "maximum ignorance"). He then applies a modified Bayesian theorem:

$$P_{\text{after}} = \frac{P_{\text{before}} \times D}{P_{\text{before}} \times D + 100\% - P_{\text{before}}}$$

In this formula the probability of God's existence after the evidence is considered is a function of the probability before times D ("Divine Indicator Scale"): 10 indicates the evidence is 10 times more likely to be produced if God exists, 2 is 2 times more likely if God exists, 1 is neutral, 0.5 is moderately more likely if God does not exist, and 0.1 is much more likely if God does not exist. Unwin then offers the following figures for six lines of evidence: *recognition of goodness* ($D = 10$), *existence of moral evil* ($D = 0.5$), *existence of natural evil* ($D = 0.1$), *intra-natural miracles* (prayers) ($D = 2$), *extra-natural miracles* (resurrection) ($D = 1$), and *religious experiences* ($D = 2$).

Plugging these figures into the formula (in sequence, where the P_{after} figure for the first computation is used for the P_{before} figure in the second computation, and so on for all six *D*s), Unwin concludes: "The probability that God exists is 67%." Remarkably, Unwin then confesses: "This number has a subjective element since it reflects *my* assessment of the evidence. It isn't as if we have calculated the value of pi for the first time."

COUNTERARGUMENT

Based on my own analysis of the evolutionary origins of morality and the sociocultural foundation of god beliefs, and starting with a 50% probability of God's existence (as Unwin does), I estimate these probabilities: recognition of goodness ($D = 0.5$), existence of moral evil ($D = 0.1$), existence of natural evil ($D = 0.1$), intra-natural miracles ($D = 1$), extra-natural miracles ($D = 0.5$), religious experiences ($D = 0.1$). With these figures, I compute the probability that God exists at 0.02, or 2%.

Regardless, this subjective component in the formula relegates the process to an entertaining exercise in thinking—on par with mathematical puzzles—but little more. In my opinion, the God question is a scientifically insoluble one. Thus, all such scientistic theologies are compelling only to those who already believe. Religious belief depends on a host of social, psychological, and emotional factors that have little or nothing to do with probabilities, evidence, and logic.

In brief summary of this section on scientific arguments for God's existence—in case you've lost the thread in the minutia of intelligent design and evolutionary theory—the details are less important than the exercise at hand, which is to demonstrate that none of these arguments leads inexorably to the conclusion that God's existence has been demonstrated.

Who Designed the Designer?

If the world is complex and looks intricately designed, and therefore the best inference is that there must be an intelligent designer, should we not then infer that an intelligent designer must itself have been designed? That is, if the earmarks of design imply that there is an intelligent designer, then the existence of an intelligent designer denotes that *it* must have a designer—a *super intelligent designer*. And by the same logic, any designer who can create a super intelligent designer must itself be a *super duper intelligent designer—ad infinitum*.

A final point on the unknowability of God and the fruitlessness of all such attempts to prove divine existence is found in the seminal work of Paul Tillich, *Systematic Theology*. The theologian declared that

> God does not exist. He is being itself beyond essence and existence. Therefore to argue that God exists is to deny him. The question of the existence of God can be neither asked nor answered. If asked, it is a question about that which by its very nature is above existence, and therefore the answer—whether negative or affirmative—implicitly denies the nature of God. It is as atheistic to affirm the existence of God as it is to deny it. God is being-itself, not *a* being.[39]

In the next chapter, we consider the ultimate known unknowable, namely why there is something rather than nothing, and I address in more detail the fine-tune argument for God's existence, as I think these two constitute the best arguments in the theist's toolkit.

12

The Truth About Existence

Why There Is Something Rather Than Nothing

■ Imagine nothing.

Go ahead, try it. Close your eyes and picture nothing. I'll wait while you work on it . . .

It's challenging, to say the least. It blows my mind when I try it. I start by visualizing the room I'm sitting in empty, then I get rid of the room itself, followed by the chair I'm sitting on and the ground on which the chair sits. At some point, I'm just floating in dark empty space bereft of galaxies, stars, planets, molecules, and atoms. But that's not even close to nothing! There is still a universe of empty space in which I am floating, along with the space and time (or space-time) in which I exist. So we have to get rid of all that as well, along with all mental and platonic concepts, all logic and mathematics, all laws and forces of nature, all concepts of deities and no actual deities, and, of course, there would be no sentient beings asking why there is something rather than nothing because there would be no sentience. At that point, there would be not just nothingness forever but not even the existence of nothingness—and no forever.

At this point, I don't even know what I'm talking about. *Nothing* is literally inconceivable.

What follows is a compendium of explanations from philosophers and scientists trying to determine the truth about the problem of existence—why there is something rather than nothing and why our universe is structured as it is to enable the existence of sentient beings to contemplate such contemplative matters.

■ Many Answers to the Existence Question

Many excellent works attempt to address this question. John Leslie's and Robert Lawrence Kuhn's *The Mystery of Existence* outlines all the thoughtful answers to the question from philosophers, scientists, and religious thinkers over the centuries.[1]

Nothing Is Something

The analytical philosopher Quentin Smith pointed out to Kuhn that it is a logical fallacy to talk about "nothing" as if it were "something"; that is, to suggest that "there might have been nothing" implies "it is possible that there is nothing." As Kuhn articulates Smith's argument:

> "There is" means "something is." So "there is nothing" means "something is nothing," which is a logical contradiction. His suggestion is to remove "nothing" and replace it by "not something" or "not anything," since one can talk about what we mean by "nothing" by referring to *something* or *anything* of which there are no instances (i.e., the concept of "something" has the property of not being instantiated). The common sense way to talk about Nothing is to talk about something and negate it, to deny that there is something.[2]

Here we encounter the restrictions that language imposes on the problem. The very act of talking about "nothing" makes it a "something," or else what are we talking about?

Nothing Would Include God's Nonexistence

In Kuhn's taxonomy of "nothings," he lists what *categories of things* might be included in "something" that would be negated by "nothing": physical, mental, platonic, and spiritual/God.

- *Physical*: all matter, energy, space and time, and all the laws and principles that govern them.
- *Mental*: all kinds of consciousness and awareness.
- *Platonic*: all forms of abstract objects (numbers, logic, forms, propositions, possibilities).
- *Spiritual/God*: all forms of religious and spiritual belief.[3]

If "nothing" means no physical objects or matter of any kind, for example, there can still be energy from which matter may arise by natural forces guided by the laws of nature. Physicists, for example, talk about empty space as seething with virtual particles, from which particle-antiparticle pairs come into existence as a consequence of the uncertainty principle of quantum physics. From this "nothingness," universes may "pop" into existence.[4]

But if "nothing" means that there is no physical, mental, platonic, or nonphysical entity of any kind, then there can be no God or gods, which means that there cannot be anything outside of nothing to create something. If God is proposed to be outside of or preexisting the "nothing" from which the "something" was created, then why can't the laws of nature that give rise to "somethings" (like universes) be outside of or preexisting nothing?

God Did It *Ex Nihilo*

For the millennia that people have been asking the existence question, the most common answer given was some version of "God did it": A creator existed before the universe and brought it into existence *ex nihilo—out of nothing*. Many people think that this is what the Bible says happened, but in fact, Genesis does not actually say that God created the universe *ex nihilo*—that is a later inference made by theologians. Genesis 1:1 reads simply: "In the beginning God created the heavens and the earth." It does not elaborate on what God made the heavens and the Earth *out of*, which theologians have presumed to be "nothing." But since theists argue that something cannot come from nothing, then out of what do they think God created the universe?

As well, there may be something lost in translation. According to *Skeptic* magazine religion editor Tim Callahan, the Hebrew word for creation in Genesis 1:1 is *bara*, which can mean create but can also mean "choose" or "divide." Callahan cites the Old Testament scholar Ellen van Wolde, who argues that the most accurate translation of *bara* is "separate," so Genesis 1:1 should read, "In the beginning God *separated* the heavens and the earth."[5] This, says Callahan, better fits the context of Genesis 1, "in which the creation is presented as a series of separations: light is created and separated from darkness, the firmament of heaven is created to separate the waters above it from the waters below it, and the separation of land from water."[6]

Even if one rejects this interpretation of Genesis 1:1 and opts for creation *ex nihilo*, this just begs the question of who or what created the creator. Theists retort that God is that which does not need to be created, but why can't the universe be in the same ontological and epistemological category as God, wherein we could simply say that the universe is that which does not need to be created? Theists counter that the universe had a Big Bang beginning and everything that begins to exist has a cause. But not everything in the universe is strictly causal, such as some quantum effects, and even though our universe in its current state can be traced back to a Big Bang beginning, that doesn't mean there was not a previous universe that gave birth to our universe through the Big Bang. And as the philosopher Rebecca Newberger Goldstein notes, applying causal reasoning within the universe to the universe itself is a category error (applying a concept from one category to another one where it doesn't belong). Determining the cause of stellar evolution within our universe, for example, tells us nothing about how the universe itself came into being. That is at the moment a known unknown, and it may be yet another known unknowable.

Theists also note that that the universe is a thing, whereas God is an agent or being. But don't things and beings all need a causal explanation? Why should God be exempt from such causal reasoning? Because, rejoins the theist, God is *super*natural—outside of space, time, and matter—whereas everything in the universe, and the universe itself, is *natural* and therefore made up of space and time, matter and energy, so God and the universe are ontologically different. But if that is so, then how would we detect God with our instruments?

If a *supernatural* deity used *natural* forces to, say, cure someone's cancer by reprogramming the cancerous cells' DNA, wouldn't that make God nothing more than a highly skilled genetic engineer? And if God used unknown *supernatural* forces to effect change in our *natural* world, how do they interact with the known forces of our universe? And if such supernatural forces could somehow stir the particles in our universe, shouldn't we be able to detect them and thereby incorporate them into our theories about the natural world? If so, wouldn't that bring God into the universe as a natural being and thus subject him to the search for a natural causal explanation for his existence?

Nothing Is Unstable, Something Is Stable

Asking why there is something rather than nothing presumes "nothing" is the natural state of things out of which "something" needs an explanation. But what if "something" is the natural state of things and "nothing" is the mystery to be solved? As the late physicist Victor Stenger notes in *The Fallacy of Fine Tuning*: "Current cosmology suggests that no laws of physics were violated in bringing the universe into existence. The laws of physics themselves are shown to correspond to what one would expect if the universe appeared from nothing. There is something rather than nothing because something is more stable."[7]

In *A Universe from Nothing*, the cosmologist Lawrence Krauss links quantum physics to Einstein's gravitational theory of general relativity to explain the origin of something from nothing: "In quantum gravity, universes can, and indeed always will, spontaneously appear from nothing. Such universes need not be empty, but can have matter and [electromagnetic] radiation in them, as long as the total energy, including the negative energy associated with gravity [balancing the positive energy of matter], is zero." Thus, Krauss concludes, "quantum gravity not only appears to allow universes to be created from nothing—meaning . . . the absence of space and time—it may require them. 'Nothing'—in this case no space, no time, no anything!—*is* unstable."[8] In his follow-up book, *The Greatest Story Ever Told—So Far*, Krauss notes that although the idea that something can come from nothing seems impossible, "this is precisely what happens with the light you are using to read this page. Electrons in hot atoms emit photons—photons that didn't exist before they were emitted—which are emitted spontaneously and without specific cause. Why is it that we have grown at least somewhat comfortable with the idea that photons can be created from nothing without cause, but not whole universes?"[9]

■ Why This Universe?

The universe appears to be finely tuned and delicately balanced to support life; change any number of physical parameters or initial conditions of the universe by even the tiniest amount, and life would not be possible. Fine-tuning implies a fine tuner, an intelligent designer, a God. There is no shortage of observations on this condition of the cosmos from leading scientists, including Stephen Hawking:

> Why is the universe so close to the dividing line between collapsing again and expanding indefinitely? In order to be as close as we are now, the rate of expansion early on had to be chosen fantastically accurately. If the rate of expansion one second after the big bang had been less by one part in 10^{10}, the universe would have collapsed after

a few million years. If it had been greater by one part in 10^{10}, the universe would have been essentially empty after a few million years. In neither case would it have lasted long enough for life to develop. Thus one either has to appeal to the anthropic principle or find some physical explanation of why the universe is the way it is.[10]

What is this "anthropic principle" to which Hawking refers? In *The Anthropic Cosmological Principle*, the physicists John Barrow and Frank Tipler explain:

> It is not only man that is adapted to the universe. The universe is adapted to man. Imagine a universe in which one or another of the fundamental dimensionless constants of physics is altered by a few percent one way or the other? Man could never come into being in such a universe. That is the central point of the anthropic principle. According to the principle, a life-giving factor lies at the center of the whole machinery and design of the world.[11]

Sir Martin Rees, Britain's Astronomer Royal, argues "our emergence from a simple Big Bang was sensitive to six 'cosmic numbers.' Had these numbers not been 'well tuned,' the gradual unfolding of layer upon layer of complexity would have been quenched."[12] These six numbers are:

Ω (omega) = 1, the amount of matter in the universe, such that if Ω was greater than 1, it would have collapsed long ago, and if Ω was less than 1, no galaxies would have formed.

E (epsilon) = 0.007, how firmly atomic nuclei bind together such that if epsilon were 0.006 or 0.008, matter could not exist as it does.

$D = 3$, the number of dimensions in which we live such that if D were 2 or 4, life could not exist.

$N = 10^{36}$, the ratio of the strength of gravity to that of electromagnetism such that if it had just a few less zeroes, the universe would be too young and too small for life to evolve.

$Q = 1/100{,}000$, the fabric of the universe, such that if Q were smaller, the universe would be featureless, and if Q were larger, the universe would be dominated by giant black holes.

λ (lambda) = 0.7, the cosmological constant, or "antigravity" force that is causing the universe to expand at an accelerating rate, such that if it were larger, it would have prevented stars and galaxies from forming.

Change these relationships, and stars, planets, and life could not exist. Thus, this is not just the best of all possible worlds, it is the *only* possible world.[13]

Counterarguments

Universe Not So Fine-Tuned for Life

The vast majority of the universe is empty space, and the vast majority of what little matter there is is completely inhospitable to life, including most planets. In the universe's 13.8-billion-year history, the anthropic conditions for life were nonexistent; it is only during this narrow slice of time that the universe is fine-tuned for life, and only a minuscule portion of the universe is hospitable.

Inconstant Constants

The various numbers invoked in the "fine-tuning" argument for our universe being special, such as the speed of light and Planck's constant, are, in fact, arbitrary numbers that can be configured in different ways so that their relationship to the other constants do not appear to be so remarkable. As well, such constants may be *inconstant* over vast spans of time, varying from the Big Bang to the present, making the universe finely tuned only *now* but not earlier or later in its history. The physicists Barrow and John Webb call these numbers the "inconstant constants," and they have demonstrated how the speed of light, gravitation, and the mass of the electron have in fact been inconstant over time.[14]

Grand Unified Theory

In order to explain our universe, we need a comprehensive theory of physics that connects the subatomic world described by quantum mechanics to the cosmic world described by general relativity. As the cosmologist Sean Carroll notes in *From Eternity to Here*:

> Possibly general relativity is not the correct theory of gravity, at least in the context of the extremely early universe. Most physicists suspect that a quantum theory of gravity, reconciling the framework of quantum mechanics with Einstein's ideas about curved spacetime, will ultimately be required to make sense of what happens at the very earliest times. So if someone asks you what really happened at the moment of the purported Big Bang, the only honest answer would be: "I don't know."[15]

That grand unified theory of everything will itself need an explanation, but it may be explicable by some other theory we have yet to comprehend out of our sheer ignorance at the moment. In the meantime, it's always okay to say "I don't know."

Boom-and-Bust Cycles

Perhaps our bubble universe is just one episode of eternal boom-and-bust cycles of expansion and contractions of the universe. Carroll argues "that space and time did exist before the Big Bang; what we call the Bang is a kind of transition from one phase to another." As such, he says, "there is no such thing as an initial state, because time is eternal. In this case, we are imagining that the Big Bang isn't the beginning of the entire universe, although it's obviously an important event in the history of our local region."[16] Although there does not appear to be enough matter in our universe to halt the expansion and bring it back into a big crunch that could launch it into a new bubble out of another Big Bang, the relevant observation here is that something existed before the Big Bang, thereby obviating the need to invoke a supernatural creator.[17]

As well, the cosmologist Kelsey Johnson, in *Into the Unknown*, argues that the Big Bang wasn't an actual explosion, as the name suggests, but rather a rapid expansion as described by inflation theory and that our concepts based on everyday life—like explosions—do not necessarily apply to the origin of the universe.[18]

Darwinian Universes

According to the cosmologist Lee Smolin, the evolution of the universe may include a Darwinian component in the form of a "natural selection" of differentially reproducing bubble universes. Like its biological counterpart, Smolin's hypothesis is that there might be a selection from different "species" of universes, each containing different laws of nature. Universes like ours will have lots of stars. This means they will have lots of black holes that collapse into singularities, a point at which infinitely strong gravity causes matter to have infinite density and zero volume, which many cosmologists believe gave birth to our universe from the Big Bang singularity. Perhaps collapsing black holes create new baby universes out of these singularities, and those baby universes with laws of nature similar to ours will be fine-tuned to life, whereas universes with radically different laws of nature that disallow stars, planets, and people will go extinct. The result of this cosmic evolutionary process would be a preponderance of universes like ours, so we should not be surprised to find ourselves in a universe fine-tuned for life.[19]

Multiple Creations Cosmology

In *The Inflationary Universe*, the cosmologist Alan Guth proposes that our universe sprang into existence from a bubble nucleation of space-time. If this process of universe creation is natural, then there may be multiple bubble nucleations that give rise to many universes that expand but remain separate from one another without any causal contact between them. Of course, if these universes were truly causally disconnected, then there is no way to get information from them, which would make this an untestable hypothesis.[20] But, again, there is much we still don't know about the cosmos, and I am encouraged by the discovery of gravitational waves, which could open up possibilities of obtaining information from other bubble universes, if they exist.

Many Worlds

According to the "many worlds" interpretation of quantum mechanics, there are an infinite number of universes in which every possible outcome of every possible choice that has ever been available, or will be available, has happened in one of those universes. This model is grounded in the bizarre findings of the famous "double-slit" experiment, in which light is passed through two slits and forms an interference pattern of waves on a surface (like throwing two stones in a pond and watching the concentric wave patterns interact, with crests and troughs adding and subtracting from one another). The spooky part comes when you send single photons of light one at a time through the two slits—they still form an interference wave pattern even though they are not interacting with other photons. How can this be?

One answer is that the photons are interacting with photons in other universes! In this many-worlds view, you could meet your doppelganger, and depending on which universe you entered, your parallel self would be fairly similar to you, a theme that has become a staple of science fiction (see, for example, Michael Crichton's *Timeline*). I am skeptical that this theory will pan out, because the idea of there being multiple versions of me and you out there—and in an infinite universe, there would be an infinite number of mes and yous—seems to me to be even less likely than the theistic alternative "God did it." Still, as Richard Feynman famously quipped, "no one understands quantum mechanics,"[21] so who am I to write off this theory considered legitimate by many quantum physicists?

Brane and String Universes

Universes may be birthed when three-dimensional "branes" (a membrane-like structure on which our universe exists) move through higher-dimensional space and collide with another brane, the result of which is the energized creation of another universe.[22] A related multiverse is derived through string theory, which by at least one calculation allows for 10^{500} possible worlds, all with different self-consistent laws and constants.[23] That's a 1 followed by 500 zeroes possible universes. The number is so large that it would be miraculous if there were not intelligent life in a number of them. In *God: The Failed Hypothesis*, Stenger created a computer model that analyzes what just 100 different universes would be like under constants different from our own, ranging from five orders of magnitude above to five orders of magnitude below their values in our universe. Stenger found that long-lived stars of at least one billion years—necessary for the production of life-giving heavy elements—would emerge within a wide range of parameters in at least half of the universes in his model.[24]

Quantum Foam Universe Creations

In this model, universes are created out of nothing, but in the scientific version of *ex nihilo*, the nothing of the vacuum of space actually contains quantum foam, which may fluctuate to create baby universes—any quantum object in any quantum state may generate a new universe, each one of which represents every possible state of every possible object.[25] In response to Hawking's outline of the fine-tuning problem, his collaborator Roger Penrose layered on even more mystery when he noted that the "extraordinary degree of precision (or 'fine tuning') that seems to be required for the Big Bang of the nature that we appear to observe . . . is one part in $_{10}10^{123}$ at least." Penrose suggested two pathways to an answer: either it was an act of God, "or we might seek some scientific/mathematical theory."[26] Hawking opted for the second with this explanation: "Quantum fluctuations lead to the spontaneous creation of tiny universes, out of nothing. Most of the universes collapse to nothing, but a few that reach a critical size, will expand in an inflationary manner, and will form galaxies and stars, and maybe beings like us."[27]

M-Theory Grand Design

Hawking continued working on this question, and he and the physicist Leonard Mlodinow presented their answer in *The Grand Design*.[28] They approach the problem from what they call "model-dependent realism," and to model the entire universe, Hawking and Mlodinow employ "M-theory," an extension of string theory that includes 11 dimensions and incorporates all five current string theory models. "M-theory is the most general supersymmetric theory of gravity," they explain. "For these reasons M-theory is the only candidate for a complete theory of the universe. If it is finite—and this has yet to be proved—it will be a model of a universe that creates itself." Although they admit that the theory has yet to be confirmed by observation, if it is, then no creator explanation is necessary because the universe creates itself.

The Multiverse

The term *multiverse*—an obvious linguistic extension of a *universe*[29]—has been a staple of science fiction through such films as *Doctor Strange in the Multiverse of Madness*, *Sliding Doors*, *Coherence*, *Run Lola Run*, and the Oscar-winning *Everything Everywhere All at Once*. There are now so many types of multiverses, in fact, that the physicist Max Tegmark has built a taxonomy of them, including two types in cosmology, the many-worlds interpretation in physics, and various mathematical versions.[30] The physicist Paul Halpern also considers multiple dimensions as possible sources for a multiverse of universes—10^{500} "ways of curling up the extra dimensions, each of which specifies a kind of universe."[31] Halpern puts it all into perspective in *The Allure of the Multiverse*: "In tandem with trying to map out the knowable, speculation about realms beyond is one of humanity's most ancient pursuits. In many cases, such as the assertion by sixteenth-century Italian philosopher Giordano Bruno that there are myriad worlds in space—which led, in part, to him being burned at the stake—such ruminations have eventually proven accurate."[32]

Predictably, theists do not like the idea of a multiverse. Cardinal Christoph Schönborn opined in the *New York Times* that "the multiverse hypothesis in cosmology [was] invented to avoid the overwhelming evidence for purpose and design found in modern science."[33] The theologian William Lane Craig insists that "the proponents of chance have been forced to postulate the existence of a World Ensemble of other universes, preferably infinite in number and randomly ordered, so that life-permitting universes will appear by chance somewhere in the Ensemble."[34] But as we have seen, the multiverse concept was not invented to hand-wave away the God hypothesis. "It is the conclusion of our best current models of cosmology based on the extremely precise observations of modern astronomy and our best knowledge of fundamental physics," explains Stenger in *God and the Multiverse*. "The multiverse is a legitimate scientific hypothesis since it seems to be an unavoidable consequence of eternal inflation, the current model of the early universe, which is based on our best observational data."[35]

The idea of a multiverse is the next natural step in our expanding knowledge of the cosmos—the Copernican revolution that overturned the medieval worldview with the Earth at the center and the stars and planets rotating close by on their crystal spheres and created within the last 10,000 years, to the early-modern worldview of the Milky Way galaxy as the entire known universe created within the last several million years, to the modern worldview of an accelerating expanding universe of some 13.8 billion years, to a multiverse of perhaps infinite age and containing possibly an infinite number of universes.

To think that all this—the universe, multiverse, or whatever it turns out to be—was created for just one species among tens of millions of species who live on one planet circling one of a couple of hundred billion stars that are located in one galaxy among hundreds of billions of galaxies, all of

Figure 12.1. A James Webb Space Telescope image of Pandora's Cluster, showing gravitational lensing, one image among many that inspires us to consider the deepest of all questions: Why is there something rather than nothing? NASA, ESA, CSA, I. Labbe (Swinburne University of Technology), R. Bezanson (University of Pittsburgh), A. Pagan (STScI). Public domain

which are in one universe among perhaps an infinite number of universes all nestled within a grand cosmic multiverse, would be provincially insular and anthropocentrically blinkered (figure 12.1). It is *not* all about us.

A Sense of Awe out of Nothing

This analysis does not exhaust the possible explanations for why there is something rather than nothing and why our universe is the way it is, but perhaps it gives one a sense that the questions are answerable through science—the best tool we have for determining the truth—and through natural and testable hypotheses and theories, without resorting to supernatural intercession.

In their book *The Battle of the Big Bang*, the physicist Niayesh Afshordi and science writer Phil Halper offer "a glimpse of science at the edge of the knowledge, past the cutoff; to show that it involves not just theoretical conjectures, equations, and experiments, but is also a human process, full of conflict and emotion: bitterness, hope, doubt, and belief." After reviewing the most prominent scientific theories for why there is something rather than nothing, what caused the Big Bang to bang, the origin of time, why the Big Bang does not prove that the universe had a beginning (it might be cyclical), and why our universe is apparently so finely tuned for matter, life, and consciousness, in the end they advise readers that "The phrase *follow the science* should really be amended to *follow the science and embrace uncertainty*." That uncertainty includes the theistic claim that the Big Bang proves the universe had a beginning and that since something cannot come from nothing there must be a deity behind it all, which Afshordi and Halper dispense thusly:

> We are on the edge of knowledge, not knowing if glories or ruin await. But while we currently cannot conclude in favor of any one model, the fact that the debate is still ongoing can have major implications for the way scientists understand cosmology. One thing we hope you appreciate from this book is that the certainty that the universe was born a finite time ago in a state of infinite density is now gone, replaced by a lineup of fascinating candidates, some that might restore an ultimate beginning and others that promise an eternal cosmos. This is the quiet revolution of twenty-first-century cosmology.[36]

It is good to reflect on the fact that the history of science is relatively young compared to the history of religion—roughly 500 versus 5,000 years—so it is premature to say that because science does not yet have a definitive explanatory theory accepted by most scientists, one is not forthcoming. There is still much we do not understand about the cosmos and everything in it. But given science's track record over the past five centuries, this only means there are remarkable and exciting new discoveries and theories yet to come. As Carl Sagan said in his 1985 Gifford Lecture Series titled *The Search for Who We Are*:

> By far the best way I know to engage the religious sensibility, the sense of awe, is to look up on a clear night. I believe that it is very difficult to know who we are until we understand where and when we are. I think everyone in every culture has felt a sense of awe and wonder looking at the sky. This is reflected throughout the world in both science and religion.[37]

Whether or not these grand mysteries are soluble by science remains an open question, but that we can even conceive of them as problems is a tribute to our species and one that gives us our name, *Homo sapiens*, Latin for *wise man*.

EPILOGUE

Like Gods The Expanding Sphere of Knowledge and My God Gambit

■ The history of science has been one long and steady replacement of unjustified false belief with justified true belief, most notably the displacement of the supernatural with the natural, the paranormal with the normal, and bad explanations with good explanations. Weather events once attributed to the supernatural scheming of demons and deities are now understood to be the product of natural forces of temperature and pressure. Plagues formerly ascribed to female witches cavorting with the devil are today known to be caused by bacteria and viruses. The causes of mental illnesses, which were previously imputed to demonic possession, are now known to stem from genes and neurochemistry. Accidents heretofore explained by fate, Karma, or providence are nowadays accredited to probabilities, statistics, and chance.

If we follow this trend to encompass all phenomena, what place is there for supernatural agents and paranormal forces? Do we know enough to know that they cannot exist? Is it possible there are unknown forces within our universe or intentional agents outside of it that we have yet to discover? According to the physicist Sean Carroll, in his book *The Big Picture*, "All of the things you've ever seen or experienced in your life—objects, plants, animals, people—are made of a small number of particles, interacting with one another through a small number of forces."[1] Once you understand the fundamental laws of nature, such as the thermodynamic arrow of time and the core theory of particles and forces, you can scale up to planets and people and even assess the likelihood that God, the soul, and the afterlife exist, which I conclude is very low.

But didn't they say that in the late nineteenth century, just before the development of the theories of relativity and quantum mechanics? Isn't the history of science strewn with the remains of failed theories like geocentrism (Earth as the center of the solar system), phlogiston (a fire-like element that causes objects to burn), miasma (the "bad air" source of disease), spontaneous generation (fully formed living organisms can abruptly arise out of inanimate matter), and the luminiferous aether (the medium filling outer space for the propagation of light)? Isn't it possible that our current best theories—as well supported as they are—may one day go the way of Aristotelian physics, Ptolemaic astronomy, the flat Earth theory, the four bodily humors theory of disease, phrenology, creationism, vitalism, alchemy, astrology, psychoanalysis, and the steady state theory of the cosmos?

As we look back on these erroneous scientific theories from centuries past with disdainful dismissal, will scientists in the 25th—or the 250th or 2,500th—century look down upon us as we do medieval physicians who believed that the four bodily humors (black bile, phlegm, blood, and yellow bile) were linked to the four elements of nature (earth, water, air, and fire) that caused the four personality temperaments (melancholic, phlegmatic, sanguine, and choleric), all of which were linked to the zodiacal signs in the heavens?

Not likely. And that's how we know we're making progress. The postmodern belief that discarded ideas mean that there is no objective truth and that all theories are equal is more wrong than all of the wrong theories combined. I have called this *Asimov's axiom*, after an observation by the science writer Isaac Asimov: "When people thought the earth was flat, they were wrong. When people thought the earth was spherical, they were wrong. But if you think that thinking the earth is spherical is just as wrong as thinking the earth is flat, then your view is wronger than both of them put together."[2]

Think of science as an expanding sphere of knowledge. As the sphere of the known expands into the ether of the unknown, the proportion of ignorance seems to grow—*the more you know, the more you know how much you don't know*. But in this mathematical metaphor, note what happens when the radius of a sphere increases: The expansion of the surface area is squared, while the increase in the volume is cubed. So as the sphere of scientific knowledge expands, the volume of the known increases by a ratio of 3:2 over the surface area of the unknown—*the more you know, the more of the unknown becomes known*. It is at this boundary where we can stake a claim of true progress in the search for truth.

Yet, it is also at the horizon where the known meets the unknown that so many of us are tempted to inject supernatural or paranormal forces to explain hitherto unsolved mysteries. We must resist the temptation, for such efforts can never succeed, not even in principle. So, I end this journey on the search for truth by returning to the definition of God as omnipotent and omniscient and the proposition that none of us are God, so absolute truth about anything will forever be beyond our reach—or will it?

■

In our search for truth using the tools of science, we make certain assumptions, one of the deepest of which is *methodological naturalism*—which holds that life, the universe, and everything are the result of natural processes in a system of material causes and effects that does not allow, or need, the introduction of *supernatural* forces or beings. Theists complain that this is too restrictive because it limits the search for God to only natural causes and that anyone who postulates that there are supernatural forces at work in the natural world are being unfairly ignored based on nothing more than an arbitrary rule in the game of science.

Okay, let's change the rules. Let's adopt into science *methodological supernaturalism*. What would that look like? How would it work? How can natural beings understand or measure something that by definition is outside of nature? And even if there is a supernatural creator God, how does said being reach into our world to stir the particles to, say, perform miracles? So far, theists are silent when I press them with such questions, along with this one: How could we distinguish an omnipotent and omniscient God or intelligent designer from an extremely powerful and really smart extraterrestrial intelligence (ETI) or a far-future human with artificial intelligence approaching omniscience? That is, if we go in search of such a being—as both theists and atheists claim to be doing in treating God as an empirical truth claim—we encounter a problem that I called (*pace* Arthur C. Clarke) Shermer's last law,[3] though I now call it my God gambit:

> *Any sufficiently advanced extraterrestrial intelligence or far-future human is indistinguishable from God.*[4]

My gambit arises from an integration of evolutionary theory, intelligent design creationism, theology, the search for extraterrestrial intelligence, and artificial intelligence and can be derived from three observations and deductions.

Observation 1: Compared to technological development, biological evolution is glacially slow because it requires generations of differential reproductive success. On evolutionary scales, time is measured in thousands and millions of years. By contrast, technological development happens in single generations or in single years, months, or even days.

Deduction 1: The odds of discovering an ETI whose biological and technological development are in lockstep with our own is virtually nil.

Observation 2: The space between galaxies is so vast (on the order of millions of light years) and the space between stars within a galaxy is so enormous (on the order of dozens or hundreds of light years) that the probability of making contact with an ETI is remote.

Deduction 2: The odds of encountering an ETI is vanishingly small, but if we did, because of the first observation and deduction, it would either be way behind us (so we would need to visit their planet to find them) or way ahead of us (so we would need to detect their radio signals, their biosignatures in their planet's atmosphere, or their techno-signatures like orbiting solar panels, interstellar probes, or, even less likely, spaceships visiting Earth).

Observation 3: Given the fact that our own science and technology have changed more in the past century than in the previous hundred centuries, we can apply Moore's law of computing power doubling every 12 to 18 months as an analogue for other technologies whose rate of change is best described as exponential.[5]

Deduction 3: Any ETI or far-future human will be so much more advanced than us that they will be, relatively speaking, indistinguishable from omniscience—not decades or centuries ahead of us, but hundreds of thousands or even millions of years more advanced.

If this were to happen, it is entirely possible that ETIs—or far-future humans—would be immortal, inasmuch as there is no known mechanism, short of the end of the universe itself trillions of years from now in our accelerating expanding cosmos,[6] to cause the extinction of all planetary and solar systems at once.[7] In the far future, with artificial intelligence so far beyond anything we can conceive of now and the concomitant science and technology applied to solving problems, civilizations may become sufficiently advanced to colonize entire galaxies, genetically engineer new life forms, terraform planets, trigger the birth of stars and new planetary solar systems through massive engineering projects, and even create new universes out of collapsing black holes at the center of which are singularities that some cosmologists think are the spark of creation.[8] Civilizations this advanced would have so much knowledge and power as to be essentially omniscient and omnipotent.[9]

If this all sounds impossibly crazy—or even hallucinatory—our distant ancestors would have felt the same way about many of the technologies we take for granted today, starting with the computer in your pocket that grants you instant access to almost all the world's knowledge and enables you to take high-resolution photographs and video, communicate with almost anyone anywhere in the world instantly, and participate in countless other activities via the internet. To our Bronze Age ancestors who created the great monotheistic religions of Judaism, Christianity, and Islam, the ability to create the universe, the world, and life seemed the province of a God-like supernatural being. Once we know the science and technology of creation, however, the supernatural becomes the natural. By this account, then, the only God that science could discover would be a natural being, an entity that exists in space and time and is constrained by the laws of nature. Thus my gambit:

> *What would we call an intelligent being capable of engineering life, planets, stars, and even universes? If we knew the underlying science and technology used to do the engineering, we would call it an extraterrestrial intelligence or a far-future human; if we did not know the underlying science and technology, we would call it God.*

Thus it is that in our search for truth, we may find that some other intelligent sentient being has already achieved omniscience, or, in the fullness of time, we may become gods ourselves.

ACKNOWLEDGMENTS

■ In my 30 years of writing books published by major trade and academic publishing houses, second to none is the team at Johns Hopkins University Press, including Laura Davulis, Ezra Rodriguez, Robert Brown, Jennifer D'Urso, and Amy Azmoun. While I love digital and audio books, I'm old-school and still love physical books—hardback and paperback—there to hold in my hands, flip their pages, and appreciate their typography, layout, design, and even paper quality, binding, and cover. Thanks to my agent, Christopher Rogers, who brought this and my previous book to fruition.

From my day job of editing and publishing *Skeptic* magazine and running the Skeptics Society, special thanks to *Skeptic* Art Director William Bull; the CSO of the Skeptics Society and producer and engineer of my podcast, Alexander Reiman; Senior Editor Frank Miele, Copy Editor Barry Bakalor, and my colleagues in running the Skeptic Research Center, Anondah Saide and Kevin McCaffree. And as always my gratitude to my late partner and cofounder of the Skeptics Society and *Skeptic* magazine, Pat Linse.

For this book, I am especially grateful to the three anonymous reviewers who offered their honest and critical comments, which contributed greatly to improving its arguments and presentation, and to colleagues and friends with whom I consulted on the many subjects covered within it, usually on my podcast that often included topics addressed in this book, including (in no particular order): Steven Pinker, Richard Dawkins, Jared Diamond, Robert Sapolsky, Emilie Caspar, Gad Saad, Michio Kaku, Paul Ehrlich, Mark Skousen, Tanya Luhrmann, Jonathan Rauch, Kennon Sheldon, Gerald Posner, Bart Ehrman, Kevin Kelly, Kieran Fox, Paul Bloom, Lee McIntyre, Jamie Q. Roberts, Nancy Segal, Avi Loeb, Christopher Chabris, Kurt Gray, Amanda Knox, Joshua Greene, Amir Raz, Guy Harrison, Dan Barker, Kelsey Johnson, Paul Seabright, Colin Wright, Jeffrey Kripal, Katherine Stewart, Will Gervais, Ben Goertzel, Helen Pluckrose, Elizabeth Weiss, Matt Ridley, Sara Imari Walker, Sebastian Junger, Jay Bhattacharya, John Mackey, Robert Powell, Neil Van Leeuwen, Marc Hauser, Bradley Campbell, Sean Carroll, Christof Koch, Tom Chivers, Lisa Kaltenegger, Bruce Hood, Annie Jacobsen, Nick Bostrom, Robert Zubrin, Lance Grande, Maggie Jackson, Eric Schwitzgebel, Samuel Wilkinson, Byron Reese, Tali Sharot, Brian Klaas, Chris Anderson, Paul Halpern, Philip Goff, Adam Frank, Garrett Graff, Yascha Mounk, Dan Ariely, Greg Lukianoff, Rikki Schlott, Niayesh Afshordi, Phil Halper, Scott Barry Kaufman, and others.

Special thanks to Daniel Dennett—the dedicatee of this book—who passed away while I was writing the final chapters on consciousness, free will, God, and existence, whose influence on my thinking on these, and many other topics, is unmeasurable.

Finally, I acknowledge the truth about the most important people in my life: my wife, Jennifer, my son, Vincent, and my daughter, Devin. Without their love, nothing else really matters.

NOTES

Prologue

1. Lauren Leatherby et al., "How a Presidential Rally Turned into a Capitol Rampage," *New York Times*, January 12, 2021, https://nyti.ms/3vl9PAP.
2. See, for example, the 1949 Supreme Court case of *Terminiello v. Chicago*.
3. William Saletan, "Republicans Still Sympathize with the Insurrection," *Slate*, April 15, 2021, https://bit.ly/3uV8jA3.
4. The documentary's webpage is here: *The Insurrectionist Next Door*, HBO, accessed April 22, 2025, https://www.hbo.com/movies/the-insurrectionist-next-door.
5. Here is a short clip with the now-famous quote: "Rumsfeld / Knowns," CNN, posted March 31, 2016, YouTube, 26 sec., accessed April 25, 2025, https://www.youtube.com/watch?v=REWeBzGuzCc. The full press conference is here: "Defense Department Briefing," C-SPAN, February 12, 2002, https://www.c-span.org/video/?168646-1/defense-department-briefing.
6. Wikipedia, "There are unknown unknowns," last modified April 9, 2025, https://en.wikipedia.org/wiki/There_are_unknown_unknowns.
7. Michael Shermer, *Why People Believe Weird Things* (1997; Henry Holt, rev. ed. 2022).

1 The Truth About Post-Truth Truthiness

1. Stephen Colbert, "Truthiness" episode, *The Colbert Report*, Comedy Central, October 17, 2005.
2. Interview with Kellyanne Conway, *Meet the Press*, NBC, January 22, 2017.

3. *Collins Dictionary*, "fake news," accessed April 4, 2025, https://bit.ly/2V7Ff7Q.
4. Steven Pinker, "Why We Are Not Living in a Post-Truth Era," *Skeptic* 24, no. 3 (2019).
5. Ian Betteridge, "TechCrunch: Irresponsible Journalism," Technovia.co.uk, February 26, 2009.
6. Pinker, "Why We Are Not."
7. Steven Pinker, *Enlightenment Now: The Case for Reason, Science, Humanism, and Progress* (Viking, 2018), 375.
8. Lee McIntyre, *Post-Truth* (MIT Press, 2018).
9. Lee McIntyre, "Why We *Are* Living in a Post-Truth Era," *Skeptic* 25, no. 1 (2020), https://www.skeptic.com/reading_room/why-we-are-living-in-a-post-truth-era/.
10. McIntyre, "Why We *Are*."
11. Jason Stanley, *How Propaganda Works* (Princeton University Press, 2015).
12. Timothy Snyder, *On Tyranny: Twenty Lessons from the Twentieth Century* (Tim Duggan Books, 2017), 71.
13. Hannah Arendt, *The Origins of Totalitarianism* (1951; Harcourt, 1994), 474.
14. Keith E. Stanovich, *The Bias That Divides Us: The Science and Politics of Myside Thinking* (MIT Press, 2021).
15. Stanovich, *The Bias That Divides Us*, 1.
16. Michael Shermer, *Why People Believe Weird Things* (1997; Henry Holt, rev. ed. 2022).
17. Stanovich, *The Bias That Divides Us*, 3–4.
18. The video of Feynman's public statement is available online: "Challenger Disaster," posted January 27, 2013, YouTube, 4 min., 14 sec., accessed April 4, 2025, https://bit.ly/2SmJltv.
19. W. P. Rogers, N. A. Armstrong, D. C. Acheson, E. E. Covert, R. P. Feynman, R. B. Holtz, D. J. Kutyna, S. K. Ride, R. W. Rummel, and J. F. Sutter. *Report of the Presidential Commission on the Space Shuttle Challenger Accident*, NASA, June 6, 1986. https://ntrs.nasa.gov/citations/19860015255.
20. Richard Feynman, "Appendix F: Personal Observations on the Reliability of the Shuttle," *Report of the Presidential Commission on the Space Shuttle Challenger Accident*, NASA, June 6, 1986.
21. Sandra Harding, *The Science Question in Feminism* (Cornell University Press, 1987), 113.
22. Norman Levitt, "More Higher Superstitions: Knowledge, Knowingness, and Reality," *Skeptic* 4, no. 4 (1997).
23. Alan Sokal, "Transgressing the Boundaries: Toward a Transformative Hermeneutics of Quantum Gravity," *Social Text* 46/47 (1996): 217–52.
24. Sokal, "Transgressing."

25. See also Sokal's book-length treatment of the hoax and its effects: Alan Sokal, *Beyond the Hoax: Science, Philosophy and Culture* (Oxford University Press, 2008).
26. Jamie Lindsay and Peter Boyle [James Lindsay and Peter Bohossian], "The Conceptual Penis as a Social Construct," *Cogent Social Sciences* 3 (2017): 1330439.
27. Gordon Pennycook and James Allan Cheyne, "On the Reception and Detection of Pseudo-Profound Bullshit," *Judgment and Decision Making* 10, no. 6 (2015): 549–63.
28. Paul Gross and Norman Levitt, *Higher Superstition: The Academic Left and Its Quarrels with Science* (Johns Hopkins University Press, 1994).
29. Naomi Oreskes, *Why Trust Science?* (Princeton University Press, 2019), 53.
30. Oreskes, *Why Trust Science?*, 53.
31. Oreskes, *Why Trust Science?*, 53.
32. " 'Post-Truth' Declared Word of the Year by Oxford Dictionaries," *BBC News*, November 16, 2016, https://bbc.in/2Vh36lt.
33. Quoted in Tom Glaisyer, "Cranking Up the Truth-o-Meter: Giving a Boost to Truth in Politics," Democracy Fund, January 13, 2016, https://bit.ly/2M8p7yK.
34. Batya Ungar-Sargon, *Bad News: How Woke Media Is Undermining Democracy* (Encounter Books, 2021).
35. Ungar-Sargon, *Bad News*.
36. Ungar-Sargon, *Bad News*. See also my podcast conversation with Ungar-Sargon: Michael Shermer, host, *The Michael Shermer Show*, podcast, episode 260, April 4, 2022, https://www.skeptic.com/michael-shermer-show/page/17/.
37. Ungar-Sargon, *Bad News*.
38. Hugo Mercier, *Not Born Yesterday: The Science of Who We Trust and What We Believe* (Princeton University Press, 2020), 257, 270–1. Quotes from Brennan are in Jason Brennan, *Against Democracy* (Princeton University Press, 2019), 8.
39. See, for example, Adam Levin, *Swiped: How to Protect Yourself in a World Full of Scammers, Phishers, and Identity Thieves* (Public Affairs, 2015).
40. Ian Kershaw, "How Effective Was Nazi Propaganda?," in *Nazi Propaganda: The Power and the Limitations*, ed. D. Welch (Croom Helm, 1983), 199.
41. Michael W. Macy, Robb Willer, and Ko Kuwabara, "The False Enforcement of Unpopular Norms," *American Journal of Sociology* 115, no. 2 (September 2009): 451–90.
42. Aleksandr Solzhenitsyn, "Part I: The Prison Industry," *The Gulag Archipelago I–II* (YMCA Press, 1973).
43. Steven Pinker, *Rationality: What It Is, Why It Seems Scarce, Why It Matters* (Penguin, 2021), 288.
44. Pinker, *Rationality*, 300.
45. Daniel DeNicola, "You Don't Have a Right to Believe Whatever You Want To,"

Aeon, May 14, 2018. See also Daniel DeNicola, *Understanding Ignorance: The Surprising Impact of What We Don't Know* (MIT Press, 2017).

46. DeNicola, "You Don't Have a Right."
47. Michael Shermer, "Factiness: Are We Living in a Post-Truth World?," *Scientific American*, March 7, 2018, https://bit.ly/2pHCzC5.

2 What Is Truth, Anyway?

1. Philip K. Dick, "How to Build a Universe That Doesn't Fall Apart Two Days Later," in *The Shifting Realities of Philip K. Dick: Selected Literary and Philosophical Writings* (Vintage, 1978).
2. We even made a video answering this question: "What Is a Skeptic?," *Skeptic*, posted September 18, 2013, 3 min., 54 sec., accessed April 7, 2025, https://youtu.be/MNCgGaeWwzw.
3. Oxford English Dictionary, "skeptic/sceptic," accessed 1997, https://www.oed.com/dictionary/sceptic_n.
4. See, for example, Donald Prothero, *Evolution: What the Fossils Say and Why it Matters*, 2nd ed. (Columbia University Press, 2017).
5. See, for example, Sean Carroll, *The Big Picture: On the Origin of Life, Meaning, and the Universe Itself* (Dutton, 2016).
6. Daniel C. Dennett, *I've Been Thinking* (W. W. Norton, 2023), 29.
7. Emphasis added. Stephen Jay Gould, "Evolution as Fact and Theory," in *Hen's Teeth and Horse's Toes* (W. W. Norton, 1994), 253–62.
8. "The Analysis of Knowledge," *Stanford Encyclopedia of Philosophy*, February 6, 2001, rev. March 7, 2017, https://plato.stanford.edu/entries/knowledge-analysis/.
9. E. L. Gettier, "Is Justified True Belief Knowledge?," *Analysis* 23, no. 6 (June 1963): 121–3.
10. Timothy Williamson, *Knowledge and its Limits* (Oxford University Press, 2000), 21.
11. Steven Pinker, *Rationality: What It Is, Why It Seems Scarce, Why It Matters* (Penguin, 2021), 40.
12. Charles Mackay, *Extraordinary Popular Delusions and the Madness of Crowds* (New York: Crown, 1841, 1852, 1980).
13. I visited Chopra's center to try out his meditation program and wrote about my experiences here: Michael Shermer, *Heavens on Earth: The Scientific Search for the Afterlife, Immortality, and Utopia* (Henry Holt, 2018), chapter 4.
14. E. S. Epel, E. Puterman, J. Lin, et al., "Meditation and Vacation Effects Have an Impact on Disease-Associated Molecular Phenotypes," *Translational Psychiatry* 6 (2016): e880, doi:10.1038/tp.2016.164. www.nature.com/tp.

15. The quote comes from Dr. Hardison's notes for the class, which I still have in my archives.
16. Carl Sagan, *The Demon-Haunted World: Science as a Candle in the Dark* (Random House, 1996), 171–3.
17. The original quote comes from a 2003 *Slate* column Hitchens wrote, which he repeated in his book: Christopher Hitchens, *God Is Not Great: How Religion Poisons Everything* (Hachette, 2007), 150. I elevated the quote into a dictum in: Michael Shermer, "The Skeptics' Skeptic," *Scientific American*, November 1, 2010, https://bit.ly/3sq0znW.
18. Carl Sagan, "Encyclopaedia Galactica," *Cosmos: A Personal Voyage*, episode 12, aired December 20, 1980, on PBS. Sagan, in fact, was quoting the lesser-known sociologist of science Marcello Truzzi, thereby confirming the observation that pithy and oft-quoted statements migrate up to the most famous person who said them, such as Mark Twain, Yogi Berra, Albert Einstein, and . . . Carl Sagan.
19. David Hume, *An Enquiry Concerning Human Understanding* (Cambridge, 1748; Repr., Cambridge University Press, 3rd ed. 1902).
20. Quoted in Patrizio E. Tressoldi, "Extraordinary Claims Require Extraordinary Evidence: The Case of Non-Local Perception, a Classical and Bayesian Review of Evidences," *Frontiers in Psychology* 2 (2011): 117.
21. I deal with these particular conspiracy claims here: Michael Shermer, *Conspiracy: Why the Rational Believe the Irrational* (Johns Hopkins University Press, 2022).
22. Michael Shermer, *The Believing Brain* (Henry Holt, 2011).
23. Michael Shermer, *Why People Believe Weird Things* (W. H. Freeman, 1997).
24. In Barry Singer and George O. Abell, *Science and the Paranormal: Probing the Existence of the Supernatural* (Scribner, 1981).
25. Philip E. Tetlock and Dan Gardner, *Superforecasting: The Art and Science of Prediction* (Broadway, 2010).
26. Gordon Pennycook, James Allan Cheyne, Derek J. Koehler, and Jonathan A. Fugelsang, "On the Belief that Beliefs Should Change According to Evidence: Implications for Conspiratorial, Moral, Paranormal, Political, Religious, and Science Beliefs," *Judgment and Decision Making* 15, no. 4 (July 2020): 476–98.
27. Gordon Pennycook and David G. Rand, "Who Falls for Fake News? The Roles of Bullshit Receptivity, Overclaiming, Familiarity, and Analytic Thinking," *Journal of Personality* (March 31, 2019), https://bit.ly/3e64QYC.
28. Steven Pinker, *Rationality: What It Is, Why It Seems Scarce, Why It Matters* (Viking, 2021).
29. Pinker, *Rationality*.
30. Cass R. Sunstein, *Going to Extremes: How Like Minds Unite and Divide* (Oxford University Press, 2009).

31. Sunstein, 2009, 20.
32. Lee McIntyre, *How to Talk to a Science Denier: Conversations with Flat Earthers, Climate Deniers, and Others Who Defy Reason* (MIT Press, 2021), 69–70.
33. Lee McIntyre, *On Disinformation: How to Fight for Truth and Protect Democracy* (MIT Press, 2023).
34. Michael Shermer, host, *The Michael Shermer Show*, podcast, episode 373, *Skeptic*, September 11, 2023, https://www.skeptic.com/michael-shermer-show/lee-mcintyre-disinformation-how-to-fight-for-truth-protect-democracy/.
35. Julia Galef, *The Scout Mindset: Why Some People See Things Clearly and Others Don't* (Portfolio, 2021).
36. Jonathan Rauch, *The Constitution of Knowledge: A Defense of Truth* (Brookings Institution, 2021).
37. Rauch, *The Constitution of Knowledge*, 100–2.
38. Rauch, *The Constitution of Knowledge*, 103–7.
39. John Stuart Mill, *On Liberty* (Dover, 1859, 2002).
40. Quoted by Christopher Hitchens, "On Free Speech," Genius, 2006, accessed April 7, 2025, https://bit.ly/2vPp4AI.
41. Michael Shermer, *Giving the Devil His Due: Reflections of a Scientific Humanist* (Cambridge University Press 2020), 7–8.
42. Michael Shermer, "It's Dogged as Does It," *Scientific American*, February 1, 2006.
43. Frank Sulloway, "Darwinian Psychobiography," *The New York Review*, October 10, 1991, https://www.nybooks.com/articles/1991/10/10/darwinian-psychobiography/.
44. In Francis Darwin, ed., *The Life and Letters of Charles Darwin*, vol. 1 (John Murray, 1887), 149.

3 The Truth About Why

1. David Hume, *An Enquiry Concerning Human Understanding*, ed. L. A. Selby Bigge (Clarendon, 1758, 1902).
2. David Hume, *A Treatise of Human Nature* (Oxford University Press, 1739, 2000). See also "David Hume: Causation," *Internet Encyclopedia of Philosophy*, accessed April 7, 2025, https://iep.utm.edu/hume-causation/.
3. You can see the episode here: "Michael Shermer Firewalking Across Hot Coals," *Skeptic*, posted June 2, 2007, YouTube, 6 min., 48 sec., accessed April 7, 2025, https://youtu.be/-W5FRl0qhOM.
4. Michael Shermer, *Why People Believe Weird Things* (W. H. Freeman, 1997), 18.
5. J. J. Ichikawa and M. Steup, "The Analysis of Knowledge," in *The Stanford Encyclope-*

dia of Philosophy, ed. E. N. Zalta (Summer 2018), Metaphysics Research Lab, Stanford University.

6. For philosophers who specialize in epistemology—the study of knowledge and how we obtain it—beliefs are "what we take to be the case or regard as true." See E. Schwitzgebel, "Belief," in *The Stanford Encyclopedia of Philosophy*, ed. E. N. Zalta (Winter 2021), Metaphysics Research Lab, Stanford University.
7. B. Dowden and N. Swartz, "Truth," *Internet Encyclopedia of Philosophy*, accessed July 23, 2023, https://iep.utm.edu/truth/.
8. S. Hetherington, "Gettier Problems," *Internet Encyclopedia of Philosophy*, accessed July 23, 2023, https://iep.utm.edu/gettier/.
9. Andrew Shtulman, *Scienceblind: Why Our Intuitive Theories About the World Are So Often Wrong* (Basic, 2017).
10. "The Scientific Method—Richard Feynman," Sképseis, posted January 20, 2013, YouTube, 1 min., 2 sec., accessed April 7, 2025, https://tinyurl.com/yrfc42ur.
11. Vincent Dethier, *To Know a Fly* (Holden-Day, 1962), 18–19.
12. Lionel Ruby, *The Art of Making Sense: A Guide to Logical Thinking*, 2nd ed. (J. B. Lippincott, 1968), 218.
13. Bertrand Russell, "On the Nature of Truth," *Proceedings of the Aristotelian Society* 7 (1906): 28–49; G. E. Moore, "Truth and Falsity," in *Selected Writings*, ed. T. Baldwin (Routledge, 1901–1902). See also Richard L. Kirkham, *Theories of Truth: A Critical Introduction* (MIT Press, 1992).
14. Karl Popper, *Conjectures and Refutations* (Routledge & Kegan Paul, 1963). See also Karl Popper, *The Logic of Scientific Discovery* (Basic, 1959).
15. Patrick Moynihan, Op-Ed, *The Washington Post*, January 18, 1983. See also sources that attribute the quote to other people: "Quote Origin: People Are Entitled to Their Own Opinions but Not to Their Own Facts," Quote Investigator, March 17, 2020, https://rb.gy/v08zza.
16. Thanks to Arthur Benjamin, professor of mathematics at Harvey Mudd College and the famous mathemagician, for this calculation.
17. You can see Randi do this trick at: Big Think "James Randi: Performing a Magic Trick." May 20, 2011: https://youtu.be/Nf6hRIbtylw?t=62.
18. You can see Lennart perform this and other card tricks at: TED2005, filmed February 2005: https://www.ted.com/talks/lennart_green_close_up_card_magic_with_a_twist.
19. There are many studies answering this question, almost all of which agree that a college degree pays off financially in the long run. For example: Kat Tretina, "Is College Worth the Cost? Pros vs. Cons," *Forbes*, June 21, 2022, https://rb.gy/885xhw. See

also Jessica Blake, "Is College Worth it? Recent Analysis Says Yes," *Inside Higher Ed*, June 22, 2023, https://rb.gy/z3o9b5; Marisol Cuellar Mejia, Cesar Alesi Perez, Vicki Hsieh, and Hans Johnson, "Is College Worth It?," Public Policy Institute of California, accessed April 8, 2025, https://rb.gy/w2ntxs; and "Rising Above the Threshold: How to Increase Equitable Postsecondary Value," Institute for Higher Education Policy, June 2023, https://rb.gy/t5cbo8.

20. Richard Boddy and Gordon Smith, *Statistical Methods in Practice: For Scientists and Technologists* (Wiley, 2009).
21. B. S. Everitt, *Cambridge Dictionary of Statistics*, 2nd ed. (Cambridge University Press, 2002), 78.
22. N. G. Waller, B. Kojetin, T. Bouchard, D. Lykken, and A. Tellegen, "Genetic and Environmental Influences on Religious Attitudes and Values: A Study of Twins Reared Apart and Together," *Psychological Science* 1, no. 2 (1990): 138–42.
23. Reported in Michael Shermer, *How We Believe: Science, Skepticism, and the Search for God*, 2nd ed. (Henry Holt, 2003).
24. Although the effect may be weak: Tyler Cowen, "The Link Between IQ and Income Is Overrated," *MarginalRevolution.com*, March 3, 2023.
25. Yoosoon Chang, Steven N. Durlauf, Seunghee Lee, and Joon Y. Park, "A Trajectories-Based Approach to Measuring Intergenerational Mobility," Becker Friedman Institute, March 22, 2023.
26. James P. Smith, "Healthy Bodies and Thick Wallets: The Dual Relation Between Health and Economic Status," *Journal of Economic Perspectives* (Spring 1999): 144–66.
27. Judea Pearl, "Simpson's Paradox, Confounding and Collapsibility," in *Causality: Models, Reasoning and Inference* (Cambridge University Press, 2009); K. J. Jager, C. Zoccali, A. MacLeod, and F. W. Dekker, "Confounding: What It Is and How to Deal with It," *Kidney International* 73, no. 3 (2008): 256–60.
28. Judea Pearl and Dana Mackenzie, *The Book of Why: The New Science of Cause and Effect* (Basic, 2018).
29. Jared Diamond and James A. Robinson, eds., *Natural Experiments of History* (Harvard University Press, 2011).
30. For more on how the uncertainty of the causal link between smoking and cancer was exploited by tobacco companies, see Naomi Oreskes and Erik M. Conway, *Merchants of Doubt: How a Handful of Scientists Obscured the Truth on Issues from Tobacco Smoke to Climate Change* (Bloomsbury, 2010).
31. Michael Greger, *How Not to Age: The Scientific Approach to Getting Healthier as You Get Older* (Flatiron, 2023).
32. Ignacio Amigo, "Shades of Blue: Blue Zones, Supposed Havens of Longevity, Have

Become a Global Brand. But Skeptics Think They Rest on Shaky Science," *Science*, November 21, 2024.

33. Nancy Segal, *Entwined Lives: Twins and What They Tell Us About Human Behavior* (Dutton, 1999).
34. Kathryn Paige Harden, *The Genetic Lottery: Why DNA Matters for Social Equality* (Princeton University Press, 2021).
35. For a highly readable and excellent overview of Bayesian statistics, see Tom Chivers, *Everything Is Predictable: How Bayesian Statistics Explain Our World* (Atria, 2024).
36. "Quote Origin: When the Facts Change, I Change My Mind. What Do You Do, Sir?," Quote Investigator, July 22, 2011, https://quoteinvestigator.com/2011/07/22/keynes-change-mind/.
37. H. Lin, "Bayesian Epistemology," in *The Stanford Encyclopedia of Philosophy*, ed. E. N. Zalta and U. Nodelman (Fall 2022), Metaphysics Research Lab, Stanford University, https://t.ly/C_7Ae.
38. A. Norman, *Mental Immunity: Infectious Ideas, Mind-Parasites, and the Search for a Better Way to Think* (Harper Wave, 2021).
39. Ed Gibney and Zafir Ivanov, "Reason's Fulcrum: How Bayesian Reasoning Can Set Us Free From the Search for Absolute Truth," *Skeptic* 28, no. 4 (2023).
40. Gibney and Ivanov, "Reason's Fulcrum."
41. Gerd Gigerenzer, *Rationality for Mortals: How People Cope with Uncertainty* (Oxford University Press, 2008).
42. Amos Tversky and Daniel Kahneman, "Judgment Under Uncertainty: Heuristics and Biases," *Science* 185 (1974): 1124–31.
43. Daniel Kahneman and Amos Tversky, "On the Reality of Cognitive Illusions," *Psychological Review* 103 (1996): 582–91; Gerd Gigerenzer, "On Narrow Norms and Vague Heuristics: A Reply to Kahneman and Tversky," *Psychological Review* 103 (1996): 592–6.
44. Leda Cosmides and John Tooby, "Are Humans Good Intuitive Statisticians After All? Rethinking Some Conclusions from the Literature on Judgment Under Uncertainty," *Cognition* 58 (1996): 1–73.
45. Amos Tversky and Daniel Kahneman, "Extensions versus Intuitive Reasoning: The Conjunction Fallacy in Probability Judgment," *Psychological Review* 90 (1983): 293–315.
46. Daniel Kahneman and Amos Tversky, "Subjective Probability: A Judgment of Representativeness," *Cognitive Psychology* 3 (1972): 430–54.
47. Dan Kahan, "Ideology, Motivated Reasoning, and Cognitive Reflection," *Judgment and Decision Making* 8 (2013): 407–24.

48. Amos Tversky and Daniel Kahneman, "Availability: A Heuristic for Judging Frequency and Probability," *Cognitive Psychology* 5 (1973): 207–32.
49. Steven Pinker, *Rationality: What It Is, Why It Seems Scarce, Why It Matters* (Viking, 2021), 156.
50. J. A. Swets, ed., *Signal Detection and Recognition by Human Observers* (Wiley, 1964); Harold Stanislaw and Natasha Todorov, "Calculation of Signal Detection Theory Measures," *Behavior Research Methods, Instruments, and Computers* 31, no. 1 (1999), 137–49; Gigerenzer, *Rationality for Mortals.*
51. Carol Tavris, "How Accurate Is the 'Cycle of Abuse'?," *Skeptic* 21, no. 2 (2017).
52. Tavris, "How Accurate Is the 'Cycle of Abuse'?"
53. Quoted in Daniel Pi, Francesco Parisi, and Barbara Luppi, "Quantifying Reasonable Doubt," *Rutgers University Law Review* 72, no. 2 (2020).
54. David Sweig, *An Abundance of Caution: American Schools, the Virus, and a Story of Bad Decisions* (MIT Press, 2025).
55. Judea Pearl and Dana Mackenzie, *The Book of Why: The New Science of Cause and Effect* (Basic, 2018), 28–30.
56. Pearl and Mackenzie, *The Book of Why*, 35. See also Judea Pearl, *Causality: Models, Reasoning and Inference* (Cambridge University Press, 2000).
57. David Deutsch, *The Beginning of Infinity: Explanations that Transform the World* (Viking, 2011).
58. Deutsch, *The Beginning of Infinity*, 32.
59. Deutsch, *The Beginning of Infinity*, 32.
60. Deutsch, *The Beginning of Infinity*, 75.

4 The Truth About Coincidences and Miracles

1. I computed the probability of my license plate configuration this way:

    The total combinations for any state is $A^B \times C^D$ where

    A = total number of allowable letters

    B = number of letters on a plate

    C = total number of allowable digits

    D = total number of digits per plate

    In California, they are 26, 3, 10, 4, which gives you 175,760,000.

    Mathematician Art Benjamin from Harvey Mudd College confirmed my calculations in an email:

    > The only change I would make is to rephrase "175,760,000 to one" to "one in 175,760,000." (Technically, the "odds" would be "175,759,999 to 1." For example

if something happens 1/4 of the time then there are 3 to 1 odds against it (not 4 to 1). Smith's numbers are fine. Technically, the probability is 1 in 2,598,960, but it's okay to round it to 1 in 3 million.

2. Gary Smith, *Standard Deviations: Flawed Assumptions, Tortured Data, and Other Ways to Lie with Statistics* (Overlook, 2014), 35–6.
3. Smith, *Standard Deviations*, 40.
4. G. S. Tune, "Response Preferences: A Review of Some Relevant Literature," *Psychological Bulletin* 61, no. 4 (1964): 286–302.
5. Amos Tversky and Daniel Kahneman, "Belief in the Law of Small Numbers," *Psychological Bulletin* 76 (1971): 105–10; Amos Tversky and Daniel Kahneman, "Judgment Under Uncertainty: Heuristics and Biases," *Science* 185 (1974): 1124–31.
6. Quoted in: Alex Bellow, "And now for something completely random," (*Daily Mail*, 2010, December 7), https://tinyurl.com/mstjamuw.
7. I generated this figure with the assistance of ChatGPT. It was inspired by similar scatterplots in Steven Pinker, *The Better Angels of Our Nature: Why Violence Has Declined* (Viking, 2011).
8. Stephen Jay Gould, "Glow, Big Glowworm," *Natural History* (December 1986).
9. Smith, *Standard Deviations*, 38–41.
10. Smith, *Standard Deviations*, 41–3.
11. Michael Shermer, "Surviving Statistics," *Scientific American*, September 2014, 94.
12. Personal correspondence, June 7, 2014.
13. David J. Hand, *The Improbability Principle: Why Coincidences, Miracles, and Rare Events Happen Every Day* (Farrar, Straus and Giroux, 2014).
14. Persi Diaconis and Frederick Mosteller, "Methods for Studying Coincidences," *Journal of the American Statistical Association* (1988): 853–61.
15. Martin Gardner repeated this story to many people, including me.
16. Tom Taylor, "How Anthony Hopkins Became the Centre of the Quantum Theory of Coincidence," *Far Out*, April 21, 2023, https://tinyurl.com/mt75dfx6.
17. Michael Shermer, *The Believing Brain* (Henry Holt, 2011).
18. Hand, *The Improbability Principle*.
19. Diaconis and Mosteller, "Methods for Studying Coincidences."
20. Hand, *The Improbability Principle*.
21. Quoted in Steven Pinker, *Rationality: What It Is, Why It Seems Scarce, Why It Matters* (Viking, 2021), 17–18.
22. L. Gillman, "The Car and the Goats," *American Mathematical Monthly* (January 1992): 3–7.

23. Marilyn vos Savant was bombarded with angry letters when she revealed the correct solution in her column: Marilyn vos Savant, "Ask Marilyn," *Parade*, September 9, 1990, February 17, 1991, July 7, 1991.
24. Pinker, *Rationality*, 20.
25. Michael Shermer, "A Drunkard's Walk Through Middle Land," *Scientific American*, October 2008, 46.
26. Thomas Gilovich, Robert Vallone, and Amos Tversky, "The Hot Hand in Basketball: On the Misperception of Random Sequences," *Cognitive Psychology* 17 (1985): 295–314.
27. "Stephen Curry Is on Fire While Eating Spicy Hot Wings," Hot Ones, posted July 27, 2023, YouTube, 27 min., 6 sec., accessed April 10, 2025, https://shorturl.at/1TaWw. David Myers, "Your Brain Looks for 'Winning Streaks' Everywhere—Here's Why," *Scientific American*, September 27, 2023.
28. Robert M. Lantis and Erik T. Nesson, "How Shots: An Analysis of the 'Hot Hand' in NBA Field Goal and Free Throw Shooting," Working Paper, National Bureau of Economic Research, 2021.
29. Konstantinos Pelechrinis and Wayne Winston, "The Hot Hand in the Wild," *PLOS ONE*, January 25, 2022.
30. J. B. Miller and A. Sanjurjo, "Surprised by the Hot Hand Fallacy? A Truth in the Law of Small Numbers," *Econometrica* 86 (2018): 2019–47. See also Amos Tversky and Thomas Gilovich, "The Cold Facts About the 'Hot Hand' in Basketball," *Chance* 2 (1989): 16–21; Amos Tversky and Thomas Gilovich, "The 'Hot Hand': Statistical Reality of Cognitive Illusion?," *Chance* 2 (1989): 31–34.
31. Myers, "Your Brain Looks for 'Winning Streaks' Everywhere."
32. Richard Hardison, *Upon the Shoulders of Giants: The Shaping of the Modern Mind* (University Press of America, 1988), 443.
33. Quoted in Hardison, *Upon the Shoulders of Giants*. See also John Scarne, *Scarne's New Complete Guide to Gambling* (Fireside, 1974, 1986); John Scarne, *The Odds Against Me: An Autobiography* (Simon and Schuster, 1966).
34. Thomas Gilovich and Gary Belsky, *Why Smart People Make Big Money Mistakes and How to Correct Them: Lessons from the New Science of Behavioral Economics* (Fireside, 2000).
35. I did this for one of my *Scientific American* "Skeptic" columns: Michael Shermer, "Miracle on Probability Street," *Scientific American*, August 2004, 32.
36. Michael Shermer, "Folk Numeracy and Middle Land," *Scientific American*, September 2008, 46.

37. Freeman Dyson, "Littlewood's Law of Miracles," *New York Review of Books*, March 25, 2004, 5.
38. Dyson, "Littlewood's Law of Miracles," 5.
39. Lee Strobel, *The Case for Miracles: A Journalist Investigates Evidence for the Supernatural* (Zondervan, 2018).
40. John W. Loftus, ed., *The Case Against Miracles* (Hypatia, 2022).
41. David Hume, *An Enquiry Concerning Human Understanding*, ed. L. A. Selby Bigge (Clarendon, 1758, 1902), 114–16.
42. Hume, *An Enquiry Concerning Human Understanding.*
43. David Kyle Johnson, "When Can We Trust Testimony?," Lecture 9, *The Big Questions of Philosophy* (The Great Courses, 2018). See also David Kyle Johnson, "Justified Belief in Miracles Is Impossible," *Science Religion and Culture* 2, no. 2 (May 2015): 62.
44. Johnson, "When Can We Trust Testimony?"
45. Loftus, *The Case Against Miracles.*
46. M. V. Kamath and V. B. Kher, *Sai Baba of Shirdi: A Unique Saint* (Jaico, 1991); Antonio Rigopoulos, *The Life and Teachings of Sai Baba of Shirdi* (State University of New York Press, 1993).
47. Joseph Pelletier, *The Sun Danced at Fátima* (Doubleday, 1983).
48. Benjamin Radford, "The Lady of Fátima & the Miracle of the Sun," LiveScience.com, May 2, 2013.
49. Radford, "The Lady of Fátima."
50. Johnson, "When Can We Trust Testimony?"

5 Religious and Mythic Truths

1. Maria Dzielska, *Apollonius of Tyana in Legend and History* (L'Erma di Bretschneider, 1986).
2. Christopher P. Jones, *The Life of Apollonius of Tyana* (Harvard University Press, 2005).
3. James A. Francis, "Truthful Fiction: New Questions to Old Answers on Philostratus' Life of Apollonius," *American Journal of Philology* 119, no. 3 (1998): 419–41.
4. Quoted in Bart Ehrman, "The Virgin Birth in Matthew and Luke," *The Bart Ehrman Blog*, December 21, 2018, https://tinyurl.com/2p96e4u9.
5. Rosemarie Taylor-Perry, *The God Who Comes: Dionysian Mysteries Revisited* (Algora, 2003).
6. George Hart, *A Dictionary of Egyptian Gods and Goddesses* (Routledge, 2006), 100.
7. *The Epic of Gilgamesh*, trans. Benjamin R. Foster (W. W. Norton, 2001).

8. David Leeming, "Flood," *The Oxford Companion to World Mythology* (Oxford University Press, 2004).
9. Michael Shermer, *How We Believe: Science, Skepticism, and the Search for God*, 2nd ed. (Henry Holt, 2003), 162.
10. Shermer, *How We Believe*, 143.
11. Oxford English Dictionary, "myth," accessed 1997, https://www.oed.com/dictionary/myth_n.
12. William Shakespeare, *The Merchant of Venice* (1600), Folger Shakespeare Library, accessed April 11, 2025, https://tinyurl.com/4ybyknsa.
13. Neil Van Leeuwen, *Religion as Make-Believe: A Theory of Belief, Imagination, and Group Identity* (Harvard University Press, 2023), 212–4.
14. Michael Baigent, Richard Leigh, and Henry Lincoln, *Holy Blood, Holy Grail* (Delacorte, 1982); Dan Brown, *The Da Vinci Code* (Doubleday / Random House, 2003).
15. Joseph Campbell, *The Hero with a Thousand Faces* (Princeton University Press, 1949).
16. Campbell, *The Hero with a Thousand Faces*, 382.
17. Joseph Campbell, *Myths to Live By* (Bantam, 1972).
18. Campbell, *Myths to Live By*, 221–2.
19. Shermer, *How We Believe*, 152.
20. Donald E. Brown, *Human Universals* (McGraw-Hill, 1991).
21. Brown, *Human Universals*, x.
22. Michael Shermer, *The Science of Good and Evil* (Henry Holt, 2003).
23. Michael Gazzaniga, *The Mind's Past* (University of California Press, 1998), 27.
24. Melvin Konner, *The Tangled Wing: Biological Constants on the Human Spirit* (Harper, 1982), 171.
25. See, for example, Joseph Campbell, *The Masks of God: Creative Mythology* (Viking, 1968), 113–23.
26. E. O. Wilson, personal correspondence, July 7, 1998.
27. Shermer, *How We Believe*, 156.
28. D. H. Miller, *Ghost Dance* (University of Nebraska Press, 1959); R. M. Utley, *The Lance and the Shield: The Life and Times of Sitting Bull* (Macmillan, 1993); S. L. A. Marshall, *Crimsoned Prairie: The Indian Wars on the Great Plains* (Scribner's, 1972).
29. Dee Brown, *Bury My Heart at Wounded Knee* (Bantam, 1970).
30. James Mooney, ed., *The Ghost Dance Religion and the Sioux Outbreak of 1890* (University of Chicago Press, 1896), 771–2, 780–1.
31. Shermer, *How We Believe*.
32. Weston La Barre, *The Ghost Dance: Origins of Religion* (Doubleday, 1970), 233–4.
33. La Barre, *The Ghost Dance*, 238–9.

34. Marvin Harris, *Cows, Pigs, Wars, and Witches: The Riddles of Culture* (Vintage, 1974), 133. See also Lamont Lindstrom, *Cargo Cult: Strange Stories of Desire from Melanesia and Beyond* (University of Hawaii Press, 1993). For a skeptical take on Cargo Cults as a subject of anthropological study, see Holger Jebens, ed., *Cargo, Cult, and Culture Critique* (University of Hawaii Press, 2004).
35. Randel Helms, *Gospel Fictions* (Prometheus, 1988).
36. Burton L. Mack, *Who Wrote the New Testament? The Making of the Christian Myth* (HarperCollins, 1995), 43.
37. Mack, *Who Wrote the New Testament?*, 226.
38. Peter Worsley, *The Trumpet Shall Sound: A Study of Cargo Cults in Melanesia* (Shocken, 1958).
39. *The Interpreter's Bible*, vol. 8 (Abingdon, 1978), 300–1.
40. *The Interpreter's Bible*, vol. 8 (Abingdon, 1978), 300–1.
41. Michael Shermer, *Heavens on Earth: The Scientific Search for the Afterlife, Immortality, and Utopia* (Henry Holt, 2018).
42. William Jennings Bryan, "Cross of Gold" speech, July 9, 1896, Democratic National Convention, Chicago. Quoted in the *San Francisco Call*, July 11, 1896, p. 3, https://tinyurl.com/myaas6ds.
43. See many studies such as this: Chunkai Li, Song Wang, Yajun Zhao, Feng Kong, and Jingguang Li, "The Freedom to Pursue Happiness: Belief in Free Will Predicts Life Satisfaction and Positive Affect Among Chinese Adolescents," *Frontiers of Psychology* 7 (2017): 2027.
44. Michael Shermer, "The Annotated Gardner: An Interview with Martin Gardner—Founder of the Modern Skeptical Movement," *Skeptic* 5, no. 2 (1997): 56–61.
45. Shermer, "The Annotated Gardner."
46. Shermer, "The Annotated Gardner."
47. Shermer, "The Annotated Gardner."
48. Shermer, "The Annotated Gardner."
49. Shermer, "The Annotated Gardner."
50. There are many sources for the 100 billion figure, but this is a good place to start: Carl Haub, "How Many People Have Ever Lived on Earth?," *Population Today* 23, no. 2 (February 1995): 4–5; see also Population Reference Bureau.
51. Shermer, *Heavens on Earth*, chapter 5.
52. Larry Shapiro, *The Miracle Myth: Why Belief in the Resurrection and the Supernatural Is Unjustified* (Columbia University Press, 2016).
53. Shapiro, *The Miracle Myth*.
54. John W. Campbell, *Cross Examined: Putting Christianity on Trial* (Prometheus, 2021),

381–2; see also Matthew S. McCormick, *Atheism and the Case Against Christ* (Prometheus, 2012), 59–60.

55. Bart Ehrman, *Jesus, Interrupted: Revealing the Hidden Contradictions in the Bible (and Why We Don't Know About Them)* (HarperOne, 2010), 171–2.
56. Ehrman, *Jesus, Interrupted*, 173–9.
57. Ehrman, *Jesus, Interrupted.*
58. John W. Loftus, ed., *The Case Against Miracles* (Hypatia, 2022).
59. Lance Grande, *The Evolution of Religions: A History of Related Traditions* (Columbia University Press, 2024), 328–9.
60. Grande, *The Evolution of Religions.*
61. Grande, *The Evolution of Religions.*
62. Bart Ehrman, *How Jesus Became God: The Exaltation of a Jewish Preacher from Galilee* (HarperOne, 2014), 2.
63. Oliver Cromwell, "To the General Assembly of the Kirk of Scotland; or, in case of their not sitting, To the Commissioners of the Kirk of Scotland," letter, August 3, 1650.

6 Historical Truths

1. The *1619 Project* in its entirety is available online: *New York Times Magazine*, accessed April 12, 2025, https://nyti.ms/39B72UL.
2. Nikole Hannah-Jones's article is available here: *New York Times Magazine*, August 14, 2019, https://nyti.ms/2SOhwKS.
3. The historians' letter and the editor's response are available online: *New York Times Magazine*, accessed April 12, 2025, https://nyti.ms/2QikuoV.
4. Attributed to Arnold Toynbee, echoing Max Plowman's earlier quip that "life is just one damn thing after another"; neither meant that history and life are random. Toynbee, in fact, believed there were patterns in history to be discerned, so his use of the phrase was antithetical. See "Quote Origin: History Is Just One Damn Thing after Another," Quote Investigator, September 16, 2015, https://quoteinvestigator.com/2015/09/16/history/.
5. Karl Popper, *The Open Society and Its Enemies* (Routledge, 1950, 1962), 473.
6. I explored and defended this interpretation of the Atlantis story here: Michael Shermer, *Heavens on Earth: The Scientific Search for the Afterlife, Immortality, and Utopia* (Henry Holt, 2018), 181–2.
7. Michael Shermer and Alex Grobman, *Denying History: Who Says the Holocaust Never Happened and Why Do They Say It?* (University of California Press, 2000, 2004).
8. Richard Evans, *In Defense of History* (W. W. Norton, 1999), 7.

9. William Whewell, *The Philosophy of the Inductive Sciences* (J. W. Parker, 1840).
10. Dwight D. Eisenhower, *Crusade in Europe* (Doubleday, 1948), 409.
11. These statistics and the others in this section were first established by the International Military Tribunal for the Far East, "Table: Estimated Number of Victims of Japanese Massacre in Nanking," document no. 1702, court exhibits, World War II War Crimes Records Collection, box 134, entry 14, record group 238, National Archives, 1948. The Nazi quote comes from C. Kröger, "Days of Fate in Nanking" (unpublished diary in the collection of P. Kröger; also in the International Military Tribunal for the Far East judgment, National Archives, 1948).
12. Iris Chang, *The Rape of Nanking: The Forgotten Holocaust of World War II* (Basic, 1997).
13. Chang, *The Rape of Nanking*, 6–7.
14. Chang, *The Rape of Nanking*, 215. The description of the "Three-all policy" is from: R. J. Rummel, *China's Bloody Century: Genocide and Mass Murder Since 1900* (Transaction, 1991), 139. The colonel's remark is quoted from: D. Wilson, *When Tigers Fight: The Story of the Sino-Japanese War, 1937–1945* (Viking, 1982), 61.
15. Chang, *The Rape of Nanking*, 219–20.
16. Hyonhee Shin, "South Korea Court Orders Japan to Compensate 'Comfort Women,' Reverses Earlier Ruling," *Reuters*, November 23, 2023.
17. Dan Fastenberg, "Japanese Sex Slavery," *Time*, June 17, 2010.
18. Fastenberg, "Japanese Sex Slavery," 201.
19. Fastenberg, "Japanese Sex Slavery." Quoted from D. Sheff, "Playboy Interview: Shintaro Ishihara—Candid Conversation," *Playboy*, October 1990, 63.
20. Chang, *The Rape of Nanking*, 201–2. Based on Yoshi Tsurumi, "Japan Makes Efforts to Be Less Insular," *New York Times*, December 25, 1990.
21. Chang, *The Rape of Nanking*, 202–3. Fujio and Okuno quoted from K. Schoenberger, "Japan Aide Quits over Remark on WWII," *Los Angeles Times*, May 14, 1988.
22. Nagano quoted from S. Moffet, "Japan Justice Minister Denies Nanking Massacre," *Reuters*, May 4, 1994.
23. Chang, *The Rape of Nanking*, 207. Quoted from "Truth in Textbooks, Freedom in Education and Peace for Children: The Struggle Against the Censorship of School Textbooks in Japan," 2nd ed., Tokyo, National League for Support of the School Textbook Screening Suit, June 1995.
24. Chang, *The Rape of Nanking*, 209. Noboru quote from the *New York Times*, November 3, 1991; Nobukatsu quote from S. Efron, "Defender of Japan's War Past," *Los Angeles Times*, May 9, 1997.
25. Quoted from R. E. Yates, "'Emperor' Film Keeps Atrocity Scenes in Japan," *Chicago Tribune*, January 23, 1988.

26. Yates, "'Emperor' Film."
27. D. Yang, "A Sino-Japanese Controversy: The Nanjing Atrocity as History," *Sino-Japanese Studies* 3, no. 1 (November 1990).
28. Chang, *The Rape of Nanking*, 212.
29. A. Brackman, *The Other Nuremberg: The Untold Story of the Tokyo War Crimes Trials* (William Morrow, 1987).
30. Jared Diamond, *Guns, Germs, and Steel: The Fate of Human Societies* (W. W. Norton, 1997).
31. Jared Diamond, *Natural Experiments of History* (Harvard University Press, 2010), 120–9.
32. Mary Lefkowitz, *Not Out of Africa: How Afrocentrism Became an Excuse to Teach Myth as History* (Basic Books, 1996), 2–3.
33. Lefkowitz, *Not Out of Africa*, 4.
34. C. M. Bernal, *Black Athena: The Afroasiatic Roots of Classical Civilization*, 2 vols. (Rutgers University Press, 1997).
35. Lefkowitz, *Not Out of Africa*, 171. See also Mary Lefkowitz and G. M. Rogers, eds., *Black Athena Revisited* (University of North Carolina Press, 1997).
36. Ken Feder, *Frauds, Myths, and Mysteries: Science and Pseudoscience in Archaeology* (Mayfield, 1996), 9–10.
37. Riane Eisler, *The Chalice and the Blade* (Harper and Row, 1987).
38. Eisler, *The Chalice and the Blade*, 17.
39. Eisler, *The Chalice and the Blade*, 18.
40. Eisler, *The Chalice and the Blade*, 20.
41. Eisler, *The Chalice and the Blade*, 43.
42. Eisler, *The Chalice and the Blade*.
43. Vine Deloria Jr., *Red Earth, White Lies: Native Americans and the Myth of Scientific Fact* (Scribner, 1995).
44. Ken Feder, "Indians and Archaeologists: Conflicting Views of Myth and Science," *Skeptic* 5, no. 3 (1997): 74–81.
45. Feder, "Indians and Archaeologists," 51–2.
46. Elizabeth Weiss, *On the Warpath: My Battles With Indians, Pretendians, and Woke Warriors* (Academica, 2024).
47. Michael Shermer, "Romance of the Vanished Past," *Scientific American*, June 2017, 75.
48. Joe Rogan, host, *The Joe Rogan Experience*, podcast, "Graham Hancock, Randall Carlson, Michael Shermer," episode 961, May 16, 2017.

49. Steven R. Holen et al., "A 130,000-Year-Old Archaeological Site in Southern California, USA," *Nature* 544 (April 27, 2017).
50. J. V. Ferraro et al., "Contesting Early Archaeology in California," *Nature* 544 (February 8, 2018).
51. S. R. Holen et al., "Broken Bones and Hammerstones at the Cerutti Mastodon Site: A Reply to Haynes," *PaleoAmerica* 4, no. 1 (2017).
52. Steven R. Holen et al., "Holen et al. Reply," *Nature* 554 (February 8, 2018).
53. Our special issue dedicated to alternative archaeologies, including Hancock's, is *Skeptic* 22, no. 3 (2017). See Marc Defant, "Conjuring Up a Lost Civilization: An Analysis of the Claims Made by Graham Hancock in *Magicians of the Gods*," *Skeptic* 22, no. 3 (2017): 32–41.
54. Personal correspondence, May 15, 2017.
55. Peter Novick, *That Noble Dream: The 'Objectivity Question' and the American Historical Profession* (Cambridge University Press, 1988).
56. James T. Kloppenberg, "Objectivity and Historicism: A Century of American Historical Writing," *American Historical Review* 94, no. 4 (1989): 1011–30.

7 Moral Truths

1. Dennis Prager, "If There Is No God, Murder Isn't Wrong," PragerU, posted March 20, 2017, YouTube, 5 min., 17 sec., accessed April 13, 2025, https://tinyurl.com/4kdnk3rv.
2. Prager, "If There Is No God."
3. Dave Rubin, "A Conversation About God and Morality: Dennis Prager & Michael Shermer," *The Rubin Report*, posted July 7, 2017, YouTube, 1 hr., 10 min., accessed April 13, 2025, https://tinyurl.com/4vb6njcx.
4. This is a rewording of Plato's famous Euthyphro's dilemma, in which he asked "whether the pious or holy is beloved by the gods because it is holy, or holy because it is beloved of the gods?" See P. Edwards, "Socrates," *Encyclopedia of Philosophy*, vol. 7 (Macmillan, 1967), 482.
5. For excellent articles on each of these and related ethical systems, see *Stanford Encyclopedia of Philosophy*, accessed April 13, 2025, https://plato.stanford.edu/.
6. David Hume, *A Treatise of Human Nature* (John Noon, 1739), 335.
7. Michael Shermer, *The Science of Good and Evil* (Times, 2003).
8. Michael Shermer, *The Moral Arc: How Science and Reason Lead Humanity Toward Truth, Justice, and Freedom* (Henry Holt, 2015).
9. Frans de Waal, *The Age of Empathy: Nature's Lessons for a Kinder Society* (Crown,

2009); Frans de Waal, *The Bonobo and the Atheist: In Search of Humanism Among the Primates* (W. W. Norton, 2013).

10. David Sloan Wilson, *Darwin's Cathedral: Evolution, Religion, and the Nature of Society* (University of Chicago Press, 2002); David Sloan Wilson, *Evolution for Everyone: How Darwin's Theory Can Change the Way We Think About Our Lives* (Delacorte, 2006); David Sloan Wilson, *This View of Life: Completing the Darwinian Revolution* (Pantheon, 2019).
11. Joshua Greene, *Moral Tribes: Emotion, Reason, and the Gap Between Us and Them* (Penguin, 2013).
12. Jonathan Haidt, *The Righteous Mind: Why Good People Are Divided by Politics and Religion* (Pantheon, 2012).
13. Kurt Gray, *Outraged! Why We Fight About Morality and Politics and How to Find Common Ground* (Pantheon, 2025).
14. Sam Harris, *The Moral Landscape: How Science Can Determine Human Values* (Free Press, 2010).
15. Steven Pinker, *The Better Angels of Our Nature* (Viking, 2011); Steven Pinker, *Enlightenment Now: The Case for Reason, Science, Humanism, and Progress* (Viking, 2018).
16. James Davison Hunter and Paul Nedelisky, *Science and the Good: The Tragic Quest for the Foundations of Morality* (Yale University Press, 2018). See also my review of their book: Michael Shermer, "Can Science Discover Moral Truths?," Henry Center, March 2, 2021. See Nedelisky's response to my review: Paul Nedelisky, "God, Science, Morality: A Reply," Henry Center, April 9, 2021.
17. Jeremy Bentham was the first to articulate the grounding principle of animal rights: Jeremy Bentham, *Introduction to the Principles of Morals and Legislation* (1823), chapter 17, footnote 122. See full text copy at Econlib, accessed April 13, 2025, http://bit.ly/1XdYerr.
18. Michael Shermer, "Scientific Naturalism: A Manifesto for Enlightenment Humanism," *Theology and Science* 15, no. 3 (June 2017). See also a critique of my manifesto: George Ellis, "Can Science Bridge the Is-Ought Gap? A Response to Michael Shermer," *Theology and Science* 16, no. 1 (December 2017). And: Michael Shermer, "A Response to George Ellis," *Theology and Science* 16, no. 1 (December 2017).
19. Data source: "Poverty," World Bank, accessed May 16, 2025, https://data.worldbank.org/topic/11, and Francois Bourguignon and Christian Morrisson, "Inequality among World Citizens: 1820–1992," *American Economic Review* 92, no. 4 (2002): 727–44.
20. See Max Roser's web page tracking progress in poverty and many other areas of human and social life: Our World in Data, accessed April 13, 2025, https://ourworldin

data.org/. See also the Cato Institute's web page: Human Progress, accessed April 13, 2025, http://humanprogress.org/.

21. Keri Geiger et al., "Progress Toward Poliomyelitis Eradication—Worldwide, January 2022–December 2023," CDC, *Weekly* 73, no. 19 (May 16, 2024): 441–6.
22. Steven Pinker, *The Better Angels of Our Nature: Why Violence Has Declined* (Viking, 2011).
23. Personal correspondence, July 28, 2011.
24. Robert Pennock, quoted in Michael Shermer, host, *The Michael Shermer Show*, podcast, episode 98, January 7, 2020, https://www.skeptic.com/michael-shermer-show/michael-shermer-with-robert-pennock-instinct-for-truth-curiosity-the-moral-character-of-science/.
25. Steven Pinker, "The Moral Instinct," *New York Times Magazine*, January 13, 2008, https://tinyurl.com/2c44x63x.
26. Robert Wright, *Nonzero: The Logic of Human Destiny* (Pantheon, 2000).
27. Wright, *Nonzero*.
28. Steven Pinker, *Rationality: What It Is, Why It Seems Scarce, Why It Matters* (Viking, 2021), 68.
29. J. Rawls, *A Theory of Justice* (Belknap/Harvard University Press, 1971).
30. Abraham Lincoln, October 15, 1858, in *The Lincoln-Douglas Debates: The First Complete, Unexpurgated Text*, ed. Harold Holzer (Fordham University Press, 2004), 55.
31. Abraham Lincoln, December 1, 1862, in *The Collected Works of Abraham Lincoln*, vol. 2, ed. Roy P. Basler (Rutgers University Press, 1953), 532.
32. Abraham Lincoln, July 1, 1854, "Lincoln on Slavery," National Park Service, April 10, 2015, https://tinyurl.com/5774ndnv.
33. Rebecca Newberger Goldstein, *Betraying Spinoza: The Renegade Jew Who Gave Us Modernity* (Nextbook/Schocken, 2006).
34. Carl Sagan, *The Demon-Haunted World: Science as a Candle in the Dark* (Random House, 1996), 424.
35. Michael Shermer, "The Sandy Hook Effect," *Skeptic* 18, no. 1 (2013), http://bit.ly/1uUZL7V.
36. Pamela K. Kohler, Lisa E. Manhart, and William E. Lafferty, "Abstinence-Only and Comprehensive Sex Education and the Initiation of Sexual Activity and Teen Pregnancy," *Journal of Adolescent Health* 42, no. 4 (April 2008): 344–51.
37. E. G. Raymond and D. A. Grimes, "The Comparative Safety of Legal Induced Abortion and Childbirth in the United States," *Obstetrics & Gynecology* 119, no. 2 (February 2012), http://bit.ly/1ikYqET.
38. Amy Deschner and Susan A. Cohen, "Contraceptive Use Is Key to Reducing Abortion Worldwide," *The Guttmacher Report on Public Policy* 6, no. 4 (October 2003).

39. L. Yoon, "GNI Per Capita Comparison Between South and North Korea, 1990 to 2023," Statista, August 15, 2024, https://tinyurl.com/4389cf4j.
40. See, for example, Jared Diamond, *Natural Experiments of History* (Harvard University Press, 2010).
41. Timothy Ferris, *The Science of Liberty: Democracy, Reason, and the Laws of Nature* (Harper, 2010).
42. For example, in the chapter on women's rights in Shermer, *The Moral Arc*; and an updated post about the Supreme Court decision overturning Roe, Michael Shermer, "Abortion: The Case for Choice," *Skeptic*, Substack, December 6, 2021.
43. Wikipedia, "List of Countries by Social Welfare Spending," last modified January 3, 2025, https://bit.ly/2H7erAE.
44. Leandro Prados de la Escosura, "World Human Development, 1870–2007," *The Review of Income and Wealth* 61 (2015): 220–47, https://bit.ly/2J3wcxm.
45. Michael Shermer, *The Moral Arc: How Science and Reason Lead Humanity Toward Truth, Justice, and Freedom* (Henry Holt, 2015).
46. Pinker, *Rationality*.
47. A comprehensive compendium of quotes from thinkers who have built this tradition may be found in Serge Bourgaine, *Enlightenment Humanism: Its Advocates Speak* (Orbis Unum, 2020).
48. Abraham Lincoln, April 4, 1864, letter to Albert G. Hodges, Library of Congress, accessed April 13, 2025, https://bit.ly/1gvohdW.
49. Michael Shermer, "Scientific Naturalism: A Manifesto for Enlightenment Humanism," *Theology and Science* 15, no. 3 (August 2017): 220–30; George Ellis, "Can Science Bridge the Is-Ought Gap? A Response to Michael Shermer," *Theology and Science* 16, no. 1 (2017): 1–5, https://bit.ly/2Eb0OPa.
50. Michael Shermer, *Giving the Devil His Due: Reflections of a Scientific Humanist* (Cambridge University Press, 2020), 237.
51. John Tooby, Leda Cosmides, and H. Clark Harrett, "The Second Law of Thermodynamics Is the First Law of Psychology," *Psychological Bulletin* 129, no. 6 (2003): 858–65.
52. Ellis, "Can Science Bridge the Is-Ought Gap?"
53. Ellis, "Can Science Bridge the Is-Ought Gap?"

■ 8 Alien Truths

1. Helene Cooper, Ralph Blumenthal, and Leslie Kean, "Glowing Auras and 'Black Money': The Pentagon's Mysterious U.F.O. Program," *New York Times*, December 16, 2017, https://nyti.ms/2SFm8Vg.

2. Bill Whitaker, "UFOs Regularly Spotted in Restricted U.S. Airspace, Report on the Phenomena Due Next Month," *CBS News*, May 16, 2021, https://cbsn.ws/3p0AHPm.
3. Mike Dash, *Borderlands: The Ultimate Exploration of the Unknown* (Overlook, 2000).
4. Leslie Kean, *UFOs: Generals, Pilots and Government Officials Go on the Record* (Harmony, 2010), 12.
5. Kean, *UFOs*, 13–14.
6. Quoted in Kean, *UFOs*, 17.
7. Robert Sheaffer, *Bad UFOs: Critical Thinking About UFO Claims* (CreateSpace Independent, 2016).
8. Kean, *UFOs*, 21.
9. Kean, *UFOs*, 11.
10. James Oberg, "UFO Book Based on Questionable Foundation," *NBC News*, August 26, 2010, https://tinyurl.com/4dx2axaw.
11. Jim Obert, "Exclusive: Russian UFO Research Revealed," Space.com, 2000.
12. Scott Kelly, "UFO 'Optical Illusions': Astronaut Scott Kelly Says It's Hard to I.D. Strange Objects in Flight," Space.com, posted June 2, 2023, YouTube, 3 min., 17 sec., accessed April 14, 2025, https://tinyurl.com/3tfxsnet.
13. Travis Walton, *Fire in the Sky: Based on the True Story* (De Capo, 1996). Film version available on Amazon.com, accessed April 14, 2025, https://tinyurl.com/yckbw9vz.
14. Michael Shermer, "Travis Walton's Alien Abduction Lie Detection Test," *Skeptic*, December 8, 2015, https://tinyurl.com/3ysxhh68.
15. Personal correspondence, May 25, 2021.
16. Ralph Blumenthal, *The Believer: Alien Encounters, Hard Science, and the Passion of John Mack* (University of New Mexico Press, 2021).
17. Whitaker, "UFOs Regularly Spotted."
18. Andrew Dyer, "Those Amazing Navy UFO Videos May Have Down-to-Earth Explanations, Skeptics Contend," *San Diego Union-Tribune*, May 29, 2021, https://bit.ly/3vQ6Zzv.
19. Tim McMillan, "The Tale of the Tape," *Popular Mechanics*, January 17, 2020, https://tinyurl.com/34dwp2dd.
20. "To the Stars: Bringing You the Future," accessed April 14, 2025, https://tothestars.media/pages/about.
21. Andrew Dyer, "U.S. Navy Says It's Tracking UFOs," *San Diego Union Tribune*, September 17, 2019, https://tinyurl.com/mpc67fym.
22. Andrew Dyer, "Pentagon Formally Releases Navy UFO Videos," *San Diego Union Tribune* April 27, 2020, https://tinyurl.com/3c2v73sd.

23. Mick West, "US Government Says UFOs Are 'Real': An Analysis of the *60 Minutes* Investigation," *Skeptic*, May 17, 2021, https://tinyurl.com/3kwv5v2h.
24. Robert Powell, *UFOs: A Scientist Explains What We Know (and Don't Know)* (Rowman & Littlefield, 2024).
25. Personal correspondence, May 14, 2024.
26. Mick West, "*Nimitz* FLIR1 'Tic-Tac' UFO Video-No Sudden Moves!," posted May 3, 2020, YouTube, 5 min., 34 sec., accessed April 14, 2025, https://tinyurl.com/98fyt7m3.
27. Mick West, "Explained: 'Go Fast' UFO Video—Not Low and Not Fast—Like a Balloon!," posted June 23, 2019, YouTube, 6 min., 42 sec., accessed April 14, 2025, https://tinyurl.com/mtbmbxvj.
28. Mick West, "Gimbal UFO: Why Does the Glare Rotate When the Horizon Does Not?," posted July 12, 2019, YouTube, 2 min., 8 sec., accessed April 14, 2025, https://tinyurl.com/yrdemb54.
29. Mick West, "Gimbal Lock and Derotation in FLIR/ATFLIR Systems," Metabunk.org, June 27, 2019, https://tinyurl.com/35xzjsda.
30. Mick West, "'Pyramid UFO'—New Footage. It's Just Bokeh, not a Pyramid," posted April 15, 2021, YouTube, 4 min., 17 sec., accessed April 14, 2025, https://tinyurl.com/bdd6yxpb.
31. Mick West, "Omaha Sphere UFO—Initial Analysis—No Sudden Moves!," posted May 15, 2021, YouTube, 4 min., 40 sec., accessed April 14, 2025, https://tinyurl.com/4tz9df43.
32. Personal correspondence, May 14, 2024.
33. René Descartes, *Meditations on First Philosophy in Which Are Demonstrated the Existence of God and the Distinction between the Human Soul and Body* (1639), "On what can be called into doubt." Available online through earlymoderntexts.com, accessed May 16, 2025, https://tinyurl.com/4n3t6hme.
34. Whitaker, "UFOs Regularly Spotted."
35. Whitaker, "UFOs Regularly Spotted."
36. George Basalla, *The Evolution of Technology* (Cambridge University Press, 1988).
37. Quoted in Basalla, *The Evolution of Technology*.
38. Matt Ridley, *How Innovation Works: And Why It Flourishes in Freedom* (Harper, 2020).
39. Ridley, *How Innovation Works*.
40. NASA Hubble Mission Team, "Hubble Reveals Observable Universe Contains 10 Times More Galaxies Than Previously Thought," Goddard Space Flight Center, October 13, 2016, https://go.nasa.gov/3yOjP2V.

41. Ann Druyan, *Cosmos: Possible Worlds* (National Geographic, 2020), 197.
42. Frank D. Drake, "Project Ozma," *Physics Today* 14, no. 4 (1961): 40–6.
43. S. Shostak, *Cosmic Company: The Search for Life in the Universe* (Cambridge University Press, 2003), 124.
44. R. Zubrin, "Galactic Society," *Analog* (April 2002): 33.
45. T. McDonough, *The Search for Extraterrestial Intelligence* (Wiley, 1987).
46. Carl Sagan's estimate comes from I. S. Shklovskii and C. Sagan, *Intelligent Life in the Universe* (Holden-Day, 1966; repr., Emerson-Adams, 1998), 413: "As an average for all technical civilizations, both short-lived and long-lived, I adopt $L \sim 10^7$ [10 million] years." This yields $N \sim 1$ million.
47. Michael Shermer, "Why ET Hasn't Called," *Scientific American*, August 2002, 33.
48. Personal correspondence, May 14, 2024.
49. For my calculation of *L*, I used the civilization chronology compiled by Northpark University historian David W. Koeller.
50. Seth Shostak, *Confessions of an Alien Hunter: A Scientist's Search for Extraterrestrial Intelligence* (National Geographic, 2009).
51. Garrett Graff, *UFO: The Inside Story of the US Government's Search for Alien Life Here and Out There* (Avid Reader / Simon & Schuster, 2023).
52. Michael Shermer, host, *The Michael Shermer Show*, podcast, episode 386, *Skeptic*, November 13, 2023, https://tinyurl.com/yrzrajm3.
53. Steven Dick, *The Plurality of Worlds* (Cambridge University Press, 1982).
54. Paul Davies, *Are We Alone?* (Basic, 1995), 135–6.
55. George Basalla, *Civilized Life in the Universe* (Cambridge University Press, 2006), 10.
56. Michael A. G. Michaud, *Contact with Alien Civilizations: Our Hopes and Fears About Encountering Extraterrestrials* (Copernicus, 2006), 347.
57. "Carl Sagan 1966 Interviewed about UFOs," Cacodemon, posted September 26, 2010, YouTube, 5 min., 59 sec., accessed April 14, 2025, https://tinyurl.com/mrnx42ec.
58. Thomas Bullard, *The Myth and Mystery of UFOs* (University of Kansas Press, 2010), 45–6, 276–7.
59. Clay Routledge, Andrew A. Abeyta, and Christina Roylance, "We Are Not Alone: The Meaning Motive, Religiosity, and Belief in Extraterrestrial Intelligence," *Motivation and Emotion* 4 (2017): 135–146, https://tinyurl.com/2s3rfkaj.
60. Routledge, Abeyta, and Roylance, "We Are Not Alone."
61. Julian Barnes, "Pentagon Review Finds No Evidence of Alien Cover-Up," *New York Times*, March 8, 2024, https://tinyurl.com/mptye2un.
62. Quoted in Graff, *UFO*, 438.

9 The Truth About Consciousness

1. Thomas Nagel, "What Is It Like to Be a Bat?," *Philosophical Review* (October 1974): 435–50.
2. David Chalmers, *The Conscious Mind: In Search of a Fundamental Theory* (Oxford University Press, 1995).
3. Nagel, "What Is It Like to Be a Bat?," 435.
4. Christof Koch, *Consciousness: Confessions of a Romantic Reductionist* (MIT Press, 2012), 1.
5. These examples, and others in the study of the psychology of essentialism and dualism, are fully developed in Bruce Hood, *SuperSense: Why We Believe the Unbelievable* (HarperOne, 2009).
6. Paul Bloom, *Descartes' Baby: How the Science of Child Development Explains What Makes Us Human* (Basic, 2004).
7. Bloom, *Descartes' Baby.*
8. The bet was a case of wine, which Christof dutifully presented to David at the annual gathering of consciousness researchers in 2023.
9. Christof Koch, *The Quest for Consciousness: A Neurobiological Approach* (Roberts & Co, 2004); Koch, *Consciousness.*
10. P. Low, "The Cambridge Declaration on Consciousness," Proceedings of the Francis Crick Memorial Conference, Churchill College, Cambridge University, July 7, 2012, 2–3, https://tinyurl.com/mrzhy4w6.
11. Anil K. Seth and Tim Bayne, "Theories of Consciousness," *Nature Reviews Neuroscience* 23 (May 3, 2022): 439–52.
12. Michael Shermer, host, *The Michael Shermer Show*, podcast, episode 430, *Skeptic*, May 5, 2024.
13. Ralph Lewis, "An Overview of the Leading Theories of Consciousness," *Psychology Today*, November 25, 2023, https://www.psychologytoday.com/us/blog/finding-purpose/202308/an-overview-of-the-leading-theories-of-consciousness.
14. Ralph Lewis, "The Predictive Brain and the 'Hard Problem' of Consciousness," *Psychology Today*, November 28, 2023, https://tinyurl.com/4n2javrs.
15. Deepak Chopra and Menas Kafatos, *You Are the Universe* (Harmony, 2017), 249.
16. Deepak Chopra and Menas Kafatos, "Reality Gets an Unlikely Savior: Infinity," *San Francisco Gate*, July 3, 2016.
17. Chopra and Kafatos, "Reality Gets an Unlikely Savior."
18. Chopra and Kafatos, *You Are the Universe*, 20.
19. Christof Koch, *Then I Am Myself the World: What Consciousness Is and How to Expand It* (Basic, 2024), 1–2.

20. Koch, *Then I Am Myself the World.*
21. Douglas Adams, *The Hitchhiker's Guide to the Galaxy* (Del Rey, 1979).
22. Ricky Williamson, "The Reality of the Mystical Experience," IAI News, October 9, 2023, https://tinyurl.com/mrxj86sj.
23. Michael Shermer, *Why People Believe Weird Things* (St. Martin's Griffin, 1997), chapter 6.
24. Williamson, "The Reality of the Mystical Experience."
25. Williamson, "The Reality of the Mystical Experience."
26. Personal correspondence, June 23, 2024.
27. Koch, *Consciousness.*
28. Donald Hoffman, "Conscious Realism and the Mind-Body Problem," *Mind & Matter* 6, no. 1 (2008): 87–121.
29. Hoffman, "Conscious Realism and the Mind-Body Problem."
30. Donald Hoffman, *The Case Against Reality: Why Evolution Hid the Truth from Our Eyes* (W. W. Norton, 2019).
31. Donald Hoffman, "Do We See Reality as It Is?," TED Talk, March 2015, 21 min., 40 sec., http://bit.ly/1TgMBiL.
32. D. Hoffman and M. Singh, "Computational Evolutionary Perception," *Perception* 41 (2012): 1073–91.
33. J. Mark, B. Marion, and D. Hoffman, "Natural Selection and Veridical Perception," *Journal of Theoretical Biology* 266, no. 4 (October 21, 2010): 504–15.
34. Donald Hoffman, "The Interface Theory of Perception: Natural Selection Drives True Perception to Swift Extinction," in *Object Categorization: Computer and Human Vision Perspectives*, ed. S. Dickinson, M. Tarr, A. Leonardis, and B. Schiele (Cambridge University Press, 2009), 148–65.
35. "The Correspondence Theory of Truth," *Stanford Encyclopedia of Philosophy*, pub. May 10, 2002, rev. May 28, 2015, https://plato.stanford.edu/entries/truth-correspondence/.
36. David Bourget and David J. Chalmers, "Philosophers on Philosophy: The 2023 PhilPapers Survey," *Philosophers' Imprint* 23, no. 11 (2023), http://philpapers.org/surveys/results.pl.
37. "Scientific Realism," *Stanford Encyclopedia of Philosophy*, pub. April 27, 2011, rev. June 12, 2017, http://stanford.io/1nqQciY.
38. Amanda Gefter, "The Evolutionary Argument Against Reality," *Quanta*, April 16, 2016, http://bit.ly/1NmFZPU.
39. Steven Pinker, *Enlightenment Now: The Case for Reason, Science, Humanism, and Progress* (Viking, 2018).

10 The Truth About Free Will

1. Benjamin Libet, "Unconscious Cerebral Initiative and the Role of Conscious Will in Voluntary Action," *Behavior and Brain Sciences* 8 (1985): 529–66.
2. John Dylan Haynes, "Decoding and Predicting Intentions," *Annals of the New York Academy of Sciences* 1224, no. 1 (2011): 9–21.
3. I. Fried, R. Mukamel, and G. Kreiman, "Internally Generated Preactivation of Single Neurons in Human Medial Frontal Cortex Predicts Volition," *Neuron* 69 (2011): 548–62. See also P. Haggard, "Decision Time for Free Will," *Neuron* 69 (2011): 404–6.
4. Sam Harris, *Free Will* (Free Press, 2012), 5.
5. Robert Sapolsky, *Determined: A Science of Life Without Free Will* (Penguin, 2023), 4.
6. Sapolsky, *Determined*, 303.
7. Sapolsky, *Determined*, 304.
8. Michael Shermer, host, *The Michael Shermer Show*, podcast, episode 379, *Skeptic*, October 17, 2023.
9. Shermer, *The Michael Shermer Show*, podcast, episode 379.
10. Sapolsky, *Determined*, 387.
11. David Bourget and David J. Chalmers, "What Do Philosophers Believe?," *Philosophical Studies* 170, no. 3 (2014): 465–500, https://philpapers.org/archive/BOUWDP.pdf.
12. Bourget and Chalmers, "What Do Philosophers Believe?"
13. Wikipedia, "Criticism of the Theory of Relativity," last modified March 1, 2025, http://bit.ly/1Sh4YUC.
14. See, for example, Harris, *Free Will*; Sapolsky, *Determined*; Daniel Dennett, *Freedom Evolves* (Viking, 2003); and Christian List, *Why Free Will Is Real* (Harvard University Press, 2019).
15. List, *Why Free Will Is Real*, 22–7.
16. Kennon Sheldon, *Freely Determined: What the New Psychology of the Self Teaches Us About How to Live* (Basic, 2022), 10–11.
17. Michael Shermer, host, *The Michael Shermer Show*, podcast, *Skeptic*, episode 376, October 3, 2023.
18. Shermer, *The Michael Shermer Show*, podcast, episode 376.
19. Kevin Mitchell, *Free Agents: How Evolution Gave Us Free Will* (Princeton University Press, 2023), x–xi.
20. Sapolsky, *Determined*, 192–3.
21. Marcel Brass and Patrick Haggard, "To Do or Not to Do: The Neural Signature of Self Control," *The Journal of Neuroscience* 27, no. 34 (2007): 9141–45.

22. Benjamin Libet, "Do We Have Free Will?," *Journal of Consciousness Studies* 6, no. 809 (1999): 47–57, 54.
23. Dennett, *Freedom Evolves*.
24. For a discussion of how the brain operates to make economic decisions that feel "free" to the decision-maker, see P. W. Glimcher, *Decisions, Uncertainty, and the Brain: The Science of Neuroeconomics* (MIT Press, 2003). See also Steven Pinker's excellent discussion on free will and determinism in Steven Pinker, *The Blank Slate: The Modern Denial of Human Nature* (Viking, 2002), 175.
25. John M. Scheb and John M. Scheb II, *Criminal Law and Procedure*, 7th ed. (Cengage Learning, 2010).
26. William H. McRaven, "University of Texas at Austin 2014 Commencement Address," May 17, 2014, accessed May 17, 2025, https://www.youtube.com/watch?v=pxBQLFLei70.
27. David Sally, "I, Too, Sail Past: Odysseus and the Logic of Self-Control," *Kyklos* 53 (2000): 173–200.
28. Walter Mischel, *The Marshmallow Test: Mastering Self-Control* (Little, Brown, 2015).
29. Walter Mischel and Ebbe B. Ebbesen, "Attention in Delay of Gratification," *Journal of Personality and Social Psychology* 16, no. 2 (1970): 329–37.
30. Inge-Marie Eigsti, Vivian Zayas, Walter Mischel, Yuichi Shoda, Ozlem Ayduk, Mamta B. Dadlani, et al., "Predicting Cognitive Control From Preschool to Late Adolescence and Young Adulthood," *Psychological Science* 17, no. 6 (June 2006): 478–84.
31. David Brooks, "Marshmallows and Public Policy," *New York Times*, May 7, 2006, https://tinyurl.com/3p9bhjck.
32. Mischel, *The Marshmallow Test*.
33. Mischel, *The Marshmallow Test*.
34. Roy Baumeister and John Tierney, *Willpower: Rediscovering the Greatest Human Strength* (Penguin, 2011).
35. Baumeister and Tierney, *Willpower*, 180.
36. Baumeister and Tierney, *Willpower*, 181.
37. Amy Alkon, *Unf*ckology: A Field Guide to Living with Guts and Confidence* (St. Martin's Griffin, 2018).
38. William James, "What Is an Emotion?," *Mind* 9 (1884): 188–205.
39. Alkon, *Unf*ckology*.
40. Richard H. Thaler, "Some Empirical Evidence on Dynamic Inconsistency," *Economic Letters* 8 (1981): 201–7.

41. Thomas Schelling, *Choice and Consequence: Perspectives of an Errant Economist* (Harvard University Press, 1984).
42. Mervyn A. Warren, *King Came Preaching: The Pulpit Power of Dr. Martin Luther King, Jr.* (Varsity, 2001), 193–4.
43. McRaven, "University of Texas at Austin 2014 Commencement Address."
44. Mischel, *The Marshmallow Test.*

11 The Truth About God

1. Phil Zuckerman, *Invitation to the Sociology of Religion* (Routledge, 2003); Rodney Stark, *One True God: Historical Consequences of Monotheism* (Princeton University Press, 2001); David. M. Wulff, *Psychology of Religion: Classic and Contemporary Views* (Wiley, 1991); Rodney Stark, *The Victory of Reason* (Random House, 2005); Pippa Norris and Ronald Inglehart, *Sacred and Secular* (Cambridge University Press, 2004).
2. William Lane Craig and Walter Sinnott-Armstrong, *God? A Debate Between a Christian and an Atheist* (Oxford University Press, 2004). Craig and Sinnott-Armstrong agreed for their debate to define God as "All-good, All-powerful, All-knowing, Eternal, Effective, and Personal" (p. 31).
3. These various positions on the God question have been outlined and defined by many writers, including: George H. Smith, *Atheism: The Case Against God* (Prometheus, 1989); Craig and Sinnott-Armstrong, *God?*; Richard Dawkins, *The God Delusion* (Houghton Mifflin, 2006); Jerry A. Coyne, *Faith vs. Fact: Why Science and Religion are Incompatible* (Viking, 2015).
4. Thomas H. Huxley, *Collected Essays*, vol. 5 (D. Appleton, 1894), 237–8.
5. *World Christian Encyclopedia*, 3rd ed., Center for the Study of Global Christianity, accessed April 16, 2025, https://tinyurl.com/4hxjuxft.
6. Thomas Aquinas, *Summa Theologica*, trans. Fathers of the English Dominican Province, rev. Daniel J. Sullivan, Great Books of the Western World (Encyclopedia Britannica, 1495/1952), 12–14.
7. Aquinas, *Summa Theologica.*
8. Aquinas, *Summa Theologica.*
9. Aquinas, *Summa Theologica.*
10. Carl Sagan, *The Varieties of Scientific Experience: A Personal View of the Search for God*, ed. Ann Druyan (Penguin, 2006), 147–68.
11. Sagan, *The Varieties of Scientific Experience*, 147–68.
12. The *Proslogion* is available online: "Medieval Sourcebook," Fordham University, accessed April 16, 2025, https://sourcebooks.fordham.edu/basis/anselm-proslogium.asp.

13. St. Anselm, *Proslogion. St. Anselm: Basic Writings*, ed. and trans. S. N. Deane (Open Court, 1962).
14. David Hume, *Dialogues Concerning Natural Religion* (1776). Available online at University of Michigan Library Digital Collections, accessed April 16, 2025, http://bit.ly/1sIsq4p.
15. Who knows, perhaps I have spawned a new syllogistic argument for the existence of Satan in the minds of those who already believe in him!
16. See also the clever takedown of the Ontological Argument in Dawkins, *The God Delusion*, 109–12.
17. Dan Barker, *Contraduction: The Hidden Fallacy That Inverts Reality* (Hypatia, 2024), 27.
18. For a deep dive into the context and nature of the argument, see James A. Connor, *Pascal's Wager: The Man Who Played Dice with God* (HarperSanFrancisco, 2006).
19. V. S. Ramachandran and Sandra Blakeslee, *Phantoms in the Brain: Probing the Mysteries of the Human Mind* (William Morrow, 1998).
20. Rebecca Newberger Goldstein, *36 Arguments for the Existence of God: A Work of Fiction* (Pantheon, 2010), 346–8.
21. Stephen C. Meyer, *Return of the God Hypothesis: Three Scientific Discoveries That Reveal the Mind Behind the Universe* (HarperOne, 2021), 7.
22. S. C. Meyer, "Word Games: DNA, Design, and Intelligence," *Touchstone* 12, no. 4 (1999): 44–50.
23. Charles Darwin, *On the Origin of Species* (John Murray, 1859), 154.
24. Michael Behe, *Darwin's Black Box: The Biochemical Challenge to Evolution* (Free Press, 1996), 39.
25. Behe, *Darwin's Black Box*, 232–3.
26. Robert Pennock, *Tower of Babel: The Evidence Against the New Creationism* (MIT Press, 1999).
27. Jerry Coyne, "God in the Details," *Nature* 383 (1996): 227–8.
28. Charles Darwin, *On the Various Contrivances by Which British and Foreign Orchids Are Fertilized by Insects, and on the Good Effects of Intercrossing* (John Murray, 1862), 348.
29. Stephen Jay Gould and Elisabeth Vrba, "Exaptation: A Missing Term in the Science of Form," *Paleobiology* 8 (1982): 4–15.
30. R. O. Prum and A. H. Brush, "Which Came First, the Feather or the Bird: A Long-Cherished View of How and Why Feathers Evolved Has Now Been Overturned," *Scientific American*, March 2003, 84–93.
31. Kevin Padian and L. M. Chiappe, "The Origin of Birds and Their Flight," *Scientific American*, February 1998, 38–47.

32. Alan Gishlick, "Evolutionary Paths to Irreducible Systems: The Avian Flight Apparatus," in *Why Intelligent Design Fails*, ed. Matt Young and Taner Edis (Rutgers University Press, 2004), 58–71.
33. Sean B. Carroll, "The Origins of Form," *Natural History* 114, no. 9 (November 2005): 58–63; Sean B. Carroll, *Endless Forms Most Beautiful: The New Science of Evo Devo* (W. W. Norton, 2005).
34. Henry Morris, *The Troubled Waters of Evolution* (Creation Life, 1974), 110.
35. Peter Atkins, *The Second Law: Energy, Chaos and Form* (W. H. Freeman, 1994).
36. Stuart Kauffman, *The Origins of Order: Self-Organization and Selection in Evolution* (Oxford University Press, 1993).
37. Richard Hardison, *Upon the Shoulders of Giants* (University Press of America, 1985).
38. Stephen D. Unwin, *The Probability of God: A Simple Calculation That Proves the Ultimate Truth* (Crown, 2003).
39. Paul Tillich, *Systematic Theology: Reason and Revelation, Being and God*, vol. 1 (University of Chicago Press, 1951), 205.

12 The Truth of Existence

1. John Leslie and Robert Lawrence Kuhn, *The Mystery of Existence: Why Is There Anything at All?* (Wiley-Blackwell, 2013). See also Jim Holt, *Why Does the World Exist: An Existential Detective Story* (Liveright, 2012).
2. Leslie and Kuhn, *The Mystery of Existence*.
3. Robert Lawrence Kuhn, "Levels of Nothing: There Are Multiple Answers to the Question of Why the Universe Exists," *Skeptic* 18, no. 2 (2013), http://bit.ly/1S7Mn9i.
4. Alex Vilenkin, *Many Worlds in One: The Search for Other Universes* (Hill and Wang, 2006).
5. Richard Alleyne, "God Is Not the Creator, Claims Academic," *The Telegraph*, October 8, 2009.
6. Tim Callahan, "The Genesis Creation Myth Is Not Unique," *eSkeptic*, April 25, 2012, http://bit.ly/1UlVqbi.
7. Victor Stenger, *God: The Failed Hypothesis* (Prometheus, 2008).
8. Lawrence Krauss, *A Universe From Nothing: Why There Is Something Rather Than Nothing* (Free Press, 2012), 169–70.
9. Lawrence Krauss, *The Greatest Story Ever Told—So Far: Why Are We Here?* (Atria, 2017).
10. Stephen Hawking, "Quantum Cosmology," in *The Nature of Space and Time*, Stephen Hawking and Roger Penrose (Princeton University Press, 1996), 89–90.

11. John D. Barrow and Frank Tipler, *The Anthropic Cosmological Principle* (Oxford University Press, 1988), vii.
12. Martin Rees, *Just Six Numbers: The Deep Forces That Shape the Universe* (Basic, 2000).
13. Michael Denton, *Nature's Destiny: How the Laws of Biology Reveal Purpose in the Universe* (Free Press, 1998).
14. John Barrow and John Webb, "Inconstant Constants," *Scientific American*, June 2005, 57–63.
15. Sean Carroll, *From Eternity to Here: The Quest for the Ultimate Theory of Time* (Dutton/Penguin, 2010), 50.
16. Carroll, *From Eternity to Here*, 51, 64.
17. Paul J. Steinhardt and Neil Turok, "A Cyclic Model of the Universe," *Science* 296, no. 5572 (May 2002): 1436–9.
18. Kelsey Johnson, *Into the Unknown: The Quest to Understand the Mysteries of the Cosmos* (Basic, 2024).
19. Lee Smolin, *The Life of the Cosmos* (Oxford University Press, 1997). See also Quentin Smith, "A Natural Explanation of the Existence and Laws of Our Universe," *Australasian Journal of Philosophy* 68 (1990): 22–43. For an elegant summary, see James Gardner, *Biocosm* (Inner Ocean, 2003).
20. Alan Guth, "The Inflationary Universe: A Possible Solution to the Horizon and Flatness Problems," *Physical Review D* 23, no. 347 (1981); Alan Guth, *The Inflationary Universe: The Quest for a New Theory of Cosmic Origins* (Addison-Wesley, 1997); Andrei Linde, "The Self-Reproducing Inflationary Universe," *Scientific American*, November 1991, 48–55; Andrei Linde, "Current Understanding of Inflation," *New Astronomy Reviews* 49 (2005): 35–41; Alex Vilenkin, *Many Worlds in One: The Search for Other Universes* (Hill and Wang, 2006).
21. Richard Feynman, *The Character of Physical Law* (MIT Press, 1967), 129.
22. Justin Khoury, Burt A. Ovrut, Paul J. Steinhardt, and Neil Turok, "Density Perturbations in the Ekpyrotic Scenario," *Physical Review D* 66, no. 046005 (2002); Jeremiah P. Ostriker and Paul Steinhardt, "The Quintessential Universe," *Scientific American*, January 2001, 46–53.
23. Raphael Bousso and Joseph Polchinski, "The String Theory Landscape," *Scientific American*, September 2004.
24. Victor Stenger, *God: The Failed Hypothesis* (Prometheus, 2007).
25. Hugh Everett, "'Relative State' Formulation of Quantum Mechanics," *Reviews of Modern Physics* 29, no.3 (1957): 454–62. Reprinted in B. S. DeWitt and N. Graham, eds., *The Many-Worlds Interpretation of Quantum Mechanics* (Princeton University

Press, 1973), 141–9. John Archibald Wheeler, *Geons, Black Holes & Quantum Foam* (W. W. Norton, 1998), 268–70.

26. Roger Penrose, *The Road to Reality: A Complete Guide to the Laws of the Universe* (Knopf, 2005), 726–32, 762–5.
27. Stephen Hawking, "The Future of Theoretical Physics and Cosmology: Stephen Hawking 60th Birthday Symposium," Lecture at the Centre for Mathematical Sciences, Cambridge, UK, January 11, 2002.
28. Stephen Hawking and Leonard Mlodinow, *The Grand Design* (Bantam, 2010).
29. Paul Halpern, *The Allure of the Multiverse: Extra Dimensions, Other Worlds, and Parallel Universes* (Basic, 2024).
30. Max Tegmark, *Our Mathematical Universe: My Quest for the Ultimate Nature of Reality* (Knopf, 2014).
31. Halpern, *The Allure of the Multiverse*, 14.
32. Halpern, *The Allure of the Multiverse*, 25.
33. Christoph Schönborn, "Finding Design in Nature," *New York Times*, July 7, 2005.
34. William Lane Craig, "Opening Speech," in *Is Faith in God Reasonable?*, ed. Paul Gould and Corey Miller (Routledge, 2014).
35. Victor Stenger, *God and the Multiverse: Humanity's Expanding View of the Cosmos* (Prometheus, 2014), 328–9.
36. Niayesh Afshordi and Phil Halper, *The Battle of the Big Bang* (University of Chicago Press, 2025), 234.
37. Carl Sagan, *The Varieties of Scientific Experience* (Penguin, 2007), 2.

Epilogue

1. Sean Carroll, *The Big Picture: On the Origins of Life, Meaning, and the Universe Itself* (Dutton, 2016), 148.
2. Michael Shermer, "Wronger than Wrong," *Scientific American*, November 2006, 40.
3. Originally presented in Michael Shermer, "Shermer's Last Law," *Scientific American*, January 2002, 33.
4. I added "or far-future humans" to acknowledge the exponential growth of technology, most notably computers and artificial intelligence, and suggest that if we extrapolated the last century of progress in technology out a thousand centuries, we might possibly be able to do what super-advanced alien civilizations can.
5. Ray Kurzweil, *The Singularity Is Near* (Penguin, 2006). See also Singularity.com, accessed April 21, 2025, http://singularity.com/.

6. Lee Smolin, *The Life of the Cosmos* (Oxford University Press, 1997); Andrew Liddle and Jon Loveday, *The Oxford Companion to Cosmology* (Oxford University Press, 2009); Steven Weinberg, *Cosmology* (Oxford University Press, 2008).
7. Freeman Dyson, "Time Without End: Physics and Biology in an Open Universe," *Reviews of Modern Physics* 51, no. 3 (July 1979).
8. James Pollack and Carl Sagan, "Planetary Engineering," in *Resources of Near Earth Space*, ed. J. Lewis, M. Matthews, and M. Guerreri (University of Arizona Press, 1993); Larry Niven, *Ringworld* (Ballentine, 1990); Olaf Stapledon, *The Starmaker* (Dover, 1968).
9. Michio Kaku, *The Future of Humanity: Terraforming Mars, Interstellar Travel, Immortality, and Our Destiny Beyond Earth* (Doubleday, 2014); Michio Kaku, *Physics of the Future* (Doubleday, 2018).

INDEX

ABOUT THE AUTHOR

Dr. Michael Shermer (michaelshermer.com) is the founding publisher and editor-in-chief of *Skeptic* magazine, since 1992 an international science magazine in print, online, and available in every bookstore in North America (skeptic.com). From 1992 through 2015, he hosted the Skeptics Society's Distinguished Science Lecture Series at Caltech, which evolved into the *Michael Shermer Show* podcast in which Dr. Shermer converses with leading scientists, scholars, and intellectuals on a wide range of topics (www.skeptic.com/michael-shermer-show/). For 18 years, he was the "Skeptic" monthly columnist for *Scientific American* in which he penned 214 consecutive monthly essays read by millions each month. His two TED Talks from the main TED stage in 2006 and 2010, viewed over 11 million times, were voted in the top 100 of the more than 2,000 TED talks, for which he was invited to deliver an All-Star TED Talk in 2014.

Dr. Shermer received his BA in psychology from Pepperdine University, his MA in experimental psychology from California State University, Fullerton, and his PhD in the history of science from Claremont Graduate University. He has taught courses in psychology and the history of science at Glendale College, Occidental College, and Claremont Graduate University. For 12 years, he was a Presidential Fellow at Chapman University, where he taught a critical thinking course titled Skepticism 101: How to Think Like a Scientist, which is also a full-length audio course for The Teaching Company's Great Courses under the same title. He is a *New York Times* best-selling author of many books:

Conspiracy: Why the Rational Believe the Irrational (2022)

Giving the Devil His Due (2020)

Heavens on Earth: The Scientific Search for the Afterlife, Immortality, and Utopia (2018)

Skeptic: Viewing the World with a Rational Eye (2016)

The Moral Arc: How Science and Reason Lead Humanity Toward Truth, Justice, and Freedom (2015)

The Believing Brain: From Ghosts and Gods to Politics and Conspiracies—How We Construct Beliefs and Reinforce Them as Truths (2011)

The Mind of the Market: Compassionate Apes, Competitive Humans, and Other Tales from Evolutionary Economics (2008)

Why Darwin Matters: The Case Against Intelligent Design (2006)

Science Friction: Where the Known Meets the Unknown (2005)

The Science of Good and Evil (2004)

In Darwin's Shadow: The Life and Science of Alfred Russel Wallace (2002)

The Borderlands of Science: Where Sense Meets Nonsense (2001)

Denying History: Who Says the Holocaust Never Happened and Why Do They Say It? (with Alex Grobman, 2000)

How We Believe: The Search for God in an Age of Science (2000)

Why People Believe Weird Things (1997; 2nd edition, 2002)